This book belongs to

John Trenkle

Neural Networks for Economic and Financial Modelling

To Anna, Rosanna and Teresio
  Luca and Gianna
  Anna, Stefano and Vanna

Neural Networks for Economic and Financial Modelling

Andrea Beltratti, Sergio Margarita
and Pietro Terna
University of Turin, Italy

INTERNATIONAL THOMSON COMPUTER PRESS
I ⓣ P An International Thomson Publishing Company

London • Bonn • Boston • Johannesburg • Madrid • Melbourne • Mexico City • New York • Paris
Singapore • Tokyo • Toronto • Albany, NY • Belmont, CA • Cincinnati, OH • Detroit, MI

Neural Networks for Economic and Financial Modelling

Copyright © 1996 Andrea Beltratti, Sergio Margarita and Pietro Terna

I ⓣ P   A division of International Thomson Publishing Inc.
The ITP logo is a trademark under licence

British Library Cataloguing-in-Publication Data
A catalogue record for this book is available from the British Library

Library of Congress Cataloging-in-Publication Data
A catalog record for this book is available from the Library of Congress

First printed 1996

Commissioning Editor: Liz Israel Oppedijk
Cover Designed by Buttons Eventures
Typeset in the UK by Florencetype Limited
Printed in the UK by Cambridge University Press

ISBN 1-85032-169-8

International Thomson Computer Press
Berkshire House
High Holborn
London WClV 7AA
UK

International Thomson Computer Press
20 Park Plaza
14th Floor
Boston MA 02116
USA

http://www.thomson.com/itcp.html

Imprints of International Thomson Publishing

Contents

Preface

With different degrees of relative intensity, all three of us are interested in both economics and computer science. A few years ago we started to study potential applications of artificial neural networks to economics, and arranged a series of seminars to discuss existing contributions. While we found many relevant examples of applications, we thought that the (at the time small) literature was characterized by an over-representation of purely financial applications, such as using artificial neural networks to predict stock prices, and an under-representation of attempts at modelling economies populated by artificial agents. We became excited about exploring such ideas.

There are two reasons why this book emphasizes theoretical applications of artificial neural networks. As already said, in the literature we found many exercises aimed at the immediate forecasting of exchange rates and stock prices, but few attempts at using interacting computer programs to create an artificial economy. Second, we thought, and found out throughout our own work, that it is not easy to generalize results obtained by econometric applications of artificial neural networks to financial time series, the results changing dramatically from one series to another, and from one sample period to another. While at the current research stage there may still be few possibilities of learning general lessons from the class of models that we present in this book, we believe that this has a great potential to change as more and more research is carried out along those lines.

This book therefore came to be written on the basis of considerations like these, followed by many passionate discussions. During the long time it took to write the book we received comments from many people, too numerous to mention. We simply thank all those who interacted with us on this research project. While the dedications appear at the front of the book, and after all the discussions we had about how to perform this research and to write this book, we want to point out that each of us is also dedicating the book to the two other co-authors.

Finally, we acknowledge financial support from various sources: the funds provided by the Italian Ministry of University and Scientific and Technological Research for the project on Financial Intermediation, the Structure of Markets and the Real Economy, the project on Applications of Artificial Neural Networks to Simulations of Economic Behaviour, and the project on Analysis and Applications of Decision Processes, and the funds provided by the Fondazione ENI Enrico Mattei for the project on Artificial Markets.

University of Turin, Italy
July 1995

Introduction

The research programme that gave rise to this book was concerned with one basic and ambitious question: is it possible to use artificial neural networks for economic research, and provide a perspective which may be useful especially in those cases in which the answers obtained from mainstream economic theories are not fully satisfactory? After a few years of work, we believe that, while still too early for a definite answer, there are some indications that one may use computer programs to study problems of great practical relevance, and obtain results which complement those already available from the economics literature.

In order to obtain some perspectives on the use of artificial neural networks in economics, we analysed two different levels: the possibility of using computer codes to represent the economic behaviour of a single agent, and the consequences of having many different codes interacting in an environment described by a few specific rules. The book reports some attempts at studying both questions. In order to provide the interested reader with a useful perspective from which to approach the following material, we make a few short comments here.

First, what is the aim of the book? We believe that the added value of the book lies mainly in the fact that it connects together different fields, such as Economics, Artificial Intelligence and Artificial Life, in order to point out interactions which may advance research in the various areas; in particular, it shows that tools representing standard practice in one discipline may be fruitfully applied to tackling other problems. We have not developed new algorithms or new economic models, but we have proposed ways of looking at economic issues, and clarified that artificial neural networks may be applied, at both a theoretical and a practical level, to relevant economic questions.

Second, to whom is the book directed? One type of reader consists of economists interested in adopting an interdisciplinary approach to the study of economic problems, and in experimenting with tools that allow a rich treatment of learning and adaptive behaviour and may help in building artificial entities (economies, organizations or individuals) useful for doing simulated experiments.

The second type consists of non-economists, perhaps computer scientists, who are looking for potential applications of artificial neural networks and the other instruments that we will review in Chapter 1. As already said, the book explores one specific tool in detail, but it is possible (and hoped) that the reading of the material will stimulate curiosity about using other approaches. Other instruments, some of which are discussed in the book, may be as useful as neural networks, or even more so. We do not intend to convey a message about the superiority of neural networks over the available alternatives. Indeed, it will be extremely useful to have future contributions comparing the various methodologies. However, we have preferred the research strategy that consists of exploring one methodology in detail across a range of models and applications rather than using many instruments for one model.

Another type of reader who may be interested in the book is the practitioner, looking for new perspectives on how to use models for day-to-day operations. Even though practical applications have not been considered in the book, some lessons can probably be learnt from the simulation models of Chapters 5, 6 and 7.

Third, we believe that the research project which may develop from this book will involve a strict integration of theory and applications, somehow blurring the distinction between pure basic research and the use of the theory for real-world phenomena. Clearly, there may be differences in the emphasis put on various characteristics: the practitioner may be interested in developing an artificial financial market to evaluate the properties of specific types of technical analyses within various environments, while the researcher may be interested in understanding whether the artificial market is able to replicate a few of the phenomena found in real markets. However, both these preoccupations may end up using the same instruments, asking similar questions, and promoting research on the part of the same group of people. This is a fascinating possibility, which would be of great relevance to both theoretical and applied researchers.

Fourth, artificial neural networks may indeed represent a flexible tool both for modelling realistic learning behaviour on the part of agents and for developing adaptive models which will prove to be extremely relevant for many problems which are very hard to study with standard economic models. In many situations economists have to use heavy simplifications in order to obtain tractable models; such simplifications are dramatic, especially in terms of the learning behaviours which are assumed on the part of the agents. In the future it may be important to study in detail the mechanics of learning and the connection between learning and actions, both for the purpose of improving a few pieces of the theory which are largely unsatisfactory in the light of results obtained with experiments, and for the purpose of building models of economies with adaptive agents.

Finally, we fully realize that we have simply started to scratch the surface of possible uses at the level of simulations of artificial financial markets. While some of our applications raise questions rather than provide answers, we hope that there will be more chances in the future to compare results from different artificial models.

Before getting to the first chapter, it may be useful to provide a general outline of the organization of the book, which is divided into three parts. The first part contains two chapters, providing some basic material for the following chapters; the second part contains two chapters concerned with carrying out experiments with artificial agents, and the third part is divided into three chapters proposing various models of artificial agents.

The first part contains some basic material about various artificial intelligence instruments, with particular regard to artificial neural networks and genetic algorithms, which will be extensively used in what follows. Some numerical examples are offered for the reader with no knowledge of such instruments. Also, there is some discussion of portions of economic theories which are relevant for the artificial models of the third part, especially issues of learning, interactions and computational costs.

The second part is about the use of artificial neural networks for doing economic experiments. Several examples are presented where economic agents modelled as neural networks are able to develop their own behavioural rules from simple consistency requirements, and show as a result fairly complex patterns of behaviour.

The third part considers interactions of artificial agents in various contexts; most applications are about financial markets, even though we also consider interactions among agents belonging to different sectors of the economy and evaluate different institutional market arrangements. The main interest of this part lies in studying issues like the consequences of heterogeneity for the dynamics of market variables, the persistence of agents' heterogeneity in situations of learning and the possibility of interpreting the actions of the agents in terms of simple behavioural rules.

Part One

Neural Networks, Genetic Algorithms and Economic Models: An Introduction

Part One

1
Artificial neural networks and genetic algorithms

Outline of the chapter

This chapter introduces the reader to the main features of artificial neural networks (ANNs) and genetic algorithms (GAs), and provide a brief survey of other learning techniques. The presentation will be kept as concise and self-contained as possible in order to make the book accessible even to readers who do not have a specific background in these techniques. Therefore the chapter will not present all the available material on artificial neural networks and genetic algorithms, since this can be found in more specific literature on the subject. For neural networks the reader can refer to Rumelhart and McClelland (1986), McClelland and Rumelhart (1986), Wasserman (1989) and Kohonen (1984), or to McClelland and Rumelhart (1988) and Caudill and Butler (1992) for a more computer-based explorative approach. Genetic algorithms are explained in detail in Holland (1992), Goldberg (1989) and Davis (1991). Simulation software for GAs is presented in Grefenstette *et al.* (1991). Finally the theoretical foundations of GAs, which will not be covered in this book, are described in Holland (1992), Rawlins (1991) and Whitley (1993).

Rather, the goal is to provide a clear and accessible presentation of the specific material that we are going to use in the economic applications we will present in the following chapters, and to mention some techniques that are not directly used in this book but may have useful applications in economic problems. Therefore references to biological aspects of neural networks and to natural genetics will be avoided as far as possible.

Section 1.1 describes the general structure of artificial neural networks, emphasizing the feed-forward architecture but also briefly describing alternative architectures. Section 1.2 then describes learning with back-propagation, the most commonly used technique, while section 1.3 describes the basic working of genetic algorithms and their use as an alternative learning algorithm that can be applied to neural networks. Finally, in section 1.4 we briefly present other learning devices.

1.1 Artificial neural networks

1.1.1 Introduction

The origin of Artificial Neural Networks can be traced back to the work of Hebb (1949), who proposed a learning law that became the ancestor of modern neural network training techniques. Subsequent developments are due to Rosenblatt (1959) and Widrow and Hoff (1960). After this brilliant start the scientific community's interest in ANNs decreased as a result of the contribution of Minsky and Papert (1969), who pointed out some of the computational limitations of the then-existing architectures. The problem was that simple networks, those with no hidden layer, could not solve a simple XOR (exclusive OR) problem. A solution was offered by a number of authors independently. The main contributions were from Werbos (1974), Parker (1985) and Le Cun (1985), who proposed a different network architecture and a supervised learning rule, the generalized Delta Rule, which could also be used for complex networks. The seminal work of Rumelhart and McClelland (1986) popularized that learning rule and suggested many applications. Parallel research streams emphasized unsupervised learning rules for neural networks (Kohonen, 1984; Grossberg, 1982). More recently, White (1992) has clarified the relationship between artificial neural networks and fields like statistics and econometrics.

Over the years many network architectures differing in their structure and learning methodology have emerged. Some of these are very general, for example feed-forward networks with back-propagation and self-organizing Kohonen maps, while others are more problem-specific, like ART networks (Carpenter and Grossberg, 1986, 1987) and Counterpropagation networks (Hecht-Nielsen, 1987). In the next sections we will limit ourselves to a description of feed-forward networks with back-propagation learning, which are the most widely diffused among researchers and the most suited to the economic applications that we discuss in the book.

1.1.2 The structure of feed-forward networks

Artificial neural networks are biologically inspired devices used for mapping a set of inputs into a set of outputs. The mapping is carried out by the processing elements, called artificial neurons or neurodes (Caudill and Butler, 1990), which are interconnected to form a network divided into layers (usually three): the input layer receives inputs from outside, the output layer sends outputs to the outside and one or more intermediate layers connect the input and output layers. The basic properties of neural networks, which are independent of the specific structure (number of layers, numbers of neurons . . .), are the following

1. Learning: the capability of the network to adapt its behaviour to the environment, or in other words to autonomously build a represen-

tation of the map from inputs to outputs on the basis of a set of examples.

2. Generalization: the ability to react in a coherent way to imperfect inputs or to inputs not explicitly seen during learning.
3. Soft degradation: the alteration or elimination of some elements of the network does not prevent it from working but only induces a smooth degradation in the performance.

In what follows we explain the most widely used architecture, known as the three-layer, fully interconnected, feed-forward network with back-propagation learning. The building blocks of this architecture are the neurons and the interconnections among them.

(a) Description of the neuron

The artificial neuron (Figure 1.1) is a processing element that:

1. receives some signals $I_0, I_1, \ldots I_k$ as inputs;
2. computes the weighted sum of all the signals that are received as inputs to generate a global net input: $net_j = \Sigma\ I_i\ w_{ji}$ (the meaning of w_{ji} will be fully described later on);

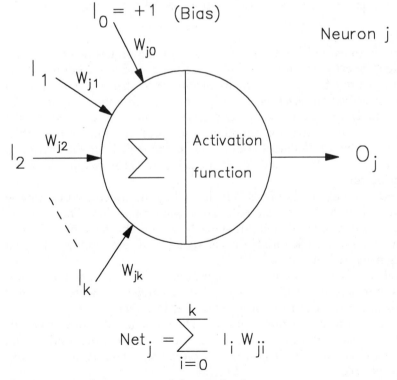

Figure 1.1 *The structure of the artificial neuron.*

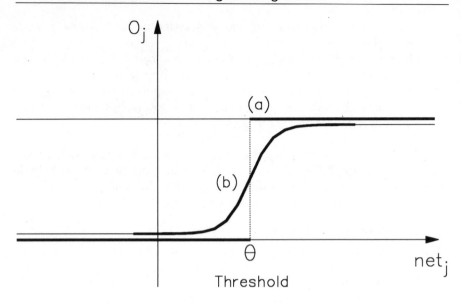

Figure 1.2 *Two activation functions: (a) Threshold; (b) Logistic.*

3. yields as output O_j a transformation of the net input by means of an activation function f, $O_j = f(net_j)$.

Analogously to natural neurons, the activation function has two main characteristics: the existence of a threshold, and upper and lower boundedness. A natural neuron fires only when its net input reaches a given threshold θ, and its activation level never surpasses a given saturation level. In order to apply the most widely used learning algorithms, based on the derivatives of the activation function, the threshold function is often approximated by a differentiable one such as the logistic or the arctan. In other applications a linear function is used. Figure 1.2 shows the threshold and logistic functions.

The existence of the threshold is replicated by introducing a bias among the inputs when the logistic is used as an activation function. This is equivalent to considering another input signal at a constant value of 1. In fact in Figure 1.1 there are k variable input signals and one input fixed signal I_0 representing the bias.

The effects of the various input signals on the neuron are not homogeneous, but depend on the strength of their connection with the source of the signals. Such a connection is represented by a weight w_{ji} going from source neuron i to destination neuron j. The absolute value of this weight represents the strength of the connection, while its sign corresponds to the nature of the connection: a positive (negative) sign reflects an excitatory (inhibitory) link.

(b) The structure of the network

Within the network, neurons are organized in layers.

1.   One input layer which receives signals from outside. Input neurons generally do not process the signals they receive but only transmit them to the subsequent layer of the network. The number of input neurons is problem-specific and depends on the amount and the type of information which is processed by the network.
2.   One or more intermediate (or hidden) layers whose neurons perform the processing described in (a) above. The number of hidden layers determines the complexity of the processing done by the network: while most applications are based on ANNs with one hidden layer, complex problems may require two or three layers. This aspect will be considered in more detail later on (see section 1.2.3).
3.   One output layer which returns signals to the outside, once the network has processed the inputs. Output neurons perform the same signal processing as described in (a) above.

The way neurons are connected fully determines the structure of the network. One of the most widely used is the so-called fully connected neural network, where all the neurons of each layer are connected with (and only with) all the neurons of the subsequent layer: input neurons with hidden neurons, and hidden neurons with output neurons (labelled inter-layer connections). Within a single layer, there is no connection from one neuron to another. When connections are oriented and the direction of information flow goes only from input to hidden and from hidden to output, the network is called a feed-forward network.

Other architectures exist which differ from the one we have described here by allowing intra-layer connections (links among neurons belonging to the same layer) or backward information flow, as in recurrent networks (Jordan, 1986). The various characteristics that we described are considered in the three-layer, feed-forward, fully connected networks that we always use in the applications considered in this book.

Their mechanism is described in the following example.

In the network of Figure 1.3, the neurons are grouped in three layers: input, hidden and output. There are four input neurons (denoted 1, 2, 3, 4), three hidden neurons (5, 6, 7) and two output neurons (8, 9). The structure is fully interconnected because each neuron in the input layer is connected with each neuron in the hidden layer, which in turn communicates directly with each neuron in the output layer. Each connection has an associated weight w_{ji}, the weight from neuron i to neuron j, which defines the strength of the connection. The information received by the neurons flows only in the forward direction, from input to hidden to output, without feedback, and bias is not considered for the sake of simplicity.

If the four inputs have values I_1, I_2, I_3 and I_4, the overall signal passed to neuron 5 is equal to:

$$net_5 = w_{51}I_1 + w_{52}I_2 + w_{53}I_3 + w_{54}I_4$$

where net_i denotes the input to the i-th neuron. Neuron 5 then transforms this linear combination of inputs by means of the logistic activation function and yields an output equal to:

$$H_5 = [1 + \exp(-net_5)]^{-1}$$

Together with the output of neurons 6 and 7, this output then forms a linear combination which is passed on to neurons 8 and 9. The signal received by neuron 8 is:

$$net_8 = w_{85}H_5 + w_{86}H_6 + w_{87}H_7$$

These neurons are again transformed by the logistic to become the final output of the neural network. The output of neuron 8 is therefore:

$$O_8 = [1 + \exp(-net_8)]^{-1}.$$

Matrix notation can be used for a concise description. If A and B are matrices that collect the values of the weights from input to hidden and from hidden to output respectively, O is the output vector of the network, I is the input vector and f is the activation function (defined over appropriate vectors), then the network can be described as:

$$O = f(f(I \cdot A) \cdot B)$$

For the example in Figure 1.3, the two matrices are respectively:

$$\underset{(4,3)}{A} = \begin{bmatrix} w_{51} & w_{61} & w_{71} \\ w_{52} & w_{62} & w_{72} \\ w_{53} & w_{63} & w_{73} \\ w_{54} & w_{64} & w_{74} \end{bmatrix} \qquad \underset{(3,2)}{B} \begin{bmatrix} w_{85} & w_{95} \\ w_{86} & w_{96} \\ w_{87} & w_{97} \end{bmatrix}$$

The weights are the devices encoding the information into the network. So, for a given structure, the behaviour of the network strictly depends on the set of weights.

White (1991) has shown in a series of important contributions that ANNs can be seen as nonlinear models. The specific functional forms used in nonlinear models imply of course that in general the function that generates the data is different from the one implied by ANNs, so that the econometric theory that needs to be used for ANNs is the one for misspecified nonlinear models (White, 1982). Their pre-specified structure notwithstanding, ANNs have the ability to approximate arbitrarily well any continuous function and its derivatives, and for this reason have been called universal approximators (Hornik et al., 1989).

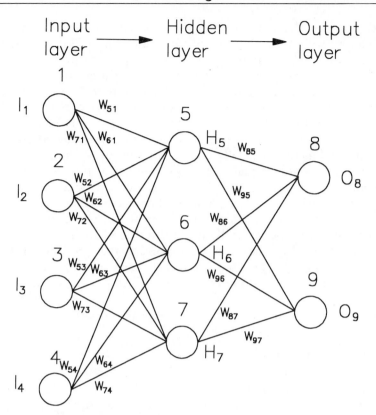

Figure 1.3 *A simple neural network (bias not shown).*

1.2 Learning in artificial neural networks

1.2.1 Main characteristics of learning

Given a specific structure chosen by the user of the network (comments on the importance of the structure for the performance of the network are contained in section 1.2.3), the aim of the learning process is to choose values of the weights so as to realize the desired mapping from inputs to outputs. In supervised learning such a mapping is learnt by reiterated presentation of a set of examples, each composed of an input and an output vector. Such learning is supervised in the sense that the output of the network is compared to a known target in order to define an error and to modify the existing weights to achieve a better performance (unsupervised learning will be described and compared to supervised learning in section 1.3.6).

Any such series of examples may be represented by a set of observations on variables at different time periods (time series), or by a set of observations on different units at the same time (cross-section). In the examples we will implicitly think of time series, and will use the subscript t to denote the observation for the t-th example. In the ANN literature the observation for a single example is called a pattern or input vector.

The standard method used in the ANN literature is the back-propagation algorithm (from now on called BP) (Rumelhart and McClelland, 1986). BP allows the network to choose its weights in order to minimize a performance function defined over the output of the network and some targets. The performance function generally used is the sum of squared errors, where the sum is taken with respect to both the number of available patterns and the number of output neurons. Other objective functions may be needed for specific problems, for example when the target is composed of a binary sequence of 0's and 1's. The error for pattern t and output neuron j is the difference between the target T_{tj} and the output of the network O_{tj}. Such output is obtained by means of the processing that was described in the previous section, and therefore involves the two matrices of the weights connecting the neurons. From now on we will collect the set of weights in a vector denoted by W.

The next section describes more precisely the mechanics of BP.

1.2.2 The back-propagation algorithm

We consider a problem with T patterns, and a network structure that includes K inputs, H hidden and J outputs. The objective function of the problem, as defined in the previous section, is therefore:

$$E(W) = \frac{1}{2} \sum_{t=1}^{T} \sum_{j=1}^{J} (T_{tj} - O_{tj})^2$$

where multiplication by ½ is introduced only for simplifying the expression of the derivatives which are computed in the learning algorithm.

The phases that characterize BP learning are the following.

1. The vector W of weights starts with initial values drawn from a uniform distribution whose range depends on the user, but is generally set at −0.5, +0.5.

2. A pattern t is presented to the network. Given the randomly assigned weights the pattern is propagated forward through the network as follows:

$$net_{th} = w_{h0} + w_{h1} I_{t1} + w_{h2} I_{t2} + \ldots + w_{hK} I_{tK} \qquad (1.1)$$

$$h = 1, 2, \ldots, H$$

$$H_{th} = [1 + \exp(-net_{th})]^{-1} \qquad (1.2)$$

$$h = 1, 2, \ldots, H$$

$$net_{tj} = w_{j0} + w_{j1} H_{t1} + w_{j2} H_{t2} + \ldots + w_{jH} H_{tH} \qquad (1.3)$$

$$j = 1, 2, \ldots, J$$

$$O_{tj} = [1 + \exp(-net_{tj})]^{-1} \qquad (1.4)$$

$$j = 1, 2, \ldots, J$$

Equation 1.1 describes how the signals I_t received from the outside are transmitted to the hidden neurons. Equation 1.2 describes the nonlinear transformation that is performed by hidden neurons by means of the logistic function. Equation 1.3 then shows how the network computes linear combinations of the outputs of the hidden neurons which are then transmitted to the output neurons. Equation 1.4 shows the way outputs are computed by the output neurons with the same nonlinear transformation through the logistic function.

3.   A set of J errors $(T_{tj} - O_{tj})$ is computed from the comparison between the target and the output computed in step (2) for pattern t. The errors are used to calculate $E_t(W)$, a global error for pattern t:

$$E_t(W) = \frac{1}{2} \sum_{t=1}^{T} (T_{tj} - O_{tj})^2 \qquad (1.5)$$

To simplify notation, from now on we will ignore the dependence of the errors on the vector of weights W and express $E_t(W)$ as E_t.

The error term is used to modify weights connecting all the various layers.

4.   The general rule for modification of the weights is:

$$\Delta_t w_{ji} = -\alpha \frac{\partial E_t}{\partial w_{ji}}$$

where α is the learning rate, a coefficient that regulates the speed of learning.

5a. When the general rule given in equation 1.6 is used for the modification of the weights connecting hidden and output layers, the global error is derived with respect to the weights connecting hidden to output. The derivatives can in general be expressed with the notation:

$$\frac{\partial E_t}{\partial w_{ji}} = \frac{\partial E_t}{\partial O_{tj}} \cdot \frac{\partial O_{tj}}{\partial w_{ji}} \qquad (1.7)$$

$$i = 0, 1, \ldots, H \quad j = 1, 2, \ldots, J$$

Index i begins at zero to take into account the presence of a bias (and its associated weight) for each output neuron. We now consider the two factors on the right-hand side of equation 1.7. From equation 1.5, the first factor is equal to:

$$\frac{\partial E_t}{\partial O_{tj}} = -(T_{tj} - O_{tj})$$

From equations 1.3 and 1.4, the second factor is equal to:

$$\frac{\partial O_{tj}}{\partial w_{ji}} = \frac{\partial O_{tj}}{\partial net_{tj}} \cdot \frac{\partial net_{tj}}{\partial w_{ji}} = O_{tj}(1 - O_{tj}) H_{ti}$$

The particularly simple expression for the second factor is due to the use of the logistic function.

5b. When the general rule given in equation 1.6 is used for the modification of the weights connecting input and hidden layers, the global error is derived with respect to the weights connecting input to hidden. The derivatives can in general be expressed with the notation:

$$\frac{\partial E_t}{\partial w_{ji}} = \frac{\partial E_t}{\partial net_{tj}} \cdot \frac{\partial net_{tj}}{\partial w_{ji}} \qquad (1.8)$$

$$i = 0, 1, \ldots, K \quad j = 1, 2, \ldots, H$$

Index i begins at zero to take into account the presence of a bias (and its associated weight) for each hidden neuron. We now consider the two factors on the right-hand side of equation 1.8. From equation 1.2, the first factor is equal to:

$$\frac{\partial E_t}{\partial net_{tj}} = H_{tj}(1 - H_{tj})$$

The second factor is equal to:

$$\frac{\partial net_{tj}}{\partial w_{ji}} = I_{tj} \sum_{k=1}^{J} (T_{tk} - O_{tk}) O_{tk}(1 - O_{tk}) w_{kj}$$

6. The cycle is repeated from step (2) by considering a different pattern, until all the patterns have been examined by the network (index t runs from 1 to T).

7. The T squared errors are summed in order to obtain a global error over all the patterns.

8. Steps 2 to 7 are repeated until the global error reaches a specified value.

1.2.3 General comments on back-propagation

Some aspects of the BP algorithm deserve comment.

(a) Learning rate

Equation 1.6 is derived from a general gradient descent algorithm. In general the coefficient that transforms the information in the first derivatives into a change in the estimated parameters is time-varying, whereas the learning rate α used in BP is fixed. Usually that coefficient is set to a small value to ensure that the network reaches a solution. A small value has the negative consequence of increasing the number of iterations necessary to obtain a solution. The learning rate may also be modified as learning takes place. White (1991) shows that decreasing α at a certain rate is necessary to ensure convergence of the algorithm.

(b) Momentum

Often equation 1.6 is modified to:

$$\Delta_t w_{ji} = -\alpha \, \frac{\partial E_t}{\partial w_{ji}} + \beta \, \Delta_{t-1} w_{ji} \qquad (1.9)$$

where β is the so-called momentum. With this formulation one introduces some degree of persistence in the modification of the weights, since the change depends on the previous change. When such a term is included the value of α can be kept higher in order to speed up convergence, since β is able to provide some stability for the search process. The inclusion of the momentum is useful in avoiding excessive oscillations of the weights, and can be justified as an approximation to a more general conjugate gradient (Battiti, 1992).

(c) BP and maximization algorithms

BP may be considered as a very special case of more general algorithms used for nonlinear problems, such as Newton–Raphson or Berndt. These algorithms are more complicated from a computational point of view, and for this reason are not suitable for ANN-based problems, given that they usually involve many weights and would become very time-consuming.

(d) Local minima

BP is a technique that performs a deterministic local search based on gradient descent, and therefore may drive the algorithm to a local minimum of the error function. A neural network which is trapped into a local minimum during learning is likely to exhibit bad performance in terms of learning and generalization capabilities. As neural networks are typically very complicated nonlinear functions of the weights, it is only natural that many local minima coexist. Different empirical rules may be followed for trying to escape from local minima:

- adding random noise to the patterns;
- reducing the learning rate;
- taking the momentum term into account;
- adding more hidden units;
- changing the initial random values of the weights.

As genetic algorithms are a global optimization technique, they are able to escape from local minima when used for ANN training (see section 1.3).

(e) Initial conditions

The previous point suggests the importance of initial conditions. In order to check for robustness of the final solution, researchers typically start the algorithm with different sets of initial weights and check whether the solutions are very different. It is also possible to use the output of the back-propagation algorithm as the initial values for the application of Newton–Raphson nonlinear least squares (White, 1992).

(f) Neuron threshold and bias

While the threshold θ of the different neurons seems to be a parameter of the problem, it is worth noting that the threshold value itself is subject to learning. For every hidden and every output neuron, the threshold is represented by the value of the weight that connects the level of the bias, I_0, set equal to one, and the neuron itself: effectively this value is added to the net input of the neuron (Figure 1.1, equations 1.1 and 1.3). Random initialization and subsequent learning extend to the whole set of weights, including weights relating to bias.

(g) On-line and off-line learning

The authors in the BP literature distinguish between on-line and off-line learning. In on-line learning the weights are changed after the presentation of each pattern, while in off-line learning the change takes place after the presentation of all the patterns of the training set.

The terminology is a little bit confusing from the point of view of recursive econometric methods, since there the term on-line learning has the very specific meaning that the time t estimates of the unknown parameters of a system are equal to the time t–1 estimates plus the modification performed on the basis of the state of the system at time t–1 and the information contained in the data for time t. In this case therefore, the updating of the signal takes place after the presentation of data for each time period, without re-elaborating the information contained in the data set for the time periods before time t. In off-line BP several iterations are in general necessary before obtaining a good estimate of the set of weights.

On-line and off-line learning each have various advantages and disadvantages (see for example Battiti, 1992). Very often the same factor is both an advantage and a disadvantage. For example, on-line learning possesses some randomness that may be useful in escaping local minima, but for the same reason may also miss some good local minimum that was being explored. In the different applications we present in the next chapters, we use on-line learning.

(h) Tuning of parameters

The main parameters of the BP algorithm are: the learning rate and the momentum (or their rate of change if they vary during learning), and the distribution of initial random weights. The values of these various parameters have to be empirically determined by the researcher, as there are no fixed rules for finding optimal values. In fact this is a very time-consuming process, as a good set of parameters for the specific problem under consideration can only be found after many trials.

(i) Choice between architectures

The choice between different architectures does not follow simple rules, but is the result of a process of trial and error. Within feed-forward networks, one important issue is the choice of the number of layers. While theoretical results (see for example Hornik *et al.*, 1989 and 1990), have shown that standard feed-forward networks with only a single hidden layer are universal approximators, many applications use ANNs with more than one hidden layer.

Moreover, even in the context of the one hidden layer ANN, another choice has to be made about the number of hidden neurons. In general, the larger the number of neurons the better the ability to learn a specific mapping through observation of a set of examples. However, in the presence of noisy data, learning in sample often takes place at the expense of a lower ability to generalize out of the set of examples that has been seen during learning. After a certain point the ANN uses the extra neurons to fit the noise in the data, and this is confusing for out-of-sample forecasting. The weight-elimination technique, described in Chapter 3, is a technique for starting from a large ANN and then reducing it to lower dimensions by assigning a cost to network complexity. White (1988) provides growth rates for network complexity that asymptotically avoid the dangers of both overfitting and underfitting the training set.

(j) Interpretation of weights

While in general it is impossible to assign specific interpretations to the individual weights, it is sometimes useful to perform statistical inference on a subset of the weights, for example to perform a test of nonlinearity (see for example Lee *et al.*, 1989) or to study causality. White's (1987) results show that standard inference procedures can be used for these purposes by using the theory of mis-specified nonlinear models.

(k) Evaluation criteria

The performance of the network after training is a very important test of the network design. Performance evaluation is generally based on some statistical indicator such as the coefficient of determination computed over the targets and the outputs of the network. This evaluation is performed in two distinct ways: in-sample and out-of-sample. The measure of in-sample performance is based on the data used during training and expresses the effectiveness of learning. The measure of out-of-sample performance is based on data not belonging to the training set. This is a measure of the generalization capability of the network. In many situations, indicators based on the effectiveness of trading strategies are preferred to statistical indicators (see Chapter 5).

(l) Knowledge representation

Representation of the knowledge acquired during training is distributed, in the sense that each concept is a pattern of activity over all the neurons. In this way each neuron is involved in representing many concepts. This characteristic confers robustness on the network but makes interpretation of self-made rules very difficult.

1.2.4 An example of back-propagation

In order to fully describe the algorithm and to make the notation of section 1.2.2 as transparent as possible we propose here a specific example for training the simple network of Figure 1.3. In order to fully explain the algorithm a bias term is considered, although not present in Figure 1.3. While realistic values may be quite different, learning rate (α) and momentum (β) are both set to 1 in order to simplify this example. The training set is made up of the following three vector pairs:

t	Input				Output	
1	0.18	0.14	0.31	0.02	0.24	0.09
2	0.14	0.01	0.87	0.06	0.85	0.11
3	0.96	0.94	0.67	0.56	0.01	0.54

In this example, only one presentation of the training set is performed. Numerical results of these three phases are reported in Figures 1.4 to 1.6 respectively. The left-hand side of the figures relates to the forward propagation of the input signal, while the right-hand side relates to the backward propagation of the error. In order to trace the different steps of the BP algorithm, the reader must follow in alphabetical order the lowercase letters enclosed in parentheses that are present in the figures. Comments in each figure explain the meaning of these letters and the dynamics of the algorithm. Repeated letters correspond to repeated use of the same data. Values are rounded to the fourth decimal place but differences in the last decimal place may occur due to rounding errors. In the three tables, I→H means 'from input to hidden' and H→O means 'from hidden to output'.

------- Forward propagation of input signal -------   ------- Backward propagation of error -------
                                                                          L.Rate   Momentum
                                                                          1.0000   1.0000

t = 1

(k) E_t 0.1052

(j) Error   -0.1675 -0.4271   (j) -0.1675 -0.4271

(i) Target   0.2400 0.0900   (l) -0.0404 -0.1067

(h) Output   0.4075 0.5171   Hidden

(g) -0.3742 0.0688   (e) 1.0000   (m) L.Rate   (n) Momentum   (o) Changes in weights H->O
                                         0.5115   -0.0404 -0.1067   0.0000 0.0000   -0.0404 -0.1067
Hidden (f)   0.4521   -0.0207 -0.0546   0.0000 0.0000   -0.0207 -0.0546
(e) 1.0000 -0.0288 0.0780   0.5981   -0.0183 -0.0482   0.0000 0.0000   -0.0183 -0.0482
    0.5115 -0.2667 0.0276   -0.0242 -0.0638   0.0000 0.0000   -0.0242 -0.0638
    0.4521 -0.1983 0.1960
    0.5981 -0.1996 -0.1871   (p) 0.0108 -0.0029   (q)   --->   (r) 0.0078 0.0020
                                          0.0080 -0.0209   --->   -0.0129 -0.0032
    Weights H->O   0.0081 0.0200   --->   0.0280 0.0067
                                                                  --->

                                                                                   (s) 0.0020 -0.0032 0.0067

(d) 0.5115 0.4521 0.5981   Input   (t) Changes due to learning rate

(c) 0.0462 -0.1919 0.3978   (a) 1.0000   0.0020 -0.0032 0.0067
                                                                0.1800   0.0004 -0.0006 0.0012
Input   0.1400   0.0003 -0.0004 0.0009
(a) 1.0000 (b) -0.0166 -0.0034 0.2991   0.3100   0.0006 -0.0010 0.0021
    0.1800   -0.1976 -0.2525 0.4848   0.0200   0.0000 -0.0001 0.0001
    0.1400   -0.2569 -0.0050 -0.1543
    0.3100   0.4120 -0.4543 0.0846   (u) Changes due to momentum
    0.0200   0.3350 -0.0801 0.3444
                                                                                    0.0000 0.0000 0.0000
    Weights I->H   0.0000 0.0000 0.0000
                                                                                    0.0000 0.0000 0.0000
                                                                                    0.0000 0.0000 0.0000
                                                                                    0.0000 0.0000 0.0000

                                                                                (v) Changes in weights I->H

                                                                                    0.0020 -0.0032 0.0067
                                                                                    0.0004 -0.0006 0.0012
                                                                                    0.0003 -0.0004 0.0009
                                                                                    0.0006 -0.0010 0.0021
                                                                                    0.0000 -0.0001 0.0001

Figure 1.4 An example of BP learning: First step.

(a) Comments on Figure 1.4

Figure 1.4 corresponds to the first phase of the algorithm, that is, the presentation to the network of the first vector of the training set (t = 1). In this first phase, weights are randomly assigned in the –0.5, +0.5 range.

Forward propagation of the input signal

1. First input vector (a) is multiplied by matrix (b) which collects the weights from input to hidden layers, giving vector (c). Note that:
   - vector (a) is the first input vector of the training set augmented by an element equal to 1 (the bias) used for simulating threshold values of hidden neurons;
   - matrix (b) is (5, 3) where 5 is the number of signals coming to each hidden neuron, and 3 is the number of hidden neurons;
   - the values of the elements of matrix (b) are the initial random assignments;
   - the three elements of vector (c) correspond to the net input of the three hidden neurons (net_{th} in equation 1.1).
2. Elements of vector (c) are processed through the logistic function giving vector (d), which collects the activation values of the hidden layer (H_{th} in equation 1.2).
3. Vector (d) is augmented by an element (bias) equal to 1 used for simulating threshold values of output neurons, giving vector (e).
4. Vector (e) is multiplied by matrix (f) of the weights W_{ij} from the hidden to the output layer, giving vector (g). Note that:
   - matrix (f) is (4 , 2) where 4 is the number of signals coming to each output neuron, and 2 is the number of output neurons;
   - the values of the elements of matrix (f) are the initial random assignments;
   - the two elements of vector (g) correspond to the net input of the two hidden neurons (net_{tj} in equation 1.3).
5. Elements of vector (g) are processed through the logistic function giving output vector (h), which collects the activation values of the output layer (O_{tj} in equation 1.4).
6. Error vector (j) is computed as the difference between the target vector (i) of the training set and the output vector (h). The correct output corresponding to input vector (a) is target vector (i), but the actual (random) output of the network is (h), which is different from (i). The resulting error is used in the following for updating the weights of the network.
7. A global error (k) for this first vector is computed (equation 1.5).

Backward propagation of the error

8. Vector (l) is computed on the basis of vector (j) by applying the transformation described in equation 1.7, that is, $(T_{tj} - O_{tj}) O_{tj} (1 - O_{tj})$.

9.   Vector (l) is multiplied by vector (e), that is to say the H_{ti} term in formulas derived from equation 1.7, to obtain the matrix (m) of changes in weights from the hidden to the output layer. Note that:
-   each element of this matrix should be multiplied by learning rate α (set to 1 in this example);
-   while in this example the extended formula in equation 1.9, which includes a momentum term, is being used, the contribution of the term including momentum is equal to 0 in the first update ($\Delta_{t-1}w_{ji} = 0$);
-   the matrix (o) of the global changes in weights from the hidden to the output layers is equal to matrix (m).

10.   Two vectors (p) and (q) are computed by multiplying vector (l) by matrix (f). They are then summed to give vector (r). Vector (s) is obtained by multiplying each term of vector (r) by the result of the transformation of the corresponding element of vector (e), as described by the first factor in equation 1.8, $e_i(1 - e_i)$, where e_i denotes the i-th element of vector (e). This is equivalent to applying the transformation described in equation 1.8 (summation term in the second factor).

Note that when using matrix (f) and vector (e) in the computations we previously described, biases are ignored as their input value e_0 equal to 1 leads to a null contribution after their transformation $e_0(1 - e_0)$.

11.   Finally, the outer product of vectors (a) and (s) is computed to obtain matrix (t), of changes in weights from the input to the hidden layer. Matrix (t) deserves the same comments we make on matrix (m) in previous step 9. Matrix (v) which collects the global changes in weights from the input to the hidden layer is equal to matrix (t).

(b) Comments on Figure 1.5

Figure 1.5 corresponds to the process of the network learning the second vector of the training set (t = 2). Only differences from the first phase are outlined and commented upon: the computations are the same, so only numerical values differ.

Forward propagation of the input signal

1.   Matrices of weights (b) and (f) are updated to reflect the changes computed in the previous phase. Updates take place as follows:

New (b) = old (b) + (v)
New (f) = old (f) + (o)

2.   Input vector (a) and target vector (i), corresponding to the second pattern, are considered.

3.   Obviously, these new data give rise to a different global error (k) for this pattern.

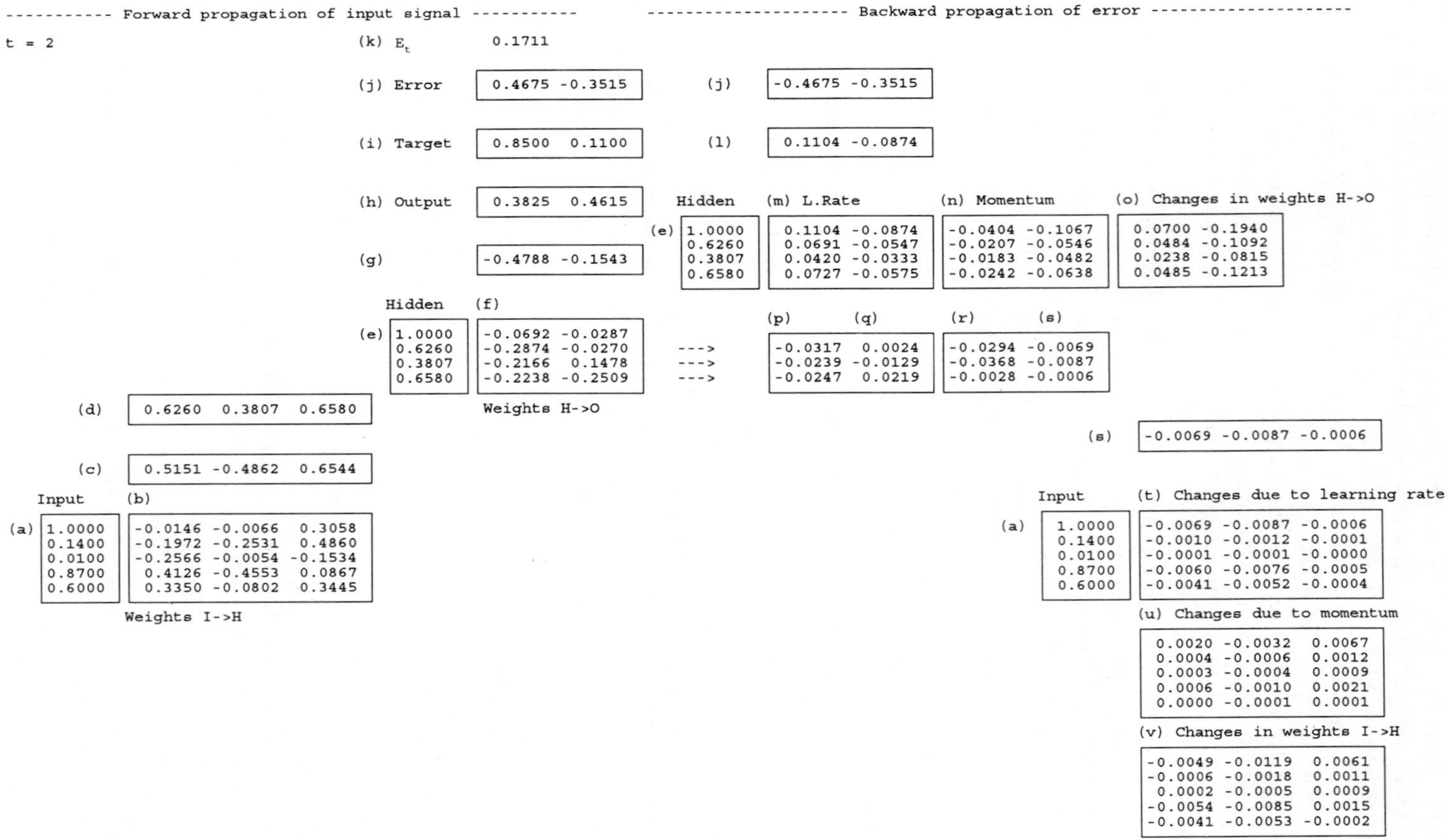

-------- Forward propagation of input signal --------   -------- Backward propagation of error --------

t = 2

(k) E_t 0.1711

(j) Error   0.4675 -0.3515   (j) -0.4675 -0.3515

(i) Target   0.8500   0.1100   (l)   0.1104 -0.0874

(h) Output   0.3825   0.4615

(o) Changes in weights H->O
```
 0.0700  -0.1940
 0.0484  -0.1092
 0.0238  -0.0815
 0.0485  -0.1213
```

(n) Momentum
```
-0.0404  -0.1067
-0.0207  -0.0546
-0.0183  -0.0482
-0.0242  -0.0638
```

(m) L.Rate
```
 0.1104  -0.0874
 0.0691  -0.0547
 0.0420  -0.0333
 0.0727  -0.0575
```

Hidden (e)
```
1.0000
0.6260
0.3807
0.6580
```

(g)   -0.4788 -0.1543

(f) Weights H->O
```
-0.0692  -0.0287
-0.2874  -0.0270
-0.2166  -0.1478
-0.2238  -0.2509
```

Hidden (e)
```
1.0000
0.6260
0.3807
0.6580
```

--->
--->
--->

(p)
```
-0.0317   0.0024
-0.0239  -0.0129
-0.0247   0.0219
```

(r) Momentum
```
-0.0294  -0.0069
-0.0368  -0.0087
-0.0028  -0.0006
```

(q)

(s)   -0.0069 -0.0087 -0.0006

(s)   -0.0069 -0.0087 -0.0006

Input (a)
```
1.0000
0.1400
0.0100
0.8700
0.6000
```

(t) Changes due to learning rate
```
-0.0069  -0.0087  -0.0006
-0.0010  -0.0012  -0.0001
-0.0001  -0.0001  -0.0000
-0.0060  -0.0076  -0.0005
-0.0041  -0.0052  -0.0004
```

(u) Changes due to momentum
```
 0.0020  -0.0032   0.0067
 0.0004  -0.0006   0.0012
 0.0003  -0.0004   0.0009
 0.0006  -0.0010   0.0021
 0.0000  -0.0001   0.0001
```

(v) Changes in weights I->H
```
-0.0049  -0.0119   0.0061
-0.0006  -0.0018   0.0011
-0.0002  -0.0005   0.0009
-0.0054  -0.0085   0.0015
-0.0041  -0.0053  -0.0002
```

(d)   0.6260   0.3807   0.6580

(c)   0.5151 -0.4862   0.6544

Input (b)
```
(a) 1.0000  -0.0146  -0.0066   0.3058
    0.1400  -0.1972  -0.2531   0.4860
    0.0100  -0.2566  -0.0054  -0.1534
    0.8700   0.4126  -0.4553  -0.0867
    0.6000   0.3350  -0.0802   0.3445
```
Weights I->H

Figure 1.5 An example of BP learning: Second step.

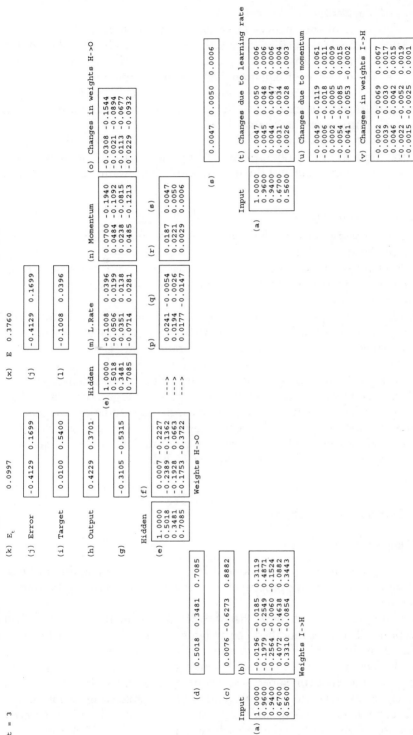

Figure 1.6 An example of BP learning: Last step.

Backward propagation of the error

4.   Matrix (o) of the changes in weights from the hidden to the output layer is no longer equal to matrix (m), but is obtained by adding matrix (m) and matrix (n) of changes due to the momentum term (the second term of equation 1.9). In the example momentum β is set to 1 and the whole previous change is included (matrix (n) is equal to old matrix (o)), while in more realistic applications only a small portion of this change is added.

5.   Similarly, the matrix (v) of the changes in weights from the input to the hidden layer is obtained by adding the matrix (t) of changes due to the learning rate and the matrix (u) of changes due to momentum.

(c) Comments on Figure 1.6

Figure 1.6 corresponds to the process of the network learning the last vector of the training set (t = 3).

This phase is similar to the previous one. The main difference lies in the fact that a global error (x) is computed over all the vectors belonging to the training set.

While our example stops after a single presentation of the training set, true applications of the BP algorithm are based on reiterated presentations of the whole training set. After each iteration the global error (x) is computed, and the algorithm stops when (x) is lower than a given value, or after a given number of iterations if this value is not reached.

BP is a supervised algorithm in the sense that targets are required to compute the errors that are used for subsequently updating weights. In the next section we present the genetic algorithm technique, which is not only an optimization tool but also an unsupervised learning technique that can be applied to ANNs' training in lieu of BP.

1.3 Genetic algorithms

1.3.1 Introduction

Genetic algorithms can be introduced from two different points of view: as an alternative learning procedure and as a more powerful optimization technique.

Regarding the former, note that the BP algorithm that was described in section 1.2 always modified the weights of the network as a function of the error, or the difference between a target and the output of the network. The algorithm therefore assumes the existence of a target, and belongs to the class of supervised learning techniques. In many cases, however, as we will see in some models in the following chapters, the target cannot be defined and one has to consider learning without supervision. GAs can be used in such situations, as they do not require a continuous availability of targets. In section 1.4 we will briefly describe other algorithms that can be used in such situations.

With regard to the class of optimization techniques, we have already observed that BP is a local optimization technique: it explores the solution space one point at a time, and is likely to be trapped in local maxima. GAs can instead be considered as global optimization algorithms, in the sense that they perform a parallel exploration of the space and are able to escape from local maxima. Therefore, GAs can be used for building models based not only on unsupervised learning, but also on supervised learning instead of the BP algorithm.

1.3.2 What is a genetic algorithm?

Goldberg (1989) defines GAs as search algorithms based on the mechanics of natural selection and natural genetics. They are inspired by Darwinian theories based on the survival and reproduction of the fittest individual in a population, and apply such principles to groups of mathematical objects, in order to find the one that is best suited to performing a specific task.

We borrow a definition from Goldberg and Holland (1988), according to whom '... genetic algorithms are probabilistic search procedures designed to work on large spaces involving states that can be represented by strings. These methods are inherently parallel, using a distributed set of samples from the space (a population of strings) to generate a new set of samples.'

In order to better describe the GAs we start by describing four important characteristics.

- Encoding of parameters: In GAs the parameters that are the object of optimization need to be encoded in terms of a string of (often binary) characters. For example, if one is looking for the maximum of a function, it is necessary to describe the space of real numbers over which the search is performed in terms of the binary representation of real-valued parameters: for example, the real number 7 is coded in a 4-bit representation as 0111. If there is more than one parameter, their binary representations are concatenated in such a way as to form a unique string. For example two real-valued parameters that have values 7 (0111) and 2 (0010) are encoded in a 8-bit string as 01110010.
- Parallelism: While standard optimization algorithms explore the solution space one point at a time, GAs simultaneously consider many points distributed in different regions of the search space. As discussed in the previous section, this characteristic confers on the GA a superiority in terms of efficiency in exploration, especially in the case of complex spaces.
- Computational requirements: The only information required by GAs is the objective function. The algorithm uses the value of the

function corresponding to each point of the domain to orient the search without needing to calculate any derivatives. GAs in fact can be applied to any kind of objective function, even if it is discontinuous, non-differentiable or non-numerical: many applications of GAs relate to different kinds of symbolic processing as described in Koza (1992a).

• Transitional rules: The exploration of the space takes place by means of stochastic transitions, contrary to what generally happens in standard gradient descent and similarly to simulated annealing (Davis, 1987). The set of potential candidates at one stage contributes to determine the set of candidates that are considered in the subsequent stage, and are selected with a probability depending on the contribution of each candidate to the objective function. The algorithm does not perform monotonic hill-climbing but can also jump to points with lower values for the objective function. In this way the algorithm can worsen the immediate values of the objective function in order to subsequently explore more promising regions of the space, without being trapped in local maxima.

We now introduce a few definitions and concepts that are useful for describing GAs in more detail.

• Individual: The single string that encodes a set of parameters;
• Population: The set of different individuals considered in the application of the algorithm;
• Fitness: The evaluation of each individual in terms of the fitness function;
• Fitness function: A transformation of the objective function which orients the evolutionary process;
• Evolution: The dynamic process that the population undergoes over time as a result of the application of genetic operators;
• Genetic operators: Operators whose repeated application allows the initial population to evolve and improve in fitness;
• Generation: The time period between different applications of genetic operators.

1.3.3 The standard genetic algorithm

There are many possible versions of genetic algorithms; in what follows we describe the one that is most often used, in terms of its various computational phases.

1. Random generation of the initial population
2. Evaluation of the fitness of the individuals
3. Selection for reproduction

4. Application of genetic operators
5. Repetition of steps 2–4

In this section we consider only a description of the various steps, while the next section describes a full example of the application of GAs.

(1) Random generation of the initial population

The process of generating the initial population consists of two steps:

- the definition of an alphabet to be used in the encoding of the parameters of the problem and the choice of a string length;
- the creation of a set of randomly generated strings, defined over this alphabet, which encode the parameters.

While actual applications use alphabets with higher cardinality, the theory of GAs relies upon the binary alphabet {0, 1}. Such a binary representation is certainly restrictive, but we will use it for a general explanation of GAs. Some examples of more general representations will be given in section 1.3.4 (c). Many examples of high-cardinality symbolic alphabets and their applications can be found in Koza (1992a).

Suppose we adopt a binary representation and want to generate a population of N individuals represented by L-bit strings (the total number of bits in the population is K = N . L). The creation of one individual belonging to the initial population takes place by randomly picking L times from the set {0, 1} with probabilities {1/2, 1/2} and concatenating the L characters to form one string. The entire population is generated by repeating this process N independent times, for a total number of K bits.

While string length may be considered as a problem-specific parameter (as it depends on the characteristics of the parameters and, in some cases, on the precision required), population size is a parameter of the GA and must be tuned empirically. It usually varies between 20 and 2000 individuals.

(2) Evaluation of the fitness of the individuals

Generally the fitness function is obtained as a transformation of the objective function of the problem (or in simple cases as the objective function itself). Each individual generated in step (1) is then evaluated using the fitness function. This operation assigns to each individual an indicator that measures how well it performs with respect to the desired target. The selection process is based on a probability which is proportional to the relative non-negative fitness of each individual. If the natural objective function given by the problem may assume negative values, the transformation must be defined in order to obtain only non-negative values. Such a mapping can be obtained by adding some positive quantity, or by scaling the objective function values. This measure of fitness is generally called raw fitness.

Normalized fitness is then computed by dividing raw fitness by the sum of the fitness values of all the individuals in the population. Note that in a framework of stochastic selection proportional to the fitness, the normalized fitness value for each individual corresponds to its probability of being selected.

(3) Selection for reproduction

Each individual has a probability of being selected given by its normalized fitness. The selection procedure is usually called roulette wheel selection, since it can be described as a wheel with slots of different sizes that are proportional to the fitness. Selected individuals are candidates for forming the new population. Note that, because of the random selection mechanism, the same individual can be selected more than once to join the new population. In the version we describe, the size of the total population remains constant, while in others it may vary.

The newly generated individuals replace the old ones to form a new population. Such a substitution may be total (generational replacement) or partial (steady state reproduction): in the former case the selection process is repeated a number of times equal to the number of individuals in the initial population, while in the latter case selections are less than the size of the population.

(4) Application of genetic operators

Crossover and mutation are the main genetic operators. They are applied on the newly formed population described at the end of step (3).

Crossover, which mimics sexual reproduction, acts on two individuals and consists of their exchanging substrings in order to generate two offspring. The two individuals that are subject to crossover are picked in various ways, either deterministically or with probabilities proportional to their fitness. The crossing point in the string is then decided by randomly choosing a position within the string.

In GA applications, crossover takes place with a certain probability, which is chosen in a range between 0.5 and 1.

Mutation simulates the errors in the transmission of genetic material from one generation to the next. This operator acts on individuals by randomly changing single characters in the string, with a probability generally set in the range $[0.001, 0.05]$. When mutation occurs, the transformation consists of changing the chosen character from 0 to 1 or vice versa.

(5) Repetition of steps 2–4

The full process is iterated for a given number of generations, resulting in an increase in the global fitness of the population. The application of fitness-based selection and of genetic operators orients the search towards regions of the space containing solutions that are more appropriate in terms of objective function. The number of generations is another parameter of the algorithm that must be tuned empirically.

1.3.4 General comments

(a) Interpretation of GA results

One of the most immediate methods for interpreting the results is to analyse various measures of fitness over time. The most significant fitness indicators, which can be compared across generations, are:

- the fitness of the individual who is the best (worst) in the last generation;
- the fitness of the best (worst) individual in each generation;
- the average fitness of the whole population.

These indicators give a first glimpse of the dynamics of the algorithm and in most cases allow one to understand whether the GA parameters need some tuning.

In order to test the efficiency and adequacy of the algorithm in solving the problem, other analyses (which are beyond the scope of this brief presentation) are usually performed, relating for example to the premature convergence of the population towards a specific region of the solution space, or to the definition of different genetic operators.

(b) Significance of results

In order to ensure the meaningfulness of the results of GAs one must take into account that GAs are a stochastic method and their performance depends on random elements. This means that a good result obtained at the end of the various generations of a single run may be due to luck rather than to achieving an effective structure, and may therefore be difficult to repeat in another context. Therefore in order to obtain more general results one needs to apply the algorithm several times, and then evaluate some measure across the various applications, as one would do in a Monte Carlo study. The measure adopted for evaluation could be the average fitness or the best fitness over the set of simulations. Of course, this is a computationally expensive method which is limited mainly by the availability of powerful computers.

(c) Length of the strings

The theory of GAs is based on fixed-length strings for encoding the parameters of the problem, but many applications require one to define variable-length strings. For example, in the case where strings represent strategies, it may well be that the length of the strings describing such strategies varies from one individual to another. The length itself may be the object of an optimization procedure comparing the effectiveness of strategies of varying complexity, rewarding simple strategies and penalizing complex ones.

(d) Non-binary strings

As stated in section 1.3.3, GA applications are often based on high-cardinality alphabets. One important application is that of ANN learning (see Chapter 5 for an example). Learning in ANNs is an optimization process over the space of the weights. Therefore the individual corresponding to a single network encodes its set of weights in a string which undergoes the evolutionary process. Weights are generally encoded in a real-value format rather than in a binary representation.

(e) ANNs structure optimization

GAs may be used not only for optimizing the set of weights of a given ANN structure, but also for optimizing the structure itself (Mühlenbein and Kindermann, 1989; Cliff, Harvey and Husbands, 1992). In this case strings encode the presence or the absence of the connection among the neurons. Weights may either assume the same fixed value, and then strings encode only the links among neurons, or they may be encoded in the strings and be the object of optimization. In both situations non-conventional architectures can emerge. This is another case where variable-length strings are necessary.

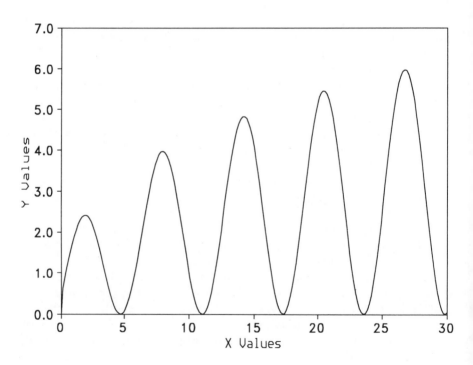

Figure 1.7 *Plot of the function* $f(X) = X^{1/3}[\sin(X) + 1]$.

1.3.5 An example of a genetic algorithm

In order to point out the details of implementation, we present a numerical example of a genetic algorithm for solving a simple function maximization problem.

We consider the function

$$f(X) = X^{1/3} [\sin(X) + 1]$$

on the domain $0 \leq X \leq 30$. From Figure 1.7 we can observe the presence of many local maxima. We now consider the different steps of the algorithm, as described in the previous section. Tables 1.1 to 1.4 describe the characteristics of the genetic population in different generations. In these tables, values are rounded to the fourth decimal place.

(1) Random generation of the initial population

The first aspect to consider is the encoding of the parameters of the problem. In our case, there is a single parameter, the variable X. We choose to encode this parameter by using a 16-bit binary string for each individual. String 0000000000000000 corresponds to X = 0 while string 1111111111111111 corresponds to X = 30. The precision of the result is proportional to the length of the string: in our example the domain is divided into $2^{16} = 65\,536$ points, corresponding to $2^{16} - 1$ intervals whose width is equal to $30/(2^{16} - 1) = 0.000\,457\,71$.

The second aspect to consider is the generation process itself. We choose a population size of 20 individuals. Each individual is built by randomly choosing 16 independent binary characters in the alphabet {0, 1} and concatenating them to a single string. The process is repeated 20 independent times to build the entire population. Table 1.1 shows the initial population. Column 1 (labelled '#') corresponds to the identification number of the individuals and column 2 (labelled 'Individuals') contains the 16-bit binary string encoding the parameter.

(2) Evaluation of the fitness of the individuals

The evaluation requires three steps:

- a conversion of the binary string to an integer decimal value in the range [0, 65 535] (Column 3);
- a scaling of this value to obtain a real value in the range [0, 30] (Column 4);
- the application of the function f(X) to this value. In our example the function does not assume negative values, and the fitness function can be defined as the function itself. Column 5, labelled 'Fitness', shows this value. This value corresponds to raw fitness.

Table 1.1 *An example of GA. Characteristics of the initial population*

#	Individuals	Decimal value	X value	Fitness	Fitness %	Σ Fitness %	Roul. wheel	Mate 1	Mate 2	Cross. point
1	1001001101001011	37707	17.2612	0.0004	0.0000	0.0000	0	0	0	0
2	0110111000111110	28222	12.9192	3.1573	0.0711	0.0711	0	0	0	0
3	1010001000111010	41530	19.0112	3.0985	0.0698	0.1410	0	0	0	0
4	1011111001101010	48746	22.3145	1.9208	0.0433	0.1842	0	0	0	0
5	1001000111100010	37346	17.0959	0.0429	0.0010	0.1852	0	0	0	0
6	1000011011110111	34551	15.8164	2.2384	0.0504	0.2356	0	0	0	0
7	1000111001011001	36441	16.6816	0.4422	0.0100	0.2456	0	0	0	0
8	0101111110010100	24468	11.2007	0.0469	0.0011	0.2467	0	0	0	0
9	1000101101101011	35691	16.3383	1.0419	0.0235	0.2701	0	0	0	0
10	0101001001100001	21089	9.6539	1.6456	0.0371	0.3072	0	0	0	0
11	0110001000101110	25134	11.5056	0.2873	0.0065	0.3137	0	0	0	0
12	0111001100000100	29444	13.4786	4.2620	0.0960	0.4097	0	0	0	0
13	1011010000000010	46082	21.0950	4.9209	0.1109	0.5206	0	0	0	0
14	0100110110001001	19849	9.0863	2.7796	0.0626	0.5832	0	0	0	0
15	0111001001111000	29304	13.4145	4.1582	0.0937	0.6769	0	0	0	0
16	0101001010101101	43357	19.8476	4.9829	0.1123	0.7892	0	0	0	0
17	0111001110011111	22991	10.5246	0.2386	0.0054	0.7945	0	0	0	0
18	1111000111100111	61927	28.3484	2.8236	0.0636	0.8582	0	0	0	0
19	1111000011111101	61693	28.2412	3.1460	0.0709	0.9291	0	0	0	0
20	1010001001100011	41571	19.0300	3.1489	0.0709	1.0000	0	0	0	0

Generation 1

Fitness Min/Avg./Max

		0.0004	2.2191	4.9829	1.0000					
				44.3830						

$(X = 19.8476)$

(3) Selection for reproduction

Two further steps are required before performing a fitness-based selection.

- A normalization of the fitness measure. The global fitness of the population is computed by summing the fitness of all individuals (at the bottom of Column 5 in Table 1.1). The normalized fitness of each individual is then computed as the ratio of its raw fitness to total fitness (Column 6).
- A summation of normalized fitness. Implementation of the roulette wheel technique for selection requires one to compute the sum of the normalized fitness over the population. This is equivalent to the cumulative percentage of the fitness (Column 7).

We choose total substitution as the generational replacement method. In our population of 20 individuals, we need to select 10 pairs of individuals for the subsequent application of genetic operators. For each selection, we select a random number from the uniform [0, 1] distribution. The individual with the cumulative fitness value directly above the generated value is selected. Table 1.2 shows how the population in generation 1 evolves and what the characteristics of the population at generation 2 are. The random numbers at the bottom of this table have been generated to select the individuals in generation 1.

For example, the first two numbers are 0.8706 and 0.6203. Searching Table 1.1 Column 7 for the fitness values directly above these numbers leads one to select individuals 19 (value 0.9291) and 15 (value 0.6769), respectively.

(4) The applying of genetic operators

The two genetic operators that we consider in this example are crossover and mutation. Once a pair of individuals is selected (this selection process is repeated 10 times), a kind of sexual reproduction is simulated by applying the crossover operator. In our example, crossover is applied with probability 1. The algorithm is the following.

- An integer random number is uniformly selected in the range [1, 15], where 15 corresponds to the length of the binary string minus 1. This value defines the crossover point, the position in the string where crossover occurs.
- The strings of the two parents are cut at a position corresponding to the crossover point.
- Two offspring are generated by interchanging the two substrings to the right of the crossover point (Figure 1.8 (a)).

Mutation is then applied with probability equal to 0.05 (1 out of 20 bits). The algorithm is the following.

Table 1.2 *An example of GA. Characteristics of the population at generation 2*

#	Individuals	Decimal value	X value	Fitness	Fitness %	Σ Fitness %	Roul. wheel	Mate 1	Mate 2	Cross. point
1	1111000011011000	61656	28.2243	3.1969	0.0465	0.0465	0	19	15	9
2	1111001001111101	62077	28.4170	2.6176	0.0381	0.0846	0	19	15	9
3	1011111001101011	48747	22.3149	1.9196	0.0279	0.1126	1	4	6	15
4	1001011011110110	38646	17.6910	0.2183	0.0032	0.1157	2	4	6	15
5	0111011100000100	30468	13.9474	4.7710	0.0694	0.1852	0	12	13	15
6	1011010000000010	46082	21.0950	4.9209	0.0716	0.2568	1	12	13	15
7	1011010000100111	46119	21.1119	4.8926	0.0712	0.3280	0	13	18	10
8	1101000111000010	53698	24.5814	1.3844	0.0201	0.3481	0	13	18	10
9	1011111001100010	48738	22.3108	1.9305	0.0281	0.3762	0	4	13	11
10	1011010000001010	46090	21.0986	4.9148	0.0715	0.4478	0	4	13	11
11	1010001001100010	41570	19.0295	3.1477	0.0458	0.4936	0	20	13	12
12	1011010000000011	46083	21.0954	4.9201	0.0716	0.5652	3	20	13	12
13	0111001100000110	29446	13.4795	4.2634	0.0620	0.6272	4	12	3	14
14	1010000000111000	41016	18.7759	2.4623	0.0358	0.6631	0	12	3	14
15	1111000111000011	61891	28.3319	2.8732	0.0418	0.7049	1	18	20	12
16	1010001001100111	41575	19.0318	3.1538	0.0459	0.7508	2	18	20	12
17	1011101101011101	47965	21.9570	2.8959	0.0421	0.7929	0	20	16	9
18	1010100101100011	43363	19.8503	4.9871	0.0726	0.8655	2	20	16	9
19	0111001101011101	29533	13.5193	4.3241	0.0629	0.9284	1	12	16	7
20	1010100100000100	43268	19.8068	4.9178	0.0716	1.0000	3	12	16	7
				68.7121	1.0000					

Generation 2   Cross 10   Mutat. 10

Random numbers

0.8706	0.6203	0.1747	0.1858	0.3420	0.4156	0.4759	0.8121	0.1415	0.4921
0.9443	0.4522	0.3576	0.0847	0.8011	0.9427	0.9691	0.7563	0.4083	0.6980

Fitness Min/Avg./Max   0.2183   3.4356   4.9871   (X = 19.8503)

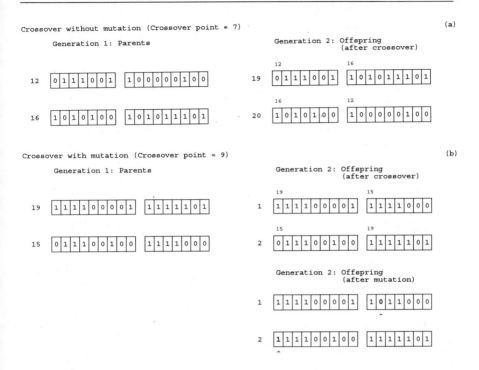

Figure 1.8 *Reproduction with crossover and mutation.*

- For each bit of the two offspring, a random number is uniformly generated in the range [0, 1].
- If this number is lower than 0.05, the value of the bit is inverted (0 becomes 1 and 1 becomes 0); otherwise the bit value does not change.

An example of crossover and mutation is shown in Figure 1.8(b). The cases in Figure 1.8 correspond to two actual transitions from generation 1 to generation 2 in the example of Table 1.1: Case (a) corresponds to the birth of new individuals 19 and 20 (whose parents were 12 and 16 of the first generation) while Case (b) relates to 1 and 2 (born from 19 and 15).

While the first seven columns of Table 1.2 refer to the characteristics of the population in generation 2, the last four columns refer to the transition from generation 1 to generation 2. Their meaning is the following.

Column 8 (Roul. wheel): number of times an individual of the previous generation has been selected. For example, the number 3 in the last row of this column states that individual 20 of generation 1

Table 1.3 An example of GA. Characteristics of the population at generation 20

#	Individuals	Decimal value	X value	Fitness	Fitness %	Σ Fitness %	Roul. wheel	Mate 1	Mate 2	Cross. point
1	1010000100000101	41221	18.8698	2.7161	0.0333	0.0333	1	16	4	3
2	1110110101110110	60790	27.8279	4.3388	0.0532	0.0865	0	16	4	3
3	1000000100010000	33040	15.1247	3.8350	0.0470	0.1335	0	1	15	15
4	1010011110010000	42896	19.6365	4.6086	0.0565	0.1900	3	1	15	15
5	1010000111110001	41457	18.9778	3.0085	0.0369	0.2269	0	14	8	7
6	1011011000010000	46608	21.3358	4.4639	0.0547	0.2817	1	14	8	7
7	1010010011110100	42228	19.3307	3.9259	0.0481	0.3298	0	14	6	2
8	1100000000010000	49168	22.5077	1.4291	0.0175	0.3473	2	14	6	2
9	1010100100010100	43284	19.8141	4.9298	0.0605	0.4078	2	16	17	4
10	1011110101110100	48500	22.2019	2.2227	0.0273	0.4350	0	16	17	4
11	1010110000100101	44069	20.1735	5.3620	0.0658	0.5008	0	19	18	6
12	1110000110110000	57776	26.4482	5.8622	0.0719	0.5727	0	19	18	6
13	1111011111001100	61388	28.1016	3.5627	0.0437	0.6164	1	4	13	2
14	1010010100010000	42256	19.3436	3.9572	0.0485	0.6649	2	4	13	2
15	1011010100010001	46353	21.2190	4.6999	0.0576	0.7225	1	9	4	6
16	1110001111100101	58341	26.7068	5.9782	0.0733	0.7958	3	9	4	6
17	1011011111100101	47077	21.5505	3.9698	0.0487	0.8445	2	16	9	3
18	1010100101110110	43382	19.8590	5.0005	0.0613	0.9058	1	16	9	3
19	0011011110010100	14228	6.5132	2.2932	0.0281	0.9339	1	8	17	9
20	1010110001110001	44145	20.2083	5.3866	0.0661	1.0000	0	8	17	9
Generation 20				81.5506	1.0000	Cross 10 Mutat. 16				
Random numbers	0.7424	0.2185 0.0271	0.6877	0.6305	0.3611 0.6292	0.3215	0.7254	0.7743	
	0.9508	0.8249 0.1812	0.5948	0.4217	0.2077 0.7581	0.4270	0.3655	0.7907	
Fitness Min/Avg./Max		1.4291	4.0775	5.9782	(X = 26.7068)				

Table 1.4 An example of GA. Characteristics of the population at Generation 35

#	Individuals	Decimal value	X value	Fitness	Fitness %	Σ Fitness %	Roul. wheel	Mate 1	Mate 2	Cross. point
1	1111010001010111	62551	28.6340	1.9825	0.0236	0.0236	0	8	3	13
2	1110100110010100	59796	27.3729	5.3773	0.0641	0.0878	0	8	3	13
3	0110001001010011	25171	11.5225	0.3064	0.0037	0.0915	2	10	7	5
4	1110000100010010	57618	26.3758	5.7950	0.0691	0.1606	1	10	7	5
5	1110011101110000	59248	27.1220	5.7498	0.0686	0.2292	2	20	12	11
6	1000101100111011	35643	16.3163	1.0868	0.0130	0.2421	1	20	12	11
7	1110010101010010	58706	26.8739	5.9473	0.0709	0.3131	2	7	14	1
8	1100000100100110	49734	22.7668	0.8498	0.0101	0.3232	1	7	14	1
9	1110010001010110	58454	26.7585	5.9775	0.0713	0.3945	0	17	14	9
10	1110000001010111	57431	26.2902	5.6966	0.0680	0.4625	1	17	14	9
11	1011010101000010	46402	21.2415	4.6566	0.0555	0.5180	0	4	19	4
12	1110111101101000	61288	28.0558	3.6972	0.0441	0.5621	1	4	19	4
13	1110010101010111	58711	26.8762	5.9463	0.0709	0.6331	0	19	17	11
14	1000100010011010	50250	23.0030	0.4328	0.0052	0.6382	2	19	17	11
15	1110100010010100	59540	27.2557	5.5717	0.0665	0.7047	1	3	15	15
16	1110010111011001	58841	26.9357	5.9148	0.0706	0.7753	0	3	15	15
17	1110011011110110	59126	27.0661	5.8097	0.0693	0.8446	3	6	5	15
18	1100000001010001	49233	22.5374	1.3572	0.0162	0.8607	0	6	5	15
19	1110010000010000	58384	26.7265	5.9789	0.0713	0.9321	2	17	5	14
20	1110000001010011	57427	26.2884	5.6943	0.0679	1.0000	1	17	5	14
				83.8285	1.0000					

Generation 35   Cross   Mutat. 19

Random numbers	0.4034	0.1266 0.4693	0.3538	0.9703	0.5610 0.3676	0.6770	0.7796 0.6590
	0.1852	0.8830 0.8766	0.7845	0.1628	0.7494 0.3224	0.2542	0.8069 0.2572

Fitness Min/Avg./Max   0.3064   4.1914   5.9789   (X = 26.7265) has been randomly selected three times in the transition from generation 1 to generation 2.

Columns 9 and 10 (Mate 1, Mate 2): The identification numbers of the parents. Individuals 1 and 2 in generation 2 are from individuals 19 and 15 in generation 1.

Column 11 (Cross. Point): The crossover point refers to the parental strings. Individuals 19 and 15 in generation 1 cross at position 9.

The number of times pair-wise crossover and mutation are performed in the transition process is shown in the same row as the total fitness. Three fitness values are shown at the bottom of Table 1.2: the minimum (fitness of the worst individual), maximum with the corresponding X value and average fitness of the generation.

(5) Repetition of steps 2–4

Steps 2 to 4 are repeated for 50 generations. In generation 35 the genetic algorithm finds the solution. Tables 1.3 and 1.4 show the characteristics of the population during generation 20 and at the end of the evolution (generation 35), respectively.

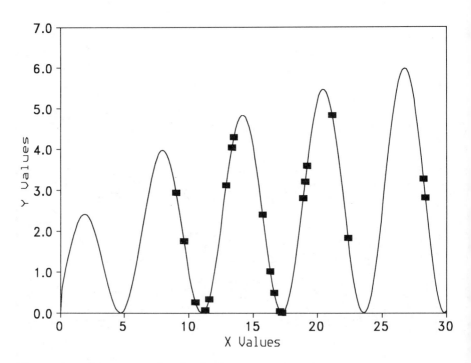

Figure 1.9 *Dispersion of individuals at generation 1.*

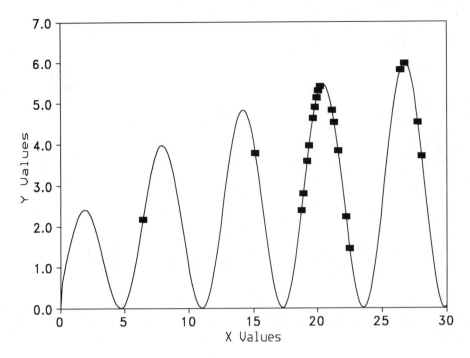

Figure 1.10 *Dispersion of individuals at generation 20.*

In order to describe the genetic evolution graphically, we plot the position of the individuals with respect to the function at generation 1, 20 and 35 in Figures 1.9 to 1.11.

These three figures deserve some comment.

- While not perfectly uniform, there is a wide dispersion of the randomly generated individuals in generation 1 (Figure 1.9). Even if there is no individual in the range [0, 9], mutation subsequently creates new individuals belonging to this interval (Figure 1.10).
- By generation 20, fitness-oriented exploration of the solution space has already oriented the search towards a local maximum (Figure 1.10).
- The genetic selective pressure allows one to escape from this local maximum and to discover and reach the global maximum, where a large concentration of individuals can be observed.
- By building 16-bit strings, we consider a solution space made of 65 535 points. In our example only 700 points (20 individuals times 35 generations) have been explored before finding the solution. Even if we want to consider the result over 10 experiments, this is equivalent to considering only about 10% of the total number of points.

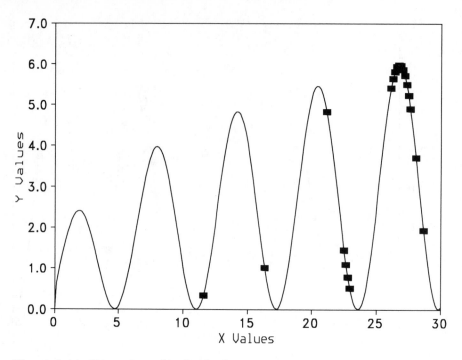

Figure 1.11 *Dispersion of individuals at generation 35.*

Finally, the dynamics of fitness over the 50 generations of the experiment are shown in Figure 1.12. The fitness of the best and the worst individual of each generation and the average fitness of the population are plotted. While the maximum fitness corresponds to the path towards the optimal solution, the increasing trend present in the average fitness reflects the concentration of the individuals near the global maximum. On the other hand, the irregular behaviour of the minimum fitness depends on the characteristics of the fitness landscape, specifically on the presence of abrupt changes in the function due to the presence of maxima and minima for neighbouring X-values.

1.3.6 Genetic algorithms for ANN learning

(a) GAs as optimization tools

As we have shown in the previous sections, genetic algorithms are an optimization tool that explicitly searches for the maximum, or the minimum, of a function over a certain domain. With respect to other optimization methods such as gradient descent, which acts as a local search mechanism, GAs perform a global search in the sense that they explore the space of

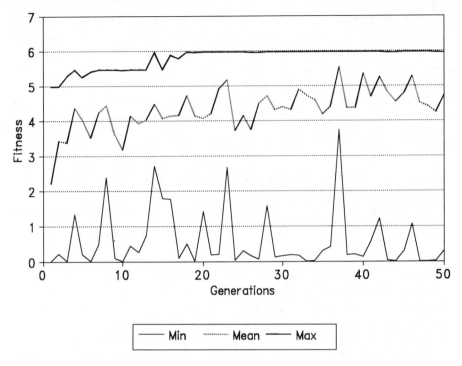

Figure 1.12 *Minimum, average and maximum fitness over 50 generations.*

solutions in a parallel way and can jump from one region of the space to another in the search for the optimal solution.

We elaborate on this point by briefly comparing GA with a local search technique. Gradient descent starts from a more or less arbitrary initial condition and then locally searches around this point for directions which show an increase in the function to be maximized. During this search, it is likely that the algorithm stops at some local maximum, around which the function decreases. GAs instead start from a set of initial conditions, and are therefore simultaneously exploring various regions. Moreover, the application of genetic operators may drive the algorithms towards regions that are not in the vicinity of the initial ones. These features ensure that GAs may easily escape from local maxima.

(b) GAs and ANNs

The relationship between GAs and learning proceeds from the similarities between learning and optimization, in the sense that learning is in general a particular type of optimization. When agents are learning the values of some parameters in order to reach some targets, they are optimizing some function that implicitly or explicitly relates the parameters to the targets. It therefore follows that GAs are also very effective learning techniques, for their ability to direct the search towards global rather than local extrema.

This observation points to the possibility of using GAs as learning tools for ANNs. BP is in fact a local technique, similar in spirit to gradient descent, and can therefore be superseded by a global technique. Of course the computational requirements of the two algorithms are different, as in general GAs require heavier computations than BP.

While GAs may be useful as learning tools for ANNs with a well-defined target because of their global nature, GAs actually may be the only feasible learning tool in those situations where the targets are not directly defined with respect to the output of the ANN in each time period. In these circumstances it is often possible to define a target that can be verified after the ANN has taken a number of actions, that is, after a few periods. In this case, the fitness definition is based on such a target.

In what follows we describe the representation of ANNs in terms of GAs, considering both absent and present targets.

(c) Representation of ANNs in terms of GAs

The binary representation used for encoding the parameters of the problem is typical of GA theory (Holland, 1992); in practical applications it is often necessary to use more sophisticated representations. In those cases the strings that represent the individuals are composed of symbols drawn from alphabets with higher cardinality. For example, if one wants to encode a strategy composed of four feasible actions, then possible characters may be 0, 1 , 2 and 3.

In the case of ANNs the problem is the codification of the weights of the network as real numbers, over which the optimization process is performed. It would certainly be possible in this case to use a binary representation of the real numbers, but it is more practical to consider each weight as a single position in the string. This is possible, provided that one defines the various genetic operators (real-valued mutation and crossover) in an appropriate and compatible way. The resulting string is obtained by:

- defining an order on the elements of the two weights matrices (from input to hidden and from hidden to output);
- concatenating the real representation of such weights.

For example, consider the simple network of Figure 1.3. The two matrices A and B defined as

$$
\underset{(4,3)}{A} = \begin{bmatrix} w_{51} & w_{61} & w_{71} \\ w_{52} & w_{62} & w_{72} \\ w_{53} & w_{63} & w_{73} \\ w_{54} & w_{64} & w_{74} \end{bmatrix} \qquad \underset{(3,2)}{B} = \begin{bmatrix} w_{85} & w_{95} \\ w_{86} & w_{96} \\ w_{87} & w_{97} \end{bmatrix}
$$

can be encoded in the following way:

Matrix (A)

w_{51}	w_{61}	w_{71}	w_{52}	w_{62}	w_{72}	w_{53}	w_{63}	w_{73}	w_{54}	w_{64}	w_{74}

Matrix (B)

w_{85}	w_{95}	w_{86}	w_{96}	w_{87}	w_{97}

(d) Genetic operators for ANNs

GAs can be applied to strings encoding ANNs' weights (or real numbers in general) provided that adequate genetic operators are defined. We now describe one of the possible ways to define these operators.

Real crossover may have two variants. The first is similar to binary crossover, in the sense that each real number is considered as a single position, and crossover can occur only between numbers and not inside the representation of the number itself. This is equivalent to considering an exchange of substrings of real numbers.

The second variant, which is less disruptive, preserves the structure of the two matrices. The full string is considered as two concatenated substrings, one for each matrix, and the crossover point is defined independently for each substring. This two-point crossover exchanges the strings between the two crossover points.

Real mutation is implemented by changing a single value by an amount drawn from a uniform random distribution over a given range.

(e) Definition of fitness

The definition of fitness varies according to whether targets are or are not available during learning.

In the first case one can still use BP, but GAs may be used due to their superior ability to locate a global, rather than a local, minimum in the error function. Then GAs are applied to the population of networks in each time period and the fitness is calculated immediately based on the squared error.

In the second case BP cannot be used, and it is replaced with a GA. The fitness is defined in terms of a measure which depends on the general structure of the problem. For example, in the case of a financial trader, a plausible measure of fitness is given by the value of the wealth that is accumulated over a certain period as a result of the application of certain possible strategies. More generally, the fitness is proportional to an indicator that defines the profitability of the strategy with respect to competitors. A full example is described in Chapter 5.

In the literature this case is called unsupervised learning, while the term supervised learning is used to denote situations in which targets are available. Therefore in general one can say that BP is supervised learning, while GAs are unsupervised learning. The latter term is a bit unfortunate, however, as it may give the idea that GAs learn some internal mapping with no intervention whatsoever by the researcher. This in fact is not true; it is more correct to say that when targets are missing, it is possible to use

GAs by defining a new delayed target that applies not to every period, but every once in a while. This means that the criterion is still given externally, as the architecture tries to adapt to that external target. The fact that the target is used every once in a while, however, confers more flexibility on this learning procedure. Therefore a more proper notation would define the application of GAs to ANNs as quasi-unsupervised learning, and limit the use of the term unsupervised learning to truly self-organizing networks (Kohonen, 1984).

In the next section we briefly present classifier systems, as an alternative to ANNs for modelling adaptive agents, and the reinforcement learning technique which can be used instead of the techniques that have been described in the previous sections of this chapter.

1.4 Other learning devices

1.4.1 Classifier systems

Classifier systems originate from the work of Holland and Reitman (1978). They belong to the Genetics-Based Machine Learning framework, as their dynamics are influenced by the application of genetic operators.

According to Goldberg (1989) 'A classifier system is a machine learning system that learns syntactically simple string rules (called classifiers) to guide its performance in an arbitrary environment.'

Although the definition does not clarify this point, classifier systems exhibit important differences with respect to rule-based systems, notably the parallel activation of rules, the learning of the strength of each rule endogenously and the autonomous creation of new rules through genetic algorithms.

Classifier systems, in a simplified version of their standard formulation, consist of several components:

1. A set of fixed-length strings (classifiers) which represent the rules. A classifier is made up of two concatenated substrings: a condition, whose representation is based on the alphabet {0, 1, #}, and an action based on {0, 1}. For example, the string 0 1 # # : 0 0 0 1 represents a classifier where 0 1 # # encodes the condition and 0 0 0 1 encodes the action. Each value in a given position assumes a specific problem-dependent meaning, while the character # is the *don't care* symbol and becomes relevant during the matching phase. Each classifier has an associated strength which is a sort of fitness of the rule and evolves over time (see later on). The initial population of classifiers may be generated randomly.

2. A system of detectors for receiving messages from the environment and performing the matching phase. Classifiers are activated if their condition matches the incoming message, on a character by character

basis, unless a *don't care* symbol is present, in which case any character in the message is a good match.

3.   An auction system for choosing a classifier to perform an action among the activated classifiers. To participate in the auction, each classifier makes a bid proportional to its strength. The selection mechanism gives preference to the fittest rule.

4.   An accounting system to update the strength of the different rules on the basis of the reward they receive after making an action. The winner of the auction posts its message and pays the amount of the bid. This amount is divided among the classifiers which contributed to its activation in the previous step. This recursive procedure is called the bucket brigade algorithm.

5.   A system of genetic algorithms for creating new rules and eliminating old ones. A GA is activated in order to introduce new operations such as specialization (transformation of general rules into more specific ones), diversification (introduction of more heterogeneity in the rule set), creation (introduction of new rules into the system when an incoming message does not match any rule) and generalization (birth of offspring from parents with high fitness through crossover).

Some attempts have been made to outline the similarities between classifier systems and neural networks (Davis, 1989; Belew and Gherrity, 1989). But classifier systems present a major drawback that limits their use in economic applications: they process discrete (mostly binary) rather than continuous entities while economic and financial models are mainly based on continuous real-valued data. Economic applications are presented by Marimon *et al.* (1990) and Nottola *et al.* (1992).

1.4.2 Reinforcement learning

While classifier systems are adaptive devices which can replace ANNs in some applications, reinforcement learning techniques may be used by themselves, or coupled to such different devices as rule-based systems, genetic algorithms and ANNs. Reinforcement learning is a form of supervised learning where the adaptive agent receives feedback from the environment which directly influences learning. This feedback generally consists of a binary reinforcement signal informing the agent that its action was right or wrong. While supervised learning is commonly likened to learning with a teacher, reinforcement learning is likened to learning with a critic, because the agent receives only an evaluation of the goodness of its action with no information about what the correct action should be.

When used jointly with ANNs, the network receives a global reward–punishment signal depending on its actions and weights are changed so as to learn an input–output mapping, called policy, which maximizes the probability of receiving a reward and minimizes that of receiving a punishment. The most rewarding actions are discovered through a trial and error search process.

A full presentation of the numerous implementations of reinforcement learning is beyond the scope of this book. We will only briefly describe some of the main techniques, and present an application in Chapter 7. Reinforcement learning is a very general framework, where the specific techniques may differ depending on the complexity of the task to be solved. The complexity is determined by the nature of the environment (deterministic or stochastic) and the timing of reward (immediate or delayed). We will present the Policy-only, Adaptive Heuristic Critic, Q-learning, Dyna and Evolutionary Reinforcement Learning architectures.

The Policy-only architecture is the simplest one. It consists of only two elements: a policy, that is, a mapping from a state to an action, and a mechanism for adjusting it. The policy can be implemented in different ways. When a neural network is used, learning takes place in a manner which accounts for the fact that targets are not directly available. Generally in this case a mechanism is implemented that updates the probability of choosing an action on the basis of the action's reward.

These simple mechanisms consider only immediate rewards, and are not effective in dealing with deferred rewards.

The Adaptive Heuristic Critic (AHC) architecture (Sutton, 1984; Barto *et al.*, 1990) takes this problem into account. The agent tries to forecast, for example with a neural network, a measure of return instead of the immediate reward value. The return for state x is defined as the expected value of the discounted value of all future rewards:

$$\text{return } (x) = E \left(\sum_{t=0}^{\infty} \gamma^t \, r_{t+1} \middle| x_0 = x \right)$$

where r_t is the reward at time t and γ is the discount rate ($0 \leqslant \gamma \leqslant 1$).

The forecast is usually based on the Temporal Difference (TD) method (Sutton, 1988) which is used in situations with delayed rewards. These situations give rise to the temporal credit assignment problem, that is, the problem of apportionment of credit and blame to each action of the sequence. TD algorithms base the apportionment of credit on the difference between temporally successive predictions. Note that a similar problem exists in classifier systems and is solved with the bucket brigade algorithm (see section 1.4.1).

The algorithm, called TD(λ), proposed by Sutton (1988) for updating the weights of the ANN-based forecaster is as follows:

$$\Delta w_t = \alpha (P_{t+1} - P_t) \sum_{k=1}^{t} \lambda^{t-k} \nabla_w P_k$$

where α is the learning rate, P_t is the output of the network at time t, w is the vector of the connection weights, $\nabla_w P_k$ is the gradient of the network output with respect to weights and λ is the discount rate ($0 \leqslant \lambda \leqslant 1$).

The updating of weights is based on errors. While conventional errors are the difference between predicted and actual values, TD errors are the difference between temporally successive predictions. This algorithm uses both the TD method for computing the errors between predictions and the BP method for changing weights in order to minimize these errors.

Q-learning (Watkins, 1989) is a further extension of the previous schemes. The forecasted return depends not only on the state but also on the action:

$$\text{return } (x, a) = E \left(\sum_{t=0}^{\infty} \gamma^t \, r_{t+1} \Big| \, x_0 = x, \, a_0 = a \right)$$

The different steps of Q-learning are:

- Observation of the current state
- Selection of an action
- Action
- Reception of immediate reward
- Learning
- Adjustment of the expected discounted reward.

The Dyna architecture (Sutton, 1990) extends traditional architectures of reinforcement learning by including an internal world model. The world model is trained to simulate the world on the basis of examples of interactions between the agent and the world. The world model is then used to test different hypotheses about the mapping (state, action → reward) that represents the reactions of the world.

Evolutionary Reinforcement Learning (ERL) (Ackley and Littman, 1991) combines genetic evolution with neural network learning to implement a form of learning based on natural selection within a population of individuals. Each individual is made up of two networks:

- an action network that maps from sensory input to behaviour;
- an evaluation network that maps from sensory input to a measure of the profitability of the situation.

The weights of the latter are inherited from parents and do not change during the lifetime of the individuals. The weights of the former change over time and are updated by a reinforcement algorithm that rewards actions leading to an increase in profitability and punishes those that lead to a decrease.

The sets of weights of the two networks are encoded in a string representing the genetic code of individuals. This approach allows one to combine adaptation due to learning and adaptation due to natural selection in a single model of adaptive agents, and to study their relative importance and reciprocal influence.

ANNs, GAs, classifier systems and reinforcement learning are the building blocks of artificial economic and financial modelling, especially when they are used in an integrated framework. Applications of some of these tools and techniques will be presented in the next chapters.

2
Economic models and decision-making

Outline of the chapter

The purpose of this chapter is to introduce the reader to some important concepts of economic analysis that represent a good starting place for exploring possible applications of artificial neural networks to economics and finance. The purpose of keeping the level of the exposition simple and self-contained is due to:

- the purpose of the chapter, which serves as one of the two intro-ductory chapters preparing the ground for a unified treatment of ANNs for economic and financial modelling;
- the necessity to maintain the description at reasonable levels of complexity, given the fact that the intended audience of the book is composed both of economists interested in ANNs and non-economists, for example researchers in computer science or engineering, who are looking for new fields of application for their models.

We want to emphasize that we are not trying to give a general survey of economic methods, but making a selective choice of some issues which are relevant for the material presented in the following chapters. As the main features of the models that we present in the book are learning and interaction among agents, in this chapter we emphasize the assumptions which are made in standard economic models about these two phenomena. In order to do this, we start in section 2.1 of this chapter with an overly simplified characterization of the description of 'the economic agent', both in a static and in a dynamic context, and then move on to describe the logic of how such agents interact. The same description is then extended in section 2.2 to situations of uncertainty, and the assumption of rational expectations is then considered in detail. The main messages obtained from these two sections is that there are strong restrictions on the behaviour of economic agents, computational abilities and structural knowledge. We believe that by weakening these restrictions it would be possible to learn much about real economies. The last two sections therefore analyse learning, both at the individual and at the organizational level, and discuss economies as complex systems, pointing out possible roles for artificial neural networks in economic models.

2.1 Some relevant features of neoclassical economic models

2.1.1 Introduction

It is obviously difficult to say exactly which models are to be considered as 'neoclassical'; the purpose of this section is simply to point out the existence of a large community of researchers using analytical models based on the following characteristics.

- The description of the economic system is based on a mathematical modelling of the individual agents in terms of maximization problems subject to various constraints. For example, the behaviour of consumers depends on preferences which are stable and independent of the environment, while the choices of firms are derived from maximization of profits.
- In large economies the interactions among agents take place by means of a set of demand and supply functions, with prices being considered as signals which make all the actions compatible. In small economies or in interpersonal interaction, agents may behave in a strategic way.
- The models make enough simplifying assumptions to allow the researcher to derive strong implications in terms of observable variables, which can then be tested by means of statistical techniques.

The next sections give an oversimplified but hopefully faithful description of some basic structures.

2.1.2 A prototype neoclassical model

According to Varian (1992), one of the most well-known textbooks in Economics, 'Microeconomics is concerned with the behaviour of individual economic units and their interactions. The two types of economic units typically considered are firms and consumers. In pursuing the study of economic units and their interactions we will utilize two major analytic techniques. The first technique involves the analysis of optimization. We will model the behaviour of economic units as optimizing behaviour. In doing this we need to specify the objectives of the unit and the constraints which it faces.' This definition captures the spirit and the methods of the mainstream research programme in Economics, with its interest in building models of economic systems that are explicitly based on optimizing the behaviours of the agents. To understand the structure of this approach, and to discuss later on some of its limitations, it is useful to start with a simplified description.

The simplest case is perhaps that of agents making decisions under certainty, that is, with complete knowledge of the environment surrounding them, of their possibilities for action and of the consequences of their actions. In this case agent i chooses the level of an instrument x, given some externally set vector of variables, z, in order to maximize the consequences of his or her actions. The consequences are described by a vector y, and the evaluation takes place by means of a function f(y, x, z). Formally:

$$\max_{x} f(y, x, z)$$

subject to:

$$y = g(x, z)$$

where g is the function connecting the external variables and the instrument with the consequences for the agent. In the case of a consumer, for example, f is a so-called utility function U (whose existence can be shown on the basis of 'reasonable' assumptions about preferences) defined over the consumption of the various goods, mapping the choices of consumption of the goods into personal satisfaction, and z is a vector composed of the prices of the goods and the income that can be spent on consumption. If there are two goods y_1 and y_2, with exogenous market prices p_1 and p_2, and if W is available income, the problem is:

$$\max U(y_1, y_2)$$

$$p_1 y_1 + p_2 y_2 = W$$

Going back to the more general formulation, one can rewrite the problem compactly by substituting the constraints into the objective function:

$$\max_{x} f(g(x, z), x, z)$$

whose first order condition is:

$$\frac{\partial f}{\partial g} \frac{\partial g}{\partial x} + \frac{\partial f}{\partial x} = 0$$

Such an equation describes the necessary (and sufficient, with proper concavity assumptions) conditions for the optimal choice of the agent. In the case of a consumer the equation allows derivation of a demand function relating the quantity demanded of the various goods to prices and income. In the case of the firm choosing the levels of factors of production that maximize profits, one finds demand as a function of the amount of production and the various prices, given the technology.

2.1.3 The intertemporal extension

One possible criticism of the model concerns its completely static nature; everything takes place simultaneously, and it is not possible to distinguish between today and tomorrow. This happens very rarely in real life. A static framework is good at describing in some cases the relation between consumption choices and the satisfaction derived from such a choice; think for example of the case of a consumer buying food at a store but already knowing the amount of pleasure that may be derived from the various types of food when eating it. In other (most) cases, however, the relation between actions and consequences takes place through time. The decision about accumulation of human capital on the part of a young person has consequences that will be clear after many years; the investment of a firm in new equipment will reveal its effectiveness when the products are sold on the market; the purchase of a financial asset like a share in a company has an uncertain payoff, and so on. In these cases a better description of the problem is the following:

$$\max_{x_0} f(x_0, y_1)$$

$$y_1 = g(x_0, z_0, z_1)$$

where the subscript indicates the time at which the event takes place. In such a framework there is an immediate (time 0) choice, call it x_0, and a consequence taking place at time 1, call it y_1, which depends on x_0 and on the values taken by exogenous variables z in both time periods. More complicated structures based on multi-period maximization are also important; the horizon may even be infinite, especially when the problems concern the whole society, for which it is difficult to establish a final date.

Problems with a finite horizon are based on solutions by backward induction: the problem is first solved for the last period, let us say period T, taking all the previous choices as given and conditioning on the levels of the stocks that are assumed to be inherited from the past. Given the optimal solution as a function of the initial stocks, one can then go to the period T-1, which can again be interpreted as a one-period maximization, taking as given the initial stocks, those left as a bequest of period T-2, but including in the objective function of the problem the evaluation of the values of the stocks that will be transmitted to time T. Such an evaluation is possible because of the computations that have already been performed for time T. By proceeding backward, one can finally get to period 1, and make a maximizing decision implicitly taking into account all the consequences for the rest of the period. We will come back to this procedure when discussing computational costs.

2.1.4 The general equilibrium of an economic system

This section has the purpose of showing how the previously described analytical machine can be used for interpreting aggregate phenomena, that is, the behaviour of the economic system as a whole. This means that, contrary to the examples of the previous section, where market variables were taken as given for the individual, the model can also explain the formation of prices and incomes on the basis of a few exogenous variables like endowments and preferences. The problem of determining the general equilibrium of an economic system has always interested economists, at least since the analysis of Smith (1776), who tried to show that the invisible hand of the market could coordinate, to the advantage of society, the activities of many different agents pursuing their own self-interest and not any collective purpose. Since the work of Walras (1954), the intuition that a competitive system would form prices that bring all the markets to equilibrium has been the subject of extensive research, pointing out various aspects of the optimality and efficiency of economies in general equilibrium.

Even though it is certainly more interesting to study models of general equilibrium with production on the part of firms, it is easier to report the main points of this approach using a model with pure exchange, where it is assumed that there are single individuals with an exogenous endowment of various goods. In this case there are C consumers and G goods in an economic system. The i-th consumer is endowed with certain quantities of the various goods, denoted by a vector $E_i = (w_{i1}, w_{i2}, \ldots, w_{iG})$. The sum of the endowments of all the consumers must be equal to the total endowment of the economy, $E_g = w_{1g} + w_{2g} + \ldots + w_{cg}$, for $g = 1, 2, \ldots, G$, where the summation is taken across consumers for each good. Given this exogenous endowment and the preferences of the various consumers, it will in general be useful to organize a process of exchange of goods across consumers to increase the utility of the agents. Given the total endowment of the economy, the initial distribution will allow for welfare-improving subsequent trades. The interesting question from the point of view of the general equilibrium of the economy is: does there exist a set of prices that simultaneously bring demand (derived from utility maximization of the various agents) and supply (equal to the exogenous endowments) into equilibrium?

Given sufficient regularity conditions on the utility functions (mainly that they give rise to continuous demand functions), it has been shown that such a vector of equilibrium prices does indeed exist. A Walrasian equilibrium is defined as a vector of prices and demands such that:

$$x_1(p, p\, E_1) + x_2(p, p\, E_2) + \ldots + x_G(p, p\, E_G) = E_1 + E_2 + \ldots + E_G$$

where $x_i(p, p\, E_i)$ is a demand function for the vector of goods on the part of the i-th agent that depends on the vector of all the prices and on the value of his or her endowment. The same theory may allow for production on the part of firms; in this case the exogenous endowments would be explained as the result of maximizing actions on the part of firms acting in competitive markets.

Among the various advantages of competitive general equilibrium pointed out by the literature, the one that is most relevant to the discussion here is related to efficiency in processing information: a system in general equilibrium forms prices that signal to producers and consumers the relative scarcity of the various goods. The amount of information processing that has to be performed by each single agent is minimized, as the only thing that the agent must do is to compute his or her optimal decisions as a function of prices.

The counterpart to this, however, is that the formation of prices must use a large amount of information. Such a formation is not explained in the competitive version of the model: since each agent takes prices as given, it is assumed that there is an external entity (the so-called auctioneer) determining the prices by means of various rounds of interactions with the agents. The auctioneer proposes a set of prices, which are then revised on the basis of the excess demand that may exist for some of the markets and the products. A different set of prices is proposed, until all the excess demands are equal to 0. The process converges to an equilibrium if the various traders are not allowed to make exchanges at false prices, that is, at prices that are not equal to equilibrium prices. Clearly this is an unsatisfactory paradigm that mainly hides the absence of clear proposals for a model of general equilibrium with price-making on the part of some agents.

What is relevant here, however, is that the competitive general equilibrium approach shows the informational role of prices without considering explicitly the mechanism which can carry out such an important job as collection of information. The fiction of the auctioneer allows many important issues connected with computational abilities and the information requirements on the part of the single agents.

The general equilibrium framework has been studied and made rigorous over the years by the work of many of the best talents of the economic profession, especially Debreu (1959) and Arrow and Hahn (1971), which laid the general model on more solid analytical grounds and extended the framework to incorporate uncertainty and dynamics. Even these extensions, however, contain some particularly unrealistic assumptions. For example, even when the model is intertemporal, it can be shown that under certain circumstances agents do all the trading at the beginning of the history of the economy, without any need for recontracting, and this makes the theory really static in spirit. This again goes back to the issue of computational and transaction costs, as pointed out by Hahn (1973), who notes that 'We thus find it reasonable to require of our equilibrium notion that it should reflect the sequential character of actual economies. But I believe that we require more than that: we want it to be sequential in an essential way. By this I mean that it should not be possible without change in content to reformulate the notion non-sequentially. This in turn requires that information processes and costs, transactions and transaction costs and also expectations and uncertainty be explicitly and essentially included in the equilibrium notion. That is what the Arrow–Debreu construction does not do.'

2.2 Uncertainty and rational expectations

The previous discussion assumed away any source of uncertainty: agents knew exactly the connection between actions and their consequences. This is extremely unrealistic in a number of cases, especially in intertemporal problems or in problems of allocation of wealth across risky financial assets. This section extends the analysis to incorporate uncertainty, first by des-cribing the microeconomic model of individual behaviour, and next by considering the hypothesis of rational expectations, the framework which is commonly used to analyse the dynamic equilibrium of economic systems subject to uncertainty.

2.2.1 The model under uncertainty

Often the relation between choices and consequences has to be described in stochastic terms; this is especially true for problems that are explicitly intertemporal in nature, in which it is difficult to know exactly the outcome of certain actions. For example, the choice of accumulation of human capital has highly uncertain returns; investing in education may or may not be useful after five or ten years, as one may obtain a specialization in a subject which may not be valuable in the light of future market oppor-tunities. Much basic R&D research has the same characteristic, due to possible shifts in preferences and technologies.

The prevalent paradigm for considering situations of uncertainty is the 'expected utility model', where agents maximize the expectation of an objec-tive function. To describe this model, suppose that there are three possible scenarios (known as states of the world) for the consequence described in section 2.1.2, that is, $f_1(y_1)$, $f_2(y_1)$ and $f_3(y_1)$, where $f_j(y_1)$ is the direct consequence of the outcome y_1 in the j-th state of the world. Suppose that the decision-maker believes that the scenarios have probabilities p_1, p_2 and p_3, with $p_1 + p_2 + p_3 = 1$. The expected utility criterion calls for maxi-mization of:

$$p_1 \, u(f_1(y_1, x_0)) + p_2 \, u(f_2(y_1, x_0)) + p_3 \, u(f_3(y_1, x_0))$$

where:

$$y_1 = g(x_1, z_0, z_1)$$

and u(.) is a von Neumann–Morgenstern utility function (such a function can be shown to exist on the basis of hypotheses about attitudes towards risky choices). The criterion therefore calls for maximization of the expected value of a utility function defined over the consequences of the actions (concavity of such a utility function implies risk aversion on the part of the agent). The criterion of choice under uncertainty is therefore an extension of the one under certainty, with many common assumptions. As Machina (1987) points out, 'the expected utility model shares many of the underlying assumptions of standard consumer theory. In each case we assume that the objects of choice, either commodity bundles or lotteries, can be unambiguously and objectively described, and that situations which ultimately imply the same set of availabilities will lead to the same choice.'

The expected utility framework can also be related easily to the Arrow–Debreu model of general equilibrium theory described in the previous section, by assuming that there is a fixed number of exogenous states of nature that may be realized with certain probabilities. The agent will then choose to purchase insurance contracts which will pay pre-specified amounts of wealth in the various states of nature.

The framework of expected utility maximization, and its use in the context of the Arrow–Debreu theory, is extremely powerful for the treatment of uncertainty, even though a number of questions can be raised at the level of both its ability to describe actual behaviour under uncertainty and its description of the economic system. In terms of compatibility between the axioms of the theory and actual behaviour, it has been noticed that in practice, humans seem to choose under conditions of uncertainty in ways that do not respect the expected utility model. Such evidence has been accumulated in a number of experiments where subjects are asked to choose among risky prospects under conditions similar to those considered by the theory. The results show that human beings deviate from the theoretical framework in many different dimensions, in that humans: (1) are influenced by the representation of the situations, (2) do not tend to have a fixed preference ordering over lotteries, (3) are differently sensitive to gains and losses, and (4) react to risky outcomes in terms of various reference points. See Allais (1953), Tversky and Thaler (1990) and Kahneman and Tversky (1979) for a more specific description of deviations from expected utility theory.

A new class of models, known as non-expected utility models, has been recently developed in order to drop one of the axioms of expected utility which seem to contrast with the empirical evidence; see Kelsey and Quiggin (1992) and Machina (1994) for a comparison of expected and non-expected utility models.

A second criticism has to do with the ability of human subjects to form probabilities of events. Even before economists started to use experiments to understand how humans actually behave in uncertain situations, Knight (1921) proposed a distinction between risk and uncertainty. Risk is a situation in which it is possible to use the empirical frequencies of past events to estimate probabilities, as has been assumed in the previous section and in this section, while in uncertain situations such an operation is not possible. Knight (1921) and many other economists regard situations of uncertainty as much more common in economics than situations of risk. Keynes (1936), for example, noted that in many economic problems such as investments in new projects, agents follow animal spirits and not a rational calculation of all possible events according to objective methods.

Another relevant criticism of the Arrow–Debreu model proposed by Kurz (1974) concerns the assumption about exogeneity of the state space.

Kurz argues that in most cases of interest to economics uncertainty is endogenously propagated through the economic system by the actions of the agents themselves, and this in turn implies the absence of markets for insurance. The consequences of this for economic theory are presented in a series of contributions discussing the theory of rational beliefs, which will be described in section 2.2.4.

2.2.2 Rational expectations

Most dynamic problems under uncertainty involve the formation of expectations at the level of the single agent. According to asset pricing models, for example, demand for a specific asset depends on the expectations of future payoffs of the asset; in macroeconomic models, expectations of inflation depend on the expected economic policy. In all these cases there are two open problems: (1) the formation of expectations on the part of each single agent (2) the relation between these expectations and the 'true' dynamic relation taking place at the level of the economic system.

One example from the theory of asset pricing may be useful in understanding the meaning of these problems, and the solution proposed by rational expectations. Suppose there are only two assets and one agent in the economy; one asset pays a fixed and known interest rate r over the period from the beginning to the end of period t, while another will pay a dividend D_{t+1} and will have a market price P_{t+1} at the end of period t. The dividend and the market price at the end of the period are stochastic, and can be described by two probability distributions. The question is: at the beginning of period t, what is the maximum price P_t that the agent is willing to pay in order to buy the risky asset? Given the supply of the asset, this amounts to calculating the equilibrium price. If the agent is not worried about buying a risky asset (technically, it is risk-neutral), then he or she will compare the expected returns from the risky and the riskless asset and will be willing to pay as a maximum price the one that makes the two alternatives indifferent, that is:

$$P_t = \frac{E_t(P_{t+1} + D_{t+1})}{1 + r}$$

In order to compute this price, the agent needs to form expectations of future dividends and prices. The initial proposal for these expectational problems was to assume the existence of reasonable rules of thumb for the formation of expectations. For example, the expectations could be static, $E_t(D_{t+1}) = D_t$, or could follow some more general adaptive scheme. In an attempt to escape the arbitrariness (inevitably) implicit in every choice of a rule of thumb, theoreticians proposed that the agent should form expectations based on the 'true' distribution that describes the probability of the variables (Muth, 1961). In the previous example this means realizing that, in a coherent theory, the model that is proposed for the explanation of stock prices at time t should also be used for time t+1, t+2 ... The agent can therefore use the arbitrage relation to explain the price of tomorrow as expectations of the prices and dividends at time t+2. By continuously substituting forward, one arrives at an equation that explains the price at time t as a function of the expectations of all the future dividends:

$$P_t = E_t((D_{t+1}/(1 + r)) + (D_{t+2}/(1 + r)^2) + \ldots)$$

This can be considered as a 'genuine' solution because an endogenous variable, the price of a financial asset, is explained on the basis of expectations of an exogenous variable, the dividend. The theory of rational expectations assumes that the agent forms expectations by using the 'true' distribution of dividends. Note that in order to do that, the agent must know not only the distribution of dividends, but also the equilibrium model that gives rise to the price as a discounted value of dividends. Rational expectations amount therefore to knowledge both of the statistical distribution of the exogenous variables and of the economic model that aggregates at the general level the actions of all the agents.

2.2.3 Structural knowledge

Clearly, the degree of realism of such a hypothesis depends on the model to which it is applied. In the case of asset prices it may be credible to assume that financial traders may be able to apply the same model for each future time period, and then compute the price as the expectations of future dividends. In other cases such a solution is hard to accept; it may strain credibility to think that firms that are forecasting the future price may know or come to learn the distribution of the price, which depends on a very complex structural model involving the actions of many different players, or that households that are forecasting inflation to decide their money demand know the underlying structure of the economy and the rule used by the government to decide the economic policy.

Doubts may arise even in the case of a simple model such as the one connecting prices and dividends. In fact, the recursion described above breaks down if at some future time there is one agent who decides to evaluate the asset on the basis of different considerations. For example, one agent may be willing to pay a large price simply because he or she believes that others will be willing to pay an even larger price in the future. Even lacking such deviations from the dynamic framework described earlier, there may be difficulties in believing that the expectations can be formed on the basis of knowledge of the true stochastic distribution of dividends. The latter is a very complicated object, as the probability density function of dividends can be affected by a variety of external variables such as the state of the economy, the profitability of firms, technological innovations and many others. It is therefore likely that any important structural change in the system will affect the distribution, and this, to the extent that agents may not be able to predict future structural changes, will make it difficult to predict future dividends. See Kurz (1994a) for a theoretical and empirical analysis of the consequences of structural changes on stock prices.

When evaluated on the grounds of realism, the hypothesis of rational expectations seems therefore to be very strong. It certainly requires an incredible computational ability on the part of the agents, who are supposed to know the structure of the economy. A natural question then becomes: can agents form rational expectations by repeated observations of the economy?

2.2.4 Statistical learning and convergence to rational expectations

Since the work of Bray (1982), a large literature has studied the logical possibility of agents forming rational expectations when their actions affect the equilibrium of the economic system. Note that this does not simply mean that, given a sufficient number of observations, agents can learn the distribution of an object whose probability density does not change with the learning actions; instead, it means that agents learn the distribution even when their actions, based on what they have learnt, affect the distribution itself.

Bray analysed a model composed of two classes of agents who want to solve a one-period two-asset portfolio problem along the lines that have been described in section 2.2.2; informed agents observe some variable that is related to the future returns of the risky asset, while uninformed agents only look at the market price of the various assets. Knowing that informed investors have superior knowledge, and that the demand of these investors will affect the market price, the uninformed agents will try to observe the relation between the market price and the return in order to deduce from the price the quality of the information of the informed agents.

In Bray's model, agents are econometricians forming expectations based on linear regressions of future returns on current prices. The estimated relation will be used to form their own expectations. Clearly, such a statistical technique is optimal only in the rational expectations equilibrium, but not in the convergence to such an equilibrium; however, OLS (ordinary least squares) may be recommended, and justifiable, on the basis of its simplicity and of a bounded rationality sort of argument. Bray shows that the equilibrium-cum-learning process converges and that the uninformed learn the correct relation if the proportion of uninformed is not too high. See Marcet and Sargent (1989) for extensions of this line of research.

While rational expectations, and all the statistical learning arguments proposed in the literature, seem to close the possibility of interesting and useful extensions to studying systems with learning agents, some new hope is offered by the theory of rational beliefs recently developed by Kurz in a series of publications; see Kurz (1994b, 1994c). The basic tenet of such a theory is that the economy is stable, meaning that it is possible to use statistical techniques for computing empirical density functions of relevant variables, but not stationary, meaning that structural breaks can happen at unpredictable future times. Kurz shows that, even with an infinite number of observations, agents may maintain different beliefs about the economy; they will not in general form rational expectations and agree on the same model of the economy. The practical implication is therefore that the agents form rational beliefs which are compatible with a multiplicity of models that cannot be rejected even on the basis of long histories of data. In this case agents may never find out the 'true' structure, but create a conventional equilibrium, which is however restricted in the long-run by its compatibility with the long run empirical density functions estimated on the basis of the actual observations. This theory proposes a vision of the economic system which is much different from the one proposed by rational expectations, and is compatible with a research project which assigns a central role to learning in the study of behaviour of economic agents.

2.3 Learning

Although the models we have described so far incorporate some learning, it is necessary to mention that such learning is simply of a statistical nature. This may also be a reflection of the fact that the microfoundations of learning behaviour are still rather vague in economics. Once learning is brought into the picture, one would like to know more about how agents learn in practice, and how they decide the appropriate investment in acquiring and processing information. Various issues which are relevant to behaviour in situations of incomplete information and uncertainty are explored next.

2.3.1 Learning and computational requirements

Computational requirements are generally ignored in the theoretical models, but are important in practice. The issue of computation can be separated into the two issues of computational costs and computational abilities. Computational costs are relevant in those cases in which an agent may know the sequences of calculations that would bring him or her to the optimal solution, but chooses not to perform all of them in the light of their costs, or in those cases in which the best sequence of calculations is not even known, and the subject stops at some stage using the available results. This has a difficult way out from the logical point of view; Conslik (1988) points out the existence of a circularity problem, according to which an optimization problem cannot fully account for the cost of its own solution.

In other cases the problem is even deeper, and is about the logic of the solution. It is sufficient to think of the intertemporal maximization model, described in section 2.1.3, where the agent is supposed to start from the last period and then work back to the initial action, to understand that the amount of computations involved in this process is incredibly large. This is not an issue of computational costs, but the more fundamental one of computational abilities.

It is not surprising that Hey (1991a) reports results from a series of experiments aimed at understanding how well agents can perform the calculations needed to compute a dynamic strategy in problems of search, savings and inventories that are optimally solved in theoretical economic work with the backward induction method. He finds that agents are usually far from optimality, even though they react to changes in some parameters in the direction that is suggested by economic theories.

These issues are particularly important in the contexts of situations where one has to learn the new environment, and the cost changes rapidly. In this sense the appropriate learning assumptions depend on the context: '. . . (the rationality hypothesis) gathers not only its force but also its very meaning from the social context in which it is embedded. It is most plausible under ideal conditions. When these conditions cease to hold, the rationality assumption becomes strained and possibly even self-contradictory. They certainly imply an ability at information processing and calculation that is far beyond the feasible and that cannot well be justified as the result of learning and adaptation' (Arrow 1986).

Given these problems, various economists have suggested that rules of thumb may be the rational reaction of agents that want to balance computational costs against the benefits of a more accurate representation of reality. The attempt is therefore to apply once again the methodology based on rationality and optimal choice, but considering various limitations. This calls into question the very notion of rationality in economics. Simon (1957) discusses bounded rationality in the following terms: 'The capacity of the human mind for formulating and solving complex problems is very small compared with the size of the problems whose solution is required for objectively rational behaviour in the real world.'

Ultimately, the attempts at considering computational costs and abilities will have to integrate with fields concerned with understanding how humans learn in practice, a position already proposed by Simon (1984): '. . . if we accept the proposition that both the knowledge and the computational power of the decision maker are severely limited, then we must distinguish between the real world and the actor's perception of it and reasoning about it. That is to say, we must construct a theory of the processes of decision. Our theory must include not only the reasoning processes but also the processes that generate the actor's subjective representation of the decision problem.'

2.3.2 Organizations

The importance of organizations in the study of economic systems derives mainly from the observation that most of the economic actors make decisions in a context that requires interactions with other agents: humans make consumption, savings and other economic decisions in the context of families, while production takes place in firms of various sizes. The predominance of organizations creates a set of important questions: what are the goals of these organizations? What are the reasons for the creation of organizations and the relations between them and markets? How do organizations work?

As far as the goals of the organizations are concerned, there is a large amount of literature that purports that firms are not simple profit maximizers; large firms may maximize the rate of sale or survival rather than simple profits. Also, the interests of the managers may be very important in determining the actions of the firms, contrary to what is assumed in the neoclassical approach (for example Pigou, 1922; Machlup, 1967) which considers the firm as a black box for making efficient production decisions.

The work of Williamson (1975) is particularly important for understanding the 'division of labor' between markets and business units from the point of view of the neoclassical theory that was described above: business organizations may perform internally a part of the activities that could in principle have been obtained from the market because of the costs involved in drawing up contracts and monitoring them to ensure they are enforced. Organizations are a response to uncertainty and to the limited computational and organizational abilities of humans in making decisions. Rather than attempting to respond to any possible contingency, it may be efficient to set up an organization that maintains flexibility with respect to the contingencies that actually occur: '. . . internal organization . . . has attractive properties in that it permits the parties to deal with uncertainty/complexity in an adaptive, sequential fashion without incurring the same types of opportunism hazards that market contracting would pose. Such adaptive, sequential decision processes economize greatly on bounded rationality. Rather than specifying the decision tree exhaustively in advance, and deriving the corresponding contingent prices, events are permitted to unfold and attention is restricted to only the actual rather than all possible outcomes.' (Williamson, 1975)

Routines are a key element in the functioning of organizations and can be understood as a reasonable reaction to a very complicated world. Nelson and Winter (1982) consider routines a '. . . relatively complex pattern of behavior . . . triggered by a relatively small number of initiating signals or choices and functioning as a recognizable unit in a relatively automatic fashion . . .'. According to such evolutionary theory (Nelson, 1995), firms may be expected to keep using the same routines, until the pressures for change coming from the interaction of the actions of the firm and the environment suggest some change. Routines also persist because they are costly, and often require irreversible investments and sunk costs. See Levitt and March (1988) for a detailed study of learning in organizations on the basis of routines.

It certainly makes sense to consider routines as reasonable reactions to complicated problems, but, to progress even further, it is interesting to ask questions about the generation of routines, an issue that is part of a more general discussion of organization learning. Newell and Simon (1972) note that to better understand routines and learning, one has to use direct observations of human behaviour in the market and in the firm.

2.3.3 Heterogeneity and interaction

Macroeconomics went through a process of deep change in the 1970s and 1980s. Earlier macroeconomic studies started from the definitions of aggregate variables, and tried to understand their relations with theories based on these variables, without going to the level of analysis of the single individuals forming the aggregate. A typical example is the Keynesian consumption function, which is more concerned with explaining the overall positive relation between consumption and income than with understanding how the aggregate relation might be derived from reasonable relations existing at the individual level.

This methodology has been severely criticized by neoclassical economists, because of lack of explanations of individual behaviour. The critique lies mainly in the possibility that the aggregate relations are subject to change with movements in the overall macroeconomic environment, as a result of the change in the behaviour of the single agents forming the aggregate. For example, if in a country subject to low inflation people on average consume 60% of their income, one cannot expect the same relation to be true if the overall inflation jumps to 35%, as each agent will revise the optimal consumption policy. The suggestion that was put forward by Lucas (1980) and others was to describe a macroeconomic system that is microfounded, where each variable can be explained in terms of aggregation of choices coming from the solution of well-specified microeconomic optimization problems, like the one described in section 2.1.2.

The strategy has its merits, but is certainly very rigid. It has forced macroeconomics to be an application of microeconomics; it is not unusual to hear that what distinguishes macroeconomics from microeconomics is not the methodology but the problems to which the models are applied. This is certainly a very restrictive view of the analysis of the aggregate, as the models that are being used are microeconomic in scope. In fact, the analysis of a microfounded economic system is achieved with the fiction of a representative agent, an entity that is supposed to describe the average person in the economy. This generally amounts to assuming that all the agents have the same preferences.

Kirman (1992) argues forcefully against this view, making the point that there is no justification for the assumption that the aggregate of individuals itself acts like an individual maximizer. Individual maximization does not engender collective rationality. It may be the case that in two situations of which the representative prefers the first to the second, every individual prefers the second to the first. Also, the sum of the behaviour of simple economically plausible agents may generate complicated dynamics, whereas constructing one individual whose behaviour has this dynamics may lead to a strange individual. Kirman calls for the necessity of an economic theory that does not necessarily aim at eliminating diversity among individuals in order to obtain well-behaved aggregates, suggesting examples where in fact the opposite is true: stability of the aggregate behaviour depends on enough diversity of the single components.

Recent economic research has begun to face this important challenge. Arthur and Lane (1991) consider a market where prospective buyers ask previous purchasers about their experience with the products they bought, and this generates an 'informational feedback' into the process that may give rise to information contagion. In Ellison and Fudenberg (1993) various technologies are chosen with rules-of-thumb that may look at the performance of the various technologies in the recent past, or at the performance of the technologies at units located near to each single agent. Similar themes are considered in Banerjee (1992) and Bikhchandani *et al.* (1992). In all these cases the behaviour of the aggregate is qualitatively different from the behaviour of each single agent, and the representative agent model cannot be used for the analysis.

2.4 Economies as complex systems

Interactions among economic agents naturally lead to viewing the economy as a complex system. One relevant factor, emphasized by Arthur (1988), is represented by increasing returns to scale. In knowledge-based industries, products are complicated to design and manufacture and require large initial investments in research and development activities. But as more production reaches the market, there is more demand directed to these products, as many users find it easier to use a system that is widespread in the market. The initial effects reinforce themselves and favour the dominance of a few standards. Clearly, this vision of the economy is very different from most of the ones presented before, since now it is recognized that the growth path of an economic system does not descend directly from some initial conditions and a deterministic law of motion. On the contrary, there may be large effects of apparently minor events, as long as these occur sufficiently early in the history of the adoption of the technology.

Arthur (1991) points out some relevant properties of economic systems dominated by these phenomena: (1) multiple equilibria, (2) possible inefficiency, (3) lock-in, (4) path-dependence. These characteristics are all due to the importance of history in these economies; small random events may be important for the long run, and may twist the system towards an inefficient equilibrium that is inferior from the point of view of welfare to other equilibria that might have been achieved given the initial conditions. Arthur (1990a) notes that such a development is common to many sciences.

This view of the economic system forces us to reconsider one issue that we have already mentioned, and to discuss two new issues that are to be considered among the most important on the agenda for future research: (1) what do we mean by complex systems? (2) how do we model economic agents that live in complex economies? (3) how do we study complex systems?

2.4.1 Complex systems

While there is a precise definition of complex systems in the mathematical literature, it is less clear what is meant by complex systems from the point of view of a social science like economics. The issue is fundamentally important. Lane (1992) proposes the study of Artificial Worlds, where basic units interact in a variety of ways to form a complex system with various rules and higher level entities. It is likely that in well-defined complex worlds, systems may tend to become more orderly.

It is interesting to compare the statements of Lane (1992), according to which '. . . the systems appear to produce their own order. The actions of lower-level entities are channelled – in effect, coordinated – by higher-level structures that themselves arise from the lower-level entities' interactions', with that of North (1991) about the importance of institutions: 'Throughout history, institutions have been devised by human beings to create order and reduce uncertainty in exchange . . . They evolve incrementally, connecting the past with the present and the future; history in consequence is largely a story of institutional evolution in which the historical performance of economies can only be understood as a part of a sequential story. Institutions provide the incentive structure of an economy; as that structure evolves, it shapes the direction of economic change towards growth, stagnation, or decline.' This comparison suggests that complex economies may be close to the view that history is fundamental in understanding evolution.

Lane (1992) also points out a fundamental criterion in deciding when a model should be defined as an artificial world, and that is when the emerging properties are not a simple forecastable consequence of the assumptions about the single units that have been introduced by the researcher. The idea is that these systems should be able to endogenously evolve institutions and meta-organizations to solve the problems that are themselves endogenously created within the models.

2.4.2 Models of learning

The issue of modelling learning has been recently considered by Arthur (1992, 1993), and is also studied in this book. In some sense this problem is at the core of the whole approach of economies as complex systems. In such complex economies, the key activity of agents is learning about other agents and about the environment, so that the way this learning is modelled becomes a fundamental component of the model. It is necessary to model the single units in simple but rigorous ways before one can make general statements about the evolution of systems composed of these units.

At this early stage, this modelling is open to many alternative possibilities; it is not necessarily true that one model will emerge as the most correct, since different learning paradigms may be useful for studying different situations. Arthur (1993) notes that in fact it may certainly be too early to select the best learning model, but that one could use computer algorithms like classifier systems and others, including ANNs as conventional learning models.

This issue also relates to the very definition of rationality. In a recent contribution, Prigogine (1993) notes that the definition of bounded rationality adopted by Simon is consonant with the recent emphasis on the study of complex systems, which is decreasing the importance of classical mechanics as a model for the other sciences. Learning is fundamental in complex systems, and the difficulty of performing such a task in a nonlinear and perhaps chaotic world can only be realistically faced with bounded rationality arguments.

The important issue then becomes the degree of computational abilities that should be imputed to the agents forming complex systems. By endowing them with too much learning ability one risks repeating the problems of models inhabited by agents with very large computational abilities, but by endowing them with too little computational and reasoning abilities there is a risk of modelling unnecessarily stupid worlds. This choice promises to be extremely difficult, and maybe impossible to solve, if not at the level of a convention among scientists.

2.4.3 The study of complex systems

Complex systems cannot be easily studied by means of standard mathematical techniques. This does not mean that they should be ignored. For example, the issue of sustainability of growth requires a proper analysis of the dynamics of systems like the economic, the environmental and the population. Researchers who want to keep mathematical tractability of the model might be tempted to ignore one dimension in order to formally consider the other two, but their results may be not very relevant to a world where the three phenomena interact in significant ways and form a general pattern that may not be captured by partial analysis.

The alternative is to use the computer for numerical simulations. There is a negative trade-off between the strength of the assumptions that are made as to the behaviour of the individual units and the need to use the computer to 'solve' the model. If the assumptions are minimal, and if therefore one wishes to study a system composed of units that behave according to patterns that are not built in by the researcher, analytical solutions often cannot be obtained.

The use of the computer to study the emergent properties of systems formed by interacting units behaving in simple ways brings about another formidable question: is there a risk of building a complex system that is as poorly understood as the real world? How does one discriminate between 'useful' and 'useless' complex models? Again, there is no univocal answer at this stage, even though it may be useful to point out the following possible uses of complex systems.

- Pedagogical devices: the artificial stock market of Arthur *et al.* (1993) or the one presented in this book might be used to train traders that are then supposed to act in the real markets.
- Sources of inspiration: emerging properties of complex systems might suggest innovative ways to look at the world.
- Artificial laboratories: Arthur (1993) argues that complex models might be useful to run experiments that cannot be run in the real world; this may be quite important when it comes to predicting the effects of economic policies, as complex systems might teach lessons about the unintended consequences of these policies.

2.4.4 Artificial neural networks and economics

We have travelled a long road that has brought us from the picture of economic agents and systems as immutable realities to the description of economic life as an ever-changing flow of relations and pieces of information. We have seen that the picture of the economy as an evolving complex system has some relevance for the way we model our economic agents: in a complex system agents have to continuously learn and adapt in order to respond to the external impulses. Their learning more complicated dynamics in some cases may increase the level of complexity of the system, in a sort of never-ending loop between internal models and actual models.

This book explores one methodology, Artificial Neural Networks, for carrying out this research programme, with a particular application to a specific sector of the economy, namely financial markets. This choice does not exclude the relevance of other instruments, some of which are briefly reviewed in what follows. Simply, we found it more useful to explore deeply the possibilities of ANNs in application to economics and finance, rather than to consider a specific problem with different methods. We also try to point out the general properties that can make ANNs applicable to other economic problems.

Why should ANNs be worthy of particular attention in the context of all the possible artificial intelligence methods? One important reason is that they are good candidates for providing us with a model of the learning behaviour of the agents, resembling, at least partially, the way economic agents learn in practice. This may provide some objective foundations that may represent a common theme for research, that might for example agree on ANNs as a paradigm to compare models and theories. As we mentioned before, however, this is only one possibility for research, and it is useful to compare it with other possible methodologies. Another important reason is that ANNs are already spreading in financial markets as important trading instruments.

Even though this chapter has been exclusively focused on general economic theory, the last chapters of the book will also consider applications that are more relevant from the point of view of the practitioner, mainly for the analysis of financial markets. One of the great advantages of the economic analysis of complex systems is to promote research that is not divorced from the problems and methods of the real world. The analysis of complex systems in fact can only be performed with instruments that are also useful to the economic agents living in the models. Sargent (1993) has argued that 'We can interpret the idea of bounded rationality broadly as a research program to build models populated by agents who behave like working economists or econometricians'. We want to push this argument even further, and suggest that in trying to do that, economists and other scientists will try to develop methodologies and instruments that will be helpful to economic agents living in actual economic systems. After all, what is more artificial than an economy populated with a representative utility-maximizer?

Part Two

Experiments with Artificial Agents

3
Neural networks and economics

Outline of the chapter

In this chapter we highlight some reasons for using connectionist tools in building economic models, and we consider issues related to the implementation and interpretation of (boundedly rational) economic agents and systems. Section 3.1 discusses the main characteristics of this approach to economic modelling, suggesting the possibility of using ANNs for doing simulated experiments based upon agents whose behaviour can be modelled in alternative ways to those familiar in neoclassical economics. The term 'simulated experiment' stands to point out that, in general, these models have no analytic solution and can only be simulated. Section 3.2 introduces ANNs as computational devices, analysing their capabilities such as classification, fuzzy information treatment, econometrics, development of expert systems on a neural basis and tools for artificial agent building. Some of these will be considered in detail in the next chapters of the book.

In section 3.3 we deal with the complex subject of interpreting implicitly developed rules in adaptive neural agents. The hidden neuron analysis is deepened to discuss both its potential and its limits, and the results are compared to those that can be obtained from cluster analysis. A section is also devoted to interpreting aggregate behaviour emerging from models of interacting agents. Finally, section 3.4 classifies models on the basis of the number of agents or populations, defined as collections of homogeneous agents, and represents an introduction to the analysis of Chapters 4 to 7.

3.1 An artificial neural network approach to economic modelling

Some of the results coming from both behavioural economics and models with artificial adaptive agents (AAAs) suggest the need to develop new tools that may be used to run simulated experiments with AAA models, mainly for explanatory purposes. Experiments or simulations are generally needed in these sorts of models for reasons that will become clearer from the reading of this and the following chapters, but that essentially are related to the nonlinearities emerging at an aggregate level as a result of interactions of learning and adaptive agents. The use of the term 'simulated experiment' instead of 'simulation' underlines the novelty of the explicit introduction of

AAAs in models. The word simulated underlines the necessity of using simulations to analyse the models, while the term experiment points out, maybe too optimistically, that the outcomes of the models come from structures populated by agents with learning mechanisms somehow resembling those used by humans.

Artificial experiments have some advantages over those conducted with human subjects (natural experiments, see Hey (1991b) for a thorough review of experimental economics). The former (1) have more possibilities of controlling the subjects, and (2) can be implemented at lower costs.

Regarding (1), the possibilities of controlling the subjects in artificial experiments are complete in terms of some key parameters of interest, while in standard experiments it is not possible to completely control the subjects. On some occasions this may create some doubts about the results; a common criticism of experimental economics in fact is about the incentives that are provided to subjects, who might behave differently in 'the real world'. This risk does not arise with software programs; of course, we do not want to deny that such artificial experiments are at the current stage only suggestive of what may be going on in the real world; hopefully in the future AAAs will be more detailed and more 'similar' to humans (see the considerations in section 3.3.6).

Regarding (2), simply note that the costs originating from software development diminish rapidly with the diffusion of more standard techniques.

Sections 3.1.1 to 3.1.5 comment on some possibilities for using ANNs for implementation of models with such AAAs. In the past few years, a large impact in the direction of introducing new tools in the field of economic research came from Santa Fe Institute; as an example, we refer to Anderson, Arrow and Pines (1988).

3.1.1 Microfoundations and realism in economics

Models with AAAs are useful for dealing with issues related to learning and interactions of agents in economic models. While standard neoclassical models, some of which were reviewed in chapter 2, are generally aimed at studying issues related to individual and aggregate behaviour of systems in steady state, models with AAAs are tailored for exactly the opposite purpose, that is, to study the dynamic evolution of systems which are not in steady state, populated by agents who try to learn as much as they can, given their computational abilities, about the environment.

One of the important open problems in dealing with such systems lies in the assumptions made about each agent and about the learning mechanism. In this book we will offer some proposals for possible solutions, even though the problem is so fundamental and complicated that we do not intend to provide solutions; rather we advance some proposals and compare them with some of the existing tools in order to promote more debate and research.

In performing such a study we start with two important issues: (1) the computational abilities of economic agents and (2) interaction.

(1) Capabilities: when full rationality is assumed, agents are supposed not only to have complete information and unlimited computational power, but also to know the true economic model explaining the consequences of their actions. As Sargent (1993) points out, they must have more knowledge than the econometrician working with the model. Little attention is devoted to learning and adaptivity of agents, which have enormous importance for their ability to survive in a continuously changing world.

(2) Interactions: In neoclassical models, agents sometimes interact only indirectly by exchanging information by prices and bargaining impersonally through market relations. Only in game theory is strategic interaction is taken into account, but with further heavy requirements for the agents' computational and reasoning ability (see the comments and the references offered in Chapter 2).

This abstractedness is often justified on the basis of the famous argument of Friedman (1953): 'Truly important and significant hypotheses will be found to have "assumptions" that are wildly inaccurate descriptive representations of reality, and, in general, the more significant the theory, the more unrealistic the assumption . . .'. However, we believe that this defence cannot be taken to the extreme; its validity depends on the problems that the theoretician wants to tackle. As we will try to argue in the book, such lack of realism is not useful in studying situations where learning is at the centre of the stage.

With respect to problems that are difficult to define and whose solutions are difficult to compute, the best reference is of course Simon and his theory of bounded rationality (Simon, 1969; Simon et al., 1992). This line of research points out that it is necessary to study the real learning procedures used by agents and organizations, almost from the point of view of case studies aimed at clarifying several different but related learning architectures.

One way to understand our proposals in this book is to consider the various models as applications of bounded rationality, implemented on the basis of ANNs rather than utility maximizing agents. Therefore we will use the tools introduced in Chapter 2 to model agents learning from the environment in the contexts of models with many interactions. As we will discuss in what follows, our description of the economic agents will be as simple as possible, and complexity will emerge from the various interactions. In order to follow the basic intuition of Artificial Life models, see section 3.3.6.

Why might one want to implement bounded rationality with ANNs? Among the many possible justifications for our emphasis on ANNs, we want to mention at this stage:

- plausibility, since ANNs imitate the structure of the brain, albeit in an oversimplified way;

- epistemological relevance, following the nonsymbolic representation, alternative to the strong AI paradigm;
- mathematical and statistical relevance, mainly in the approximation of functions;
- architectural relevance, leading to parallel hardware implementations in a straightforward way.

The relative merits of ANNs with respect to other possible candidates from the artificial intelligence literature can be better appreciated by introducing connectionism and then comparing various possible tools.

3.1.2 Connectionism and ANNs

The connectionist framework involves many different structures, such as classifier systems (CSs, described in sections 1.4.1 and 3.1.3), genetic algorithms (see section 1.2) and artificial neural networks. The last, already discussed at length in Chapter 1, have a central place in connectionism. The term 'connectionism' was popularized in Feldman and Ballard (1982) and was then adopted to avoid the criticism against neural models, which was widespread at that time. It synthesizes the idea of setting up models of 'nodes' linked by connections where information of any kind is stored.

However, it is interesting to note that until the middle of the 1980s, most of the AI community was highly averse to neural networks, because of the apparently conclusive critique of Minsky and Papert (1969 and 1988). An anecdote, reported in Anderson and Rosenfeld (1988), may go a long way towards explaining the general attitude: the meaning of the name of the Widrow and Hoff algorithm, ADALINE, was originally ADAptive LInear NEuron, but was changed to ADAptive LINear Element to avoid the unpopularity of neural networks.

Currently, the main characteristics of connectionism can be defined in terms of its functions. A connectionist structure, such as an ANN, is (1) parallel, (2) subsymbolic, (3) self-organizing, (4) fault tolerant and (5) redundant.

(1) Here we emphasize the distribution of computing tasks among 'nodes' or processing units, linked by connections: links are present both in true connectionist systems and in artificial ones. Neurons in a neural network, processing units in an ANN, human agents in an economic system, living beings in an ecological structure, processing units in a massively parallel computer, etc. are examples of parallelism. Parallel tasks can be independent or interacting: the latter is the most common situation. Nature also is massively parallel: parallelism ensures rapidity in reactions, in reasoning capabilities, in pattern recognition ability etc., despite the fact that the brain itself is composed of slow-operating neurons. Neurons are slow, but highly nonlinear efficiency effects emerge when employing many of them simultaneously.

(2) Subsymbolic representation of knowledge is a more abstract concept. In a connectionist structure, either in an artificial or in a natural one, knowledge is not stored in an explicit or symbolic way (Hinton *et al.*, 1986). In an ANN, each weight or hidden neuron does not independently play a role identifiable with a specific meaning or task; each weight contributes together with other weights, by neuron activity and interaction, to produce results. A result can be an action, a pattern recognition, an information retrieving operation, etc. It follows that knowledge is distributed in a subsymbolic way among the weights in an ANN, or among the synapses in a true neural network. An example of distributed information is shown in Figure 3.4 (in section 3.3.5), where links between inputs and outputs follow multiple and also unexpected paths.

Also, in our brains, knowledge is not stored in a systemic repertoire of symbols, meanings and itemized pieces of culture, but in a distributed way, through synapses linking neurons. Similarly, in an ANN acting as an Expert System (see section 3.2.2) the responses to specific situations depend neither on a single weight nor on a delimited group acting in a specialized way. The responses are stored in many weights, each of them being useful in building up different responses.

This description of the structure of knowledge storage and representation does not absolutely agree with the tradition that, since Aristotle, through Boole and until the so-called strong AI, has been spreading an unreal interpretation of the activity of the mind. The mind, considered separately from the brain, was supposed to employ something analogous to formal logic in elaborating symbols upon which both thoughts and beliefs were supposed to be based (the title chosen by Boole for his fundamental 1854 work, 'An Investigation of the Laws of Thought, on Which Are Founded the Mathematical Theories of Logic and Probabilities', is very revealing). Similar considerations hold today, albeit presented in a more subtle way, in the Artificial Intelligence field, which partially overlaps with cognitivism.

With ANN and connectionism, we are far from the formal structures of facts and rules of traditional AI. As we can easily recognize, formal logic can be a subsidiary tool in reasoning, not the ordinary mechanism: in connectionism we have no explicit symbols or concept and, as a strong consequence, no explicit rules operating upon them. Also, in social and natural organizations, the distributed and subsymbolic storage of knowledge is recognizable at different levels. For example, the competitiveness of a firm involves a large array of interpersonal links that exist inside and outside each organization. Where and how is the competence of the firm stored? It is distributed in small pieces of individual capabilities and interpersonal links. Let us notice that each of them is apparently useless in doing anything if examined alone.

To make the same point in a more specific way, an analogy can be drawn with econometric specifications like equation 3.1 or 3.2 below, where we have some parameters such as a_1 and a_2, or α and β, with definite meanings: a_1 and a_2 measure the direct links among x_1 and x_2, respectively, and y; in the same way, α and β respectively measure the elasticity between the dependent variable and the independent ones.

$$y = a_0 + a_1 x_1 + a_2 x_2 \tag{3.1}$$

$$y = a x_1^{\alpha} x_2^{\beta} \tag{3.2}$$

On the contrary we cannot establish any clear meaning for any single parameter if we adopt a connectionist approach as in equation 3.3 below, where we describe an ANN with two input neurons (# 1, 2), three hidden neurons (# 3, 4, 5), one output neuron (# 6), plus the 0 neuron representing the bias (see section 1.2.3):

$$y = f[w_{60} + w_{63} f(w_{30} + w_{31} x_1 + w_{32} x_2) +$$

$$w_{64} f(w_{40} + w_{41} x_1 + w_{42} x_2) + w_{65} f(w_{50} + w_{51} x_1 + w_{52} x_2)] \tag{3.3}$$

with

$$f(x) = 1/(1 + \exp (x))$$

Let us take for instance the w_{32} parameter (or 'weight'); it links x_2 to y, but it is easy to point out that w_{42} and w_{52} do the same; furthermore, the effect of $w_{52} \cdot x_2$ is applied to the first hidden neuron, giving $f(w_{30} + w_{31}$ $x_1 + w_{32} x_2)$, linked to y by w_{63}. In simple terms, we cannot attribute an explicit meaning to w_{32} or to the other parameters, because we have here a distributed representation that is hard to interpret in terms of its components.

The ANN critics claim that with these tools it is impossible to manage tasks involving symbolic representation. But then we can ask the following question: are symbolic representations and symbolic reasoning truly necessary to solve those tasks? An answer is suggested in section 3.2.1, to which the reader is referred.

A final remark: the subsymbolic characteristic does not fully apply to CSs, which develop rules with explicit meaning to elaborate data.

(3) Self-organization is a widely diffused quality of structures in the actual world. Prigogine's work (Prigogine and Stengers, 1984) has drawn our attention to 'self-organizing structures' in natural and social domains: Impersonal structures in the actual economic world, like the market, are run by a lot of self-organizing people; the links among neurons in our brain are the outcome of autonomous self-developed processes, etc. In these cases, we observe the emergence of a complex learning process, with a sort of trial and error procedure: bargaining agents develop relations that may even end up creating markets; the emergence of the synapses among brain neurons is the consequence of the interaction with other subjects and with the environment, etc.

When we train an ANN or develop another connectionist structure with a proper algorithm, we let a synthetic type of self-organization appear. The flexibility of ANNs is a direct consequence of the internal distributed organization, which is also very important in numerical approximation tasks. But such an organization cannot be produced 'by hand': this was in fact the original critique of multi-layer ANN, where it seemed impossible to establish the weights except in very simple cases. Back-propagation (introduced in Chapter 1) implements this trial and error learning method and can be interpreted as a process of organization of the various components of the network, starting with a randomly set ANN to finish with a well-shaped one. This is synthetic self-organization.

(4) Fault tolerance and (5) redundancy are characteristics generated by the distributed representation framework described above. Faults and errors in the 'hardware' – true electronic hardware, brain, social organization – do not usually lock a connectionist system because parallelism and subsymbolic representation allow the mechanism to run in a defective way. We strengthen the phenomenon if we allow redundancy in the hardware (for example, more hidden nodes, more agents in an organization, etc.).

For example, in a function like equation 3.3, we can to some extent arbitrarily modify one or more parameters without significantly modifying the output of the function. Indeed, each parameter contains only a small portion of information (here, the measure of the effects of x_1 and x_2 upon y). In other terms, connectionist models avoid the brittleness typical of traditional AI and of traditional computer applications.

From the previous description, it should now be apparent why ANNs are the most typical connectionist tool. With ANNs we can set up complex adaptive systems, exploiting their learning capability to a large degree. We can also have connectionist macro structures built upon connectionist micro ones. As the power of an ANN is stored in the connections among neurons, the links among neural agents, established (often self-established) in an adaptive interacting model, memorize the knowledge and the mechanisms from which the characteristics of the synthetic system arise.

3.1.3 Other approaches: expert systems and classifier systems

Among the other approaches that can be considered for implementing economic models with bounded rational agents, we mention expert systems (ESs) and classifier systems.

A wide definition of an ES is 'a computer program that performs a task normally done by a human expert' (Gallant, 1993). Technically, an ES is a software tool containing rules and information related to a knowledge domain; a tool that we can query for aid and advice. ESs are coded in computer macrolanguages or employ specialist shells, with meta-rules governing the interaction between the rules and the knowledge related to a specific domain. Famous examples (Gallant, 1993) of ESs are: MYCIN, diagnosing microbial diseases of the blood; Prospector, which helps in discovering minerals; Internist-I, able to diagnose 500 diseases based upon 3500 symptoms and containing 15 person-years of human expert work; R1/XCON, whose task is configuring computers. In economics and finance

ESs are now widely used; for example, to evaluate risks in credit assignment, to manage funds, to evaluate investments etc. An analysis of ESs in business is reported in Beerel and Horwood (1993). See also Trippi and Turban (1990).

All these ESs work on the basis of an input data set, such as symptoms or the geological characteristics of a site or customer needs etc., to which they apply a system of rules that yields their responses. The process of input acquisition can be interactive or batch; inputs and outputs can be more or less user friendly, with or without the evaluation of probability judgements; however, the kernel of any ES is the capability of linking inputs to outputs by rules derived from experts' work.

This successful AI field has produced many important results, with products based upon specialized software (the so-called inferential engine) managing rules of the IF – THEN – ELSE-type or true/false tables or more sophisticated lists of cases. The construction of inferential engines incurs heavy costs, but the engines are mostly reusable in different applications. The production of the knowledge base related to a specific application is generally as costly as the production of the engine, but it is only partially reusable. An important cost comes from the formalization of experts' knowledge. Experts can often only express their know-how in an unaware and vague way, despite their capability of reacting correctly in real-world situations. Interacting with 'knowledge engineers', the experts rationalize their information, often changing their minds during the process, but this activity is expensive. This is natural, as anyone can easily verify by attempting to formalize with a set of facts and rules a subject about which he or she has specific competencies or abilities. More generally, we are here dealing with the difficulty of understanding what knowledge is and how it is stored in the mind (Dreyfus and Dreyfus, 1986).

ESs are certainly useful for coding the rules governing the behaviour of artificial economic agents. If we want to build an artificial agent wired with behavioural rules and calibrated with more or less adherence to the bounded rationality principles, able to act and interact in an artificial environment, one possibility is to put those requirements into an ES. The problem is that, by construction, a behavioural model based upon an ES has a high degree of intrinsic rigidity, as with this kind of tool we can only build agents acting on the basis of a priori defined rules, without the ability to develop new rules which is so important for many economic problems.

CSs are certainly more powerful. We can easily discover analogies between ESs and CSs, as they are both based upon rules, coded by the experimenter in ESs or self-developed by learning in CSs. It is also easy, from the point of view of learning abilities, to discover differences. ESs are characterized by a high degree of rigidity, even if some learning capability is allowed; mainly, the kernel of an ES is always the product of an *ex ante* human activity. CSs are built upon learning, employing mechanisms which yield the appearance of links among variables; links are built as rules, in a form that allows the meaning of each link to be explicit or nearly explicit; in Marimon *et al.* (1990) we can see an example of interpretation of the rules developed by CSs. Models with CS-based agents can be highly useful in economics: certainly, they are more powerful than ES-based ones, which suffer mainly from the absence of learning capabilities.

If at present our choice is in favour of ANNs and GAs based upon ANNs, it is mainly because the following well-known characteristics of CSs conflict with our research goals:

- the complexity of the CS mechanism and that of the related learning strategies;
- the large role of subjective experimenters' choices in building CSs;
- the presence of a symbolic structure in CSs, inducing them to be less flexible than the other connectionist tools;
- the rigidity in dealing with continuum values, a process that is easy with ANNs and difficult with other tools such as CSs; obviously, this difficulty increases using tools such as ESs.

This is not however a dogmatic rejection, but a choice related to the results obtained in our work. It is also possible to link CSs and ANNs together from the point of view of learning (Belew and Gherrity, 1989).

3.1.4 Learning with bounded rationality

In this section we introduce learning processes in economic applications, as these are in our opinion central to many situations in the real world, where agents have to learn continuously to adapt their behaviour to the changing environment and to the consequences of other agents' behaviour.

As we have already remarked in Chapter 2 and in section 3.1.1, learning is not considered in problems where choices are made among a known set of possibilities, with a known outcome for each of them or with known probability distributions. It is not difficult to mention economic problems where learning is relevant, for example in cases where agents have to discover their possible choices, or in cases where their payoffs depend on the actions of other agents, or in cases of intertemporal optimization where the alternatives become less and less defined with the growing length of the planning horizon.

In this book we want to consider learning from the point of view of the bounded rationality research programme; as Arthur (1990b) points out: 'In designing a learning system to represent human behaviour in a particular context, we would be interested not only in reproducing human rates of learning, but also in reproducing the "style" in which humans learn, possibly even the ways in which they might depart from perfect rationality. The ideal, then, would not simply be learning curves that reproduce human learning curves to high goodness-of-fit, but more ambitiously, learning behaviour that could pass the Turing test of being indistinguishable from human behaviour with its foibles, departures and errors, to an observer who was not informed whether the behaviour was algorithm-generated or human-generated.' (See also Arthur, 1991.)

In order to implement this ideal target without falling into the trap of creating models that are too complicated to be managed, we consider artificially intelligent agents founded upon algorithms which can be modified by a trial and error process. In one sense our agents are even simpler than those considered in neoclassical models, as their targets and instruments are not as powerful as those assumed in those models. From another point of view, however, our agents are much more complex, due to their continuous effort to learn the main features of the environment with the available instruments.

This emphasis on building models populated with 'reasonably complex' agents is also aimed at creating theoretical structures which are closer to real structures. One fundamental objection which can be raised about models with perfect foresight agents is that in practice agents seem to have limited planning horizons and limited computational abilities, and that for many problems the solutions of theoretical models are not implementable. On the contrary, the solutions derived from models where agents have realistic abilities may shed more light on actual decision processes and global solutions.

Agents calibrated with this kind of limitation, but also with adaptation capabilities, can be the basis upon which to build large interacting models, like those of the following chapters, which arise directly from the economic or financial framework, or like the more abstract models of the Artificial Worlds (AW) literature (Lane, 1993a and 1993b). AWs are a class of models designed to give insights about emergent hierarchical organizations. Many systems, in chemistry and biology as well as in human society, appear to have the capability of achieving, over time, more complex organization. Mainly, emerging organizations are hierarchical. That is, the systems are composed of a number of different levels, each of them consisting of entities that interact with the others. For example, economic activities involve interaction between individual decision-makers, firms and households, industries, and national economies.

In such a setting, attention is directed towards discovering and interpreting the consequences emerging in aggregate results or in individual behaviour when the artificial agents are put together, with a set of rules defining the environment. These consequences can be unforeseeable or simply unforeseen; in both cases, the experimenters learn about the situations underlying their models (see section 3.3.6). While AWs are generally populated with pieces of replicating software codes or of rules useful for playing the evolutionary prisoner's dilemma (see references in section 3.3.6), in our models we mainly consider economic agents interacting in settings that can be interpreted in a market framework. Obviously, artificial results can only be truly understood by keeping in mind the specific structure they come from.

To summarize, we make three basic assumptions (see also Bourgine *et al.* 1991): (1) agents are learning and evolving ones; (2) they have bounded rationality; (3) they build representations of other agents' behaviour and interact.

3.1.5 Implementing bounded rationality with neural networks

After analysing ANNs and mentioning bounded rationality, we now want to discuss some points related to the implementation of the bounded rationality framework with artificial agents. We believe this is a useful step in the direction of putting realism into the processes of simulating human economic behaviour, as ANNs allows us to implement computer programs that share some of the characteristics of the working of the human mind, some of which are well described in the following quotation from Kosko (1992): 'We reason with scant evidence, vague concepts, heuristic syllogisms, tentative facts, rules of thumb, principles shot through with exceptions, and an inarticulable pantheon of inexact intuitions, hunches, suspicious, beliefs, estimates, guesses, and the like.'

We are therefore trying to evolve AAAs that behave like human beings, with errors, irrationalities and inconsistencies, but also with regularities, possibly self-developed. ANNs are proper for this task because they can not only interpolate the learned examples, but also introduce some degree of uncertainty in their replies, like humans do (see section 3.2.1). To store patterns into the structure of an ANN is like memorizing what in psychology are called 'chunks'; things that we know about a subject, for example the more common actions that one can choose in a typical economic situation. This is very realistic because commonly (always?) human subjects also, in order to outline decisions, actions and inferences, either recall 'chunks' or interpolate among them, without solving complex cognitive problems.

ANNs are instruments that allow an endogenous creation of this sort of decision process, as the rules that are implicit in the nodes of the network are formed on the basis of a series of examples; this is not true with other systems like CSs, where the rules are explicitly handled. Also note that as a consequence of our imposing some general learning rules rather than a rigid learning approach, our agents will in general not be all similar to each other, but will show a certain heterogeneity, which will be useful for generating realistic economic situations.

In the process of endowing ANNs with a behavioural interpretation in a bounded rationality framework, it is important to discuss the learning method which will be generally assumed in our models.

In our models, learning takes place contemporaneously with the acting phase, a choice that enables us to analyse the interactions between learning and acting.

Rules development follows weight determination which, in this kind of learning and acting model, presents a certain degree of indefiniteness.

As the data are commonly generated on-line, the training set is 'open' and training is not repeated on the same patterns, but always on newly generated ones; the process of data generation and learning is repeated for a reasonable number of days (cycles); this number is never 'large', or comparable to that of the learning cycles employed in a usual back-propagation training task. Thus a problem arises concerning the significance of the weights which are, in many cases, certainly under-trained.

A solution could be to repeat the learning each 'day' upon the set generated from the beginning of the experiment up to the present time or cycle; alternatively, the learning iteration could be set up at a regular interval of n days. The problem with these forms of mixed training is the computational time. Other considerations concerning this subject will be developed in Chapter 4, where we define the concepts of short- and long-term learning.

Finally, with regard to the main problem of the interpretation of the behaviour, we observe that a generalized 'ready to apply' tool is at present missing. So in sections 3.3.1, 3.3.2 and 3.3.3 we describe a heuristic method useful for discovering rules in neural agents, namely implicit rules developed during ANN learning or, in other terms, agents' adaptation. These are not the classic IF – THEN – ELSE rules of traditional AI, wired into agents or developed by evolving methods like CSs: mainly we will discover continuous causal links between input data and output responses in agents.

3.2 The development of computational devices with ANNs

With a suitable set of data and with a sufficient number of hidden neurons, we can train neural networks to make, in principle, virtually any type of feasible computation or classification.

The computation may concern, for example, forecasts, support decisions or the responses of a simulated agent to environmental situations or to other agents' actions. If the training is based upon a set of data containing pairs of input and output vectors (each pair is a pattern, in the neural jargon), there are no technical differences among these situations.

3.2.1 ANNs as computational devices and their interpretation as reasoning systems

ANNs are computational devices. An ANN uses numerical operations (nonlinear transformations of sums of input) to perform classifications, comparisons, forecasts, knowledge retrieval from neural knowledge bases, actions etc. The same is true of many other systems, for example when we use an IF construct in a computer macrolanguage or in an ES shell, since behind the execution of the instruction there is a lot of arithmetic.

Here we want to concentrate on the possibilities of interpreting ANNs as reasoning agents, because, even though in the models introduced in the next chapters neural agents perform numerical operations by mapping inputs into outputs, in many cases the resulting system can be understood as an artificial reasoning system, acting on the basis of rules that have been learned or self-developed.

How is it possible to interpret systems based on calculations as reasoning systems? This is a crucial issue, because our target is to construct learning agents which can behave in an economically plausible way without endowing them with all the necessary rules from the very beginning. An answer to the previous question can be given by noting that in computational terms, reasoning consists 'simply' in mapping inputs into a vector of possible responses, one of which is chosen. A large share of the product of the brain activity that we call intelligence (in short, the mind–brain output) is indeed made up of choices or, more closely, classifications. When we 'think', we mainly apply old rules to new data. What kind of rules? Certainly, in most of the cases, we do not use the rule-based reasoning system (IF–THEN–ELSE rules etc.) or the syllogism apparatus. The last one is the way of traditional AI, which has achieved very important results, but suffers high costs and complexity.

Natural intelligence certainly employs rules and syllogism, but only as subsidiary means of reasoning, used if one is faced with a difficult choice, or whenever more formal instruments may be needed (for example, a handbook or an ES).

The interpretation of ANNs as reasoning agents that we are proposing here is enhanced by the possibility of viewing ANNs as fuzzy systems. ANNs are certainly not fuzzy systems by themselves, but can reproduce their operating characteristics.

The term 'fuzzy' is used here with the same meaning it has in the fuzzy logic definition, where by fuzzy logic we mean the modern computational logic applied to intermediate continuous values from true to false. This is a very interesting characteristic which can be exploited to simulate, when necessary, the vagueness of many human attitudes and decisions. This makes ANNs even more adept at reproducing the kind of human behaviour we were describing before. ANNs have an advantage over fuzzy systems: they learn by example, while fuzzy logic requires a lot of careful hand-tuning.

A simple example of this connection between ANNs and fuzzy logic is the execution of multiplications. Humans perform them by recalling the exact values that have been stored in the memory, a result that in turn can be obtained by practising upon operations like the result of 7 times 8 or 8 times 5 etc. Such a practice can take place only in a limited range. The result can be emulated by an ANN with K output nodes whose values are 0 or 1; all outputs are 0, apart from the one whose position corresponds to the correct value.

Obviously, neither our minds nor an ANN can accomplish the exact evaluation of operations like 1234 times 98786, but only estimate a rough result; for example, in our case, to guess that the result is more likely to be in the range 110 000–120 000 than 120 000–130 000, without being able to say exactly in which one. In the same way, we can train an ANN to map into a vector of response whose range is between 0 and 1, one for each interval chosen, the results of the possible multiplications for a large range of inputs, admitting multiple fuzzy responses for the values that are near the edge of two intervals. For example, we can obtain 0 as the output of the node corresponding to the 100 000–110 000 range, 0.6 related to 110 000–120 000 range and 0.8 for the 120 000–130 000 range, etc.

Beyond the interpretation possibilities that we have described, the connection between ANNs and fuzzy systems is very important from the point of view of neural computation, and allows us to look at the similarity between ANNs and fuzzy systems founded upon fuzzy sets (Kosko, 1992) from at least two viewpoints: (1) the capability of dealing with wrong information; (2) the possibility of defining the multidimensional output of an ANN as a vector of fuzzy units, in which each value shows the degree of membership of an object in a fuzzy set. An example in the field of diagnosis systems will clarify the two matters: with fuzzy systems and with neural networks we can treat inexact patterns that have to be classified; with the same tools, we can ascribe multiple diagnoses to patterns, with different membership values.

3.2.2 Neural expert systems

ANNs can also be used to perform tasks which are usually implemented by ESs. We call these ANNs 'neural expert systems' (NESs) to emphasize this use; however, there are no differences between ANNs and NESs, either in terms of structure or in terms of algorithms; we emphasize here the use of NESs from an applied point of view and also for building models of agents.

In other terms, by building NESs we apply ANNs to problems mainly based on true/false input – output values, in some cases with the necessity of dealing with fuzzy outputs (see section 3.2.1).

Decision support systems, classification algorithms and rule-based control systems are all special cases of ESs. We have already defined (section 3.1.3) ESs as computer programs performing tasks normally done by human experts, and have pointed out their costs both in the construction of inferential engines and in the production of the knowledge base related to a specific application. If the rules were known, it would be easy to build an ES. This is the ideal situation which we would encounter when building a true ES with the collaboration of an expert who knew exactly the rules applying to the various cases; as mentioned in section 3.1.3, however, note that often experts do not know the rules exactly, see Dreyfus and Dreyfus (1986). Even assuming that such an ideal situation is encountered, there is a cost problem, due to the time required to implement all the necessary facts and rules, which in practical applications can be of the order of several thousands. Moreover, if the 'true' number of rules is one thousand, for example, one should also consider that such rules are not discovered immediately, but by means of a trial and error process involving the discovery of unforeseen and unforeseeable interrelations among rules, and the possibility that the experts may change their minds many times during the analysis. With an NES the results are not likely to be fully comparable with those of a true ES, but the cost is a small fraction of the previous ones. We prepare examples, or patterns; we can change our minds adding other cases or eliminating some of the earlier ones. The consequence is only that we have to train our network again; if we have already identified the correct parameters, such as learning rate, momentum and hidden node number, we need only the computer time necessary for running the training algorithm.

Summarizing, with Baum (1988), an ANN trained with a back-propagation algorithm, when applied to an ES '. . . performs as well as many human constructed expert systems or classification algorithms . . . It has the advantage . . . of being easy to implement, and requiring little human time, although it may require considerable computer time.'

Table 3.1 *The random training set of the NES*

x_1	x_2	x_3	x_4	x_5	y_1	y_2	y_3
1	0	1	0	1	0	0	1
1	1	0	0	1	1	1	0
1	0	1	0	0	0	0	1
1	1	0	1	0	1	1	0
1	0	0	1	0	1	0	0
1	1	0	1	1	1	1	1
0	1	0	1	1	0	0	1
1	1	1	0	0	0	1	1
1	0	0	1	1	1	0	1
0	0	0	1	1	0	0	1
0	1	1	1	1	0	0	1
0	0	1	0	1	0	0	1
0	1	1	1	0	0	0	0
1	0	0	0	1	1	0	0
0	0	1	0	0	0	0	1
1	1	1	0	1	0	1	1
0	1	0	1	0	0	0	0
1	0	1	1	1	0	0	1
0	0	0	0	0	0	0	0
1	1	0	0	0	1	1	0
1	1	1	1	0	0	1	0
0	0	0	1	0	0	0	0
1	1	1	1	1	0	1	1
0	1	0	0	1	0	0	0

As an example, in Table 3.1 we show a training set with 24 patterns of five inputs (from x_1 to x_5) and three outputs (y_1, y_2, y_3); all values are binary; inputs are randomly generated, while outputs are produced according to the following three rules:

IF x_1 = 1 AND x_3 = 0 THEN y_1 = 1

IF x_1 = 1 AND x_2 = 1 THEN y_2 = 1

IF (x_3 = 1 AND x_4 = 0) OR (x_4 = 1 AND x_5 = 1) THEN y_3 = 1

These simple rules give results of (apparently) high complexity. If we know them, it is very easy to write an ES reproducing the same responses; if we ignore them, one possibility consists of training an ANN, to produce an NES.

To replicate a situation with a lack of data, we use a sample from the set of the 32 possible cases; the training involves only 24 patterns, that is, 75% of the total. (If we trained the ANN upon the whole set of cases, the responses that we obtained would be perfect; however, knowing all the possible cases is not a common situation). With this partial training set and a run of 2400 cycles, that is, 100 epochs times 24 patterns, we easily obtain a perfect response from the training set.

With regard to the verification set, containing the remaining eight cases, we can see the responses of the network in the Table 3.2. If we employ four hidden nodes, the performance is feeble (see the three starred results), but if we raise their number, for example to eight, the results are good.

Contrary to the example, in building an NES it is useful to employ all the known patterns, without reserving a group of them for validation purposes; if other cases are possible, but with unknown responses, we can generate the responses of the network to them, repeating the experience by increasing the number of hidden nodes up to the stabilization of the network outputs. As we will see in the XOR example, in section 3.3.1, an excess of hidden nodes in a qualitative network does not create nega-

Table 3.2 *The validation set of the NES and related outputs with 4 or 8 hidden nodes*

x_1	x_2	x_3	x_4	x_5	y_1	y_2	y_3	y_1 (4 h.n.)	y_2	y_3	y_1 (8 h.n.)	y_2	y_3
0	0	0	0	1	0	0	0	0.07	0	0.15	0.01	0	0.03
0	0	1	1	0	0	0	0	0	0	0.05	0	0	0.11
0	0	1	1	1	0	0	1	0	0	1	0	0	1
0	1	0	0	0	0	0	0	0.01	0	0	0	0	0
0	1	1	0	0	0	0	1	0	0	0*	0	0.07	0.91
0	1	1	0	1	0	0	1	0	0	0.55*	0	0.06	0.99
1	0	0	0	0	1	0	0	0.90	0.03	0	1	0.02	0
1	0	1	1	0	0	0	0	0	0	1*	0	0	0.14

tive consequences. However, for interpretative purposes (see section 3.3.5) it is probably convenient if the number of hidden nodes does not increase excessively.

In actual cases of NES implementation, the training is generally founded upon a set of examples taken from experience; examples can also be constructed artificially with the aid of a human expert or from technical literature. These are not, however the only ways: for example, the knowledge can be extracted from artificially generated data.

There are several conditions and limitations that we have to check carefully in the training phase, like avoiding overfitting (see section 3.3.4) or assuring a wide coverage of the data space (obviously we cannot expect good inference in empty space), but in most cases, with the correct learning parameter, NESs learn and perform as well as ESs. We want to emphasize that the result is obtained for a small fraction of the costs involved in traditional ES building. For a wide ranging and accurate introduc-tion see Gallant (1993); some experiments are reported in Looney (1993).

NESs can also replace ESs in building interacting systems made with artificial agents driven by rule. This kind of NES can be developed by building the data necessary for training with the aid of economic rules, used to generate input – output pairs. Here we would have each neural network representing a small expert system trained to reproduce responses that incorporate rules. With independently trained NESs, founded upon different sets of initial weights, we can also reproduce differentiation among agents.

3.2.3 Building economic and financial models with ANNs

It is possible to define at least three ways of building economic and financial models with ANNs: two are models of agents and the third operates without implicit or explicit definition of agents.

1. Models with agents that use ANNs to form expectations. In the examples we will present in Chapters 6 and 7 the agents (the ANNs) estimate the future price and then act on the basis of such a forecast.
2. Model with agents, whose behavioural rules are implicitly and autonomously settled by ANNs, acting and trained in an interactive way (see Chapters 6 and 7).

    As we have already mentioned at the beginning of this chapter, these models can be used for performing experiments in artificial adaptive systems; by implementing controlled modifications to the environment or to the decision rules it is possible to derive plausible explanations of actual economical mechanisms. It is difficult, but not impossible, to derive predictions: think, for example, of a computer model resembling some social system of interest, or of the possibility that some of the experiments result in system behaviour that had not been either observed in practice or even thought of theoretically. This might push other researchers to study that system in new directions, and might also suggest practical interventions aimed at reducing (increasing) the likelihood of the negative (positive) scenario coming out of the simulation. Some scientific theories are useful in the same way, not by making precise predictions, but by suggesting that new phenomena might happen. An example is Darwin's theory of evolution, which does not predict when a new species appears, but clarifies the mechanism by which this happens. For an introductory discussion of these subjects, see Waldrop (1992).

3. The third kind of model is founded upon the direct use of ANNs to map inputs to outputs, interpolating or generalizing data or making forecasts, with ANNs intended as econometric tools.

3.3 Understanding behaviour

One fundamental problem in promoting the use of ANNs for theoretical and practical applications lies in the so-called 'black box' trap: end users are averse to using tools that work in ways which are not completely understood. We are not referring to the mechanics of ANNs, which are in fact well known, but to the implementation of the prescriptions coming from ANNs. For example, why should a financial trader buy and sell securities on the basis of the suggestion of an ANN, if its structure cannot be understood in terms of simple rules?

Even though it should be remembered that to understand the contents of either an NES or an ANN we have to take into account the main characteristics of connectionism, that is, the subsymbolic and distributed representation of meanings, it is certainly necessary to give answers to such questions. In fact, in many senses this may be the most useful research area of the whole ANNs field.

Here we try to propose some possibilities, which may be suggestive of future explorations. We start by introducing the techniques of hidden neurons (or nodes) interpretation and cluster analysis. Then we discuss a more general tool consisting of the evaluation of derivatives between input and output variables in ANNs. With regard to the possibility of simplifying networks to help interpretation, the following section proposes a method for reducing weight number. Finally, true rules discovery is proposed, both following a quantitative heuristic related to a single ANN analysis and introducing considerations useful in reading complex interaction phenomena in models containing many agents.

```
- - - - - - - - - - - - - - - - - - - - - - - - - - - -

XOR      Input 1      Input 2      Output

           T            T            F

           F            T            T

           T            F            T

           F            F            F

- - - - - - - - - - - - - - - - - - - - - - - - - - - -
```

(T=true; F=false)

Figure 3.1 *The XOR function.*

3.3.1 Interpretation of hidden neurons

A useful way to introduce the role of hidden neurons (or nodes) and their interpretation, is to review a classic problem, which has often been considered as a test for ANNs: the XOR Boolean function or exclusive-OR function. In Figure 3.1 we have the truth table of the function, with the four possible cases.

To review the XOR problem, we introduce an ANN scheme known as a perceptron (Rosenblatt, 1958), a modified pattern associator with linear threshold output units. A pattern associator is a simple two-layer (input and output) network, with modifiable connections (see Figure 3.2, network 1 or 2). In a perceptron we employ a transfer function of the type

$$f(x) = 0 \text{ if } x < 0; f(x) = 1 \text{ if } x \geq 0 \qquad (3.4)$$

where x is the sum of the weighted inputs of the neuron including the bias term (see section 1.2.3).

It is well known that it is not possible to solve the XOR problem with such a structure; we cannot find a solution, because of the following four inequalities:

$$w_{30} + 0 \ w_{31} + 0 \ w_{32} < 0 \qquad (3.5)$$

$$w_{30} + 1 \ w_{31} + 1 \ w_{32} < 0 \qquad (3.6)$$

$$w_{30} + 1 \ w_{31} + 0 \ w_{32} \geq 0 \qquad (3.7)$$

$$w_{30} + 0 \ w_{31} + 1 \ w_{32} \geq 0 \qquad (3.8)$$

where 0 and 1 are the two inputs (0 = false; 1 = true); w_{31} and w_{32} are the weights linking inputs to outputs and w_{30} is the bias (see network 1 of Figure 3.2).

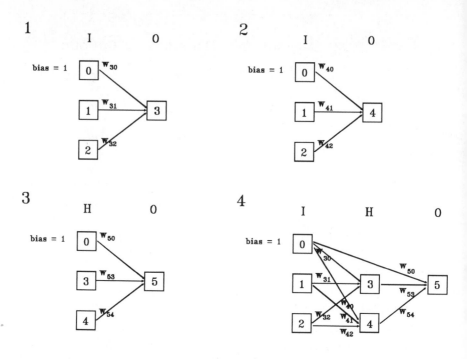

Figure 3.2 *Three perceptron structures combined in a three-layer network.*

Applying the transfer function (3.4), if the sum on the left of the inequalities is either equal to or greater than 0, then the output is 1 (true); otherwise it is 0 (false). A solution of 3.5 to 3.8 in w_{30}, w_{31}, w_{32} does not exist.

Instead, it is possible to construct perceptrons able to recognize specific cases among the four possible ones ($I_1 = 0$, $I_2 = 0$; $I_1 = 1$, $I_2 = 1$; $I_1 = 1$, $I_2 = 0$; $I_1 = 0$, $I_2 = 1$; where I_1 and I_2 are the inputs of the perceptron). The simplest way is described with the help of Figure 3.2, which illustrates a three-layer ANN (network 4) with two perceptrons in the first level, linked by a third one as a second level. Hidden neurons are simultaneously the outputs of the first and second perceptrons and the inputs of the third.

1   We build a perceptron recognizing the 'true-false' case $I_1 = 1$, $I_2 = 0$. Choosing $w_{30} = -1$, $w_{31} = 1$, $w_{32} = -1$ and applying the transfer function (3.4) to a structure like 1 in Figure 3.2, we have:

$$O_3 = f(w_{30} + I_1 \, w_{31} + I_2 \, w_{32})$$

from which:

$$O_3 = 1 \text{ iff } I_1 = 1 \text{ and } I_2 = 0$$

2   In the same way, we obtain a perceptron that recognizes the 'false–true' case $I_1 = 0$, $I_2 = 1$. Referring to the network 2 of Figure 3.2, with $w_{40} = -1$, $w_{41} = -1$, $w_{42} = 1$, always adopting (3.4), we have:

$$O_4 = f(w_{40} + I_1 \, w_{41} + I_2 \, w_{42})$$

which gives:

$$O_4 = 1 \text{ iff } I_1 = 0 \text{ and } I_2 = 1$$

3   Now we replace O_3 with H_3 and O_4 with H_4. Introducing the weights w_{50}, w_{53}, w_{54}, linking the bias and the H nodes (hidden) to the output O_5, we have network 3 of Figure 3.2. With $w_{50} = -1$, $w_{53} = 1$, $w_{54} = 1$, we have an OR logic function applied to H_3 and H_4:

$$O_5 = f(w_{50} + H_3 \, w_{53} + H_4 \, w_{54})$$

which gives:

$$O_5 = 1 \text{ iff } (H_3 = 1 \text{ and } H_4 = 0) \text{ or } (H_3 = 0 \text{ and } H_4 = 1)$$

Joining networks 1, 2 and 3 of Figure 3.2 we obtain network 4 which performs the XOR logic function; indeed network 1 recognizes the case $I_1 = 1$, $I_2 = 0$, giving $H_3 = 1$ in this case only and $H_3 = 0$ in the other ones; network 2 recognizes $I_1 = 0$, $I_2 = 1$, giving $H_4 = 1$ in this case and $H_4 = 0$ otherwise; network 3 performs OR upon the outputs of the hidden nodes, so:

$$O_5 = 1 \text{ iff } (I_1 = 1 \text{ and } I_2 = 0) \text{ or } (I_1 = 0 \text{ and } I_2 = 1)$$

This example points out that it is possible to give an interpretation to the structure of an ANN; here the meaning of the hidden nodes (H_3 and H_4) is in fact clear and explicit. However, it is fair to say that this is not easy in the context of problems which are more complicated and require the construction of an ANN with the heuristic methods that are commonly used in practice. Such heuristic methods do not necessarily develop the simplest rules and the simplest hidden node meanings which replicate a well-shaped human reasoning. Besides this, distributed representation of internal meanings certainly emerges when the structure is a little more complex than those examined in this section (see section 3.3.5 and Figure 3.4).

A second example illustrates this difficulty; here we look for a solution to the XOR problem with the same general method that is used in practice when estimating ANNs, that is, analysing data coming from an unknown structural data generating process.

Neurons and weights have the same meanings as those of the Figure 3.2, network 4; g( ) is the logistic transfer function (3.11). Here, with two hidden nodes:

$$O_5 = g(z \, B) \tag{3.9}$$

$$\text{with } z = (1 \ H_3 \ H_4)$$

and

$$(H_3 \ H_4) = g(x \ A) \tag{3.10}$$

where $x = (1 \ I_1 \ I_2)$

with weights (values obtained by applying the back-propagation algorithm to the XOR data described before and rounded off):

$$A = \begin{bmatrix} w_{30} & w_{40} \\ w_{31} & w_{41} \\ w_{32} & w_{42} \end{bmatrix} = \begin{bmatrix} 1.8 & 4.6 \\ -7.8 & -3.3 \\ -7.8 & -3.3 \end{bmatrix}$$

$$B = \begin{bmatrix} w_{50} \\ w_{53} \\ w_{54} \end{bmatrix} = \begin{bmatrix} -3.0 \\ -6.7 \\ 6.6 \end{bmatrix}$$

and

$$g(w) = 1/[1 + \exp(-w)]. \tag{3.11}$$

We can easily obtain the following outcomes:

I_1	I_2	H_3	H_4	O_5
0	0	0.9	1	0
1	1	0	0.1	0
1	0	0	0.8	1
0	1	0	0.8	1

Such an estimated ANN certainly solves the XOR problem, but is a very complicated one. The first hidden value is specific to the $I_1 = 0$ and $I_2 = 0$ case; it is equivalent to the Boolean function [(NOT I_1) AND (NOT I_2)] which we can also write as [NOT (I_1 OR I_2)]. The second hidden value is more general: it acts as [NOT (I_1 AND I_2)]. The rule linking the two hidden values recognizes only the $H_3 = 0$ and $H_4 = 1$ case, which equivalent to [(NOT H_3) AND H_4]. NB: the value 0.8 is equivalent to 1 in a Boolean use; the 0.1 value is equivalent to 0; the arithmetic of our ANNs properly acts in this way, via the logistic function.

Increasing the number of hidden nodes, we find that more hidden nodes perform the same task, but also with permutations of meanings and with some nodes that do not perform any task at all in the overall structure.

With three hidden nodes (weights are numbered in a way consistent with the preceding case; by increasing the number of hidden nodes, we shift the number identifying the output one):

I_1	I_2	H_3	H_4	H_5	O_6
0	0	1	0.8	0.6	0
1	1	0.1	0	0	0
1	0	0.8	0	0	1
0	1	0.8	0	0	1

With four hidden nodes:

I_1	I_2	H_3	H_4	H_5	H_6	O_7
0	0	0.9	0.2	0.9	0.9	0
1	1	0	0	0.2	0.2	0
1	0	0	0	0.7	0.7	1
0	1	0	0	0.8	0.6	1

With five hidden nodes:

I_1	I_2	H_3	H_4	H_5	H_6	H_7	O_8
0	0	0.8	0.5	1	0.2	0.6	0
1	1	0	0	0.1	0	0.1	0
1	0	0	0	0.8	0	0.3	1
0	1	0	0	0.8	0	0.4	1

We observe that it would be possible to find two matrices of weights by which (3.9) and (3.10) perform the XOR calculation, reproducing the simple direct meanings that we can ascribe to H_3 and H_4 in the perceptron scheme seen above. For example, the following weights run perfectly; let us observe that they are bigger than those used in perceptrons, because here we must generate inputs from which the logistic transfer function (3.11) could produce outputs near 0 or 1.

$$A = \begin{bmatrix} w_{30} & w_{40} \\ w_{31} & w_{41} \\ w_{32} & w_{42} \end{bmatrix} = \begin{bmatrix} -5 & -5 \\ 10 & 10 \\ 10 & -10 \end{bmatrix}$$

$$B = \begin{bmatrix} w_{50} \\ w_{53} \\ w_{54} \end{bmatrix} = \begin{bmatrix} -5 \\ 10 \\ 10 \end{bmatrix}$$

We can conclude that the inspection of hidden neurons produced by back-propagation is possible, but not meaningful in a genuine way: the rules that we can extract, analysing input to hidden and hidden to output weights separately, can be highly 'artificial', like here. They run perfectly, but they can be unnatural from the point of view of human reasoning and simplicity. As we will see in the next section, however, with cluster analysis this 'unnatural' internal structure can shed light on the structure of the problems we are dealing with.

In more general terms, as we have anticipated in section 3.1.2 and will see in Figure 3.4, hidden cell values are strictly related to the distributed or subsymbolic representation of internal meanings and so they are very hard to interpret directly.

With Gallant (1993) we can observe that effectively the 'interest in what the intermediate cells compute seems to have tapered off over the last few years'. But the problem of hidden nodes interpretation cannot be forgotten, both working in the direction of artificial behaviour interpretation and employing ANNs in function approximation. In this last case, each hidden node behaves like a function whose shape, added to those produced by the other hidden nodes, cooperates in approximating the goal function. A meaningful analysis of this aspect is in Smith (1993).

3.3.2 Cluster analysis

Cluster analysis is a statistical technique founded upon the idea of measuring the distances, in a given metric, between points in a multi-dimensional space. Applying it, we can form several groups, or clusters, of vectors. For each cluster it is of interest to investigate the characteristics of the patterns associated with the clustered vectors; in several cases we will discover a 'name' or meaning for clusters grouping patterns that represent situations, objects etc. with a strong common character. By also examining clusters of clusters, a complete hierarchical classification can emerge.

All this is of great interest from a cognitive point of view, because it can explain how the ANN makes inferences about patterns, assimilating them internally to different clusters; however, it does not give any direct meaning to single hidden nodes. Cluster analysis is on the contrary very consistent with the idea of distributed representation of meanings among the hidden nodes, because what we are measuring is distance between vectors, without specifically considering any single hidden node.

So, cluster analysis applied to the hidden nodes chiefly lights up the structural organization of the patterns, adding elements to the knowledge that we obtain by applying cluster analysis directly to the input vectors of the same patterns; that is, to their structure.

In the following example we consider the input values of the XOR problem and the hidden node values of the networks p (perceptron) and b (back-propagation). Data come from section 3.3.1.

I_1	I_2	H_{3p}	H_{4p}	H_{3b}	H_{4b}
0	0	0	0	0.9	1
1	1	0	0	0	0.1
1	0	0	1	0	0.8
0	1	1	0	0	0.8

Applying cluster analysis to the data of columns I_1 and I_2 we obtain result 'I' of Figure 3.3; with the data of columns H_{3p} and H_{4p} or H_{3b} and H_{4b} we have respectively the results 'H p' and 'H b' of the same figure. (In the figure, the reported values are always the input ones.)

Looking at these results, we can observe that by clustering the input vectors we obtain no useful data interpretation. On the contrary, the clusters arising from the analysis of the hidden nodes of the perceptron identify the two cases with 'false' output. However, the third case is the most meaningful: by clustering the hidden vectors produced by the artificial rules of back-propagation (see section 3.3.1) we can see useful information emerge, with the three cases that are similar to the 'true' OR responses linked together, but also with a clear identification of the two XOR true cases.

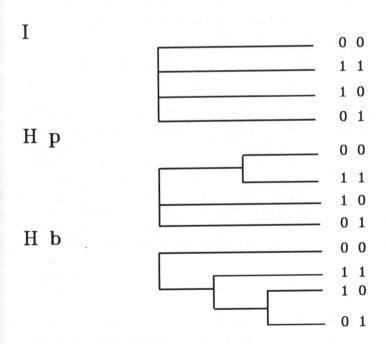

Figure 3.3 *Clustering the XOR problem in three different ways.*

3.3.3 Derivatives between outputs and inputs

When considering ANNs as functions mapping inputs into outputs, it is natural to refer to the partial derivatives of the outputs with respect to the inputs. Due to the nonlinear structure of ANNs, all the hidden and output values are influenced by the modification of an input value and these modifications also depend on the value of the other input elements. Refenes and Azema-Barac (1993) suggest a way to avoid the necessity of considering the values of each input element, substituting the exact effects of the weights linking input and hidden nodes (which depend in the input values) with a sort of fixed estimation founded upon a linear combination of the same weights, but our method seems to be more straightforward from the computational point of view.

The use of derivatives between outputs and inputs is also natural because back-propagation involves the use of derivatives of the error as a function of the weights. By using the data on such derivatives we can immediately compute $\partial_{On}/\partial_{Im}$ (Baum, 1988).

$$\frac{\partial_{On}}{\partial_{Im}} = O_n(1 - O_n) \sum_{j=1}^{K} [w_{nj} H_j (1 - H_j) w_{jm}]$$

where O_n represents a generic output element and I_m a generic input element; K is the number of true hidden nodes, which are globally K+1 with the bias node, numbered 0; the summation index goes from 1 to K; w_{nj} is the weight linking the j-th hidden node to the n-th output node; H_j is the activation of the j-th hidden node; w_{jm} is the weight linking the m-th input node to the j-th hidden node.

To calculate the derivatives we can use all inputs set conventionally to 0.5, since they are scaled between 0 and 1 in our applications. Outputs are also scaled, between 0 and 1, or between 0.1 and 0.9 to help learning.

When derivatives show a clear meaning, as in the examples of section 3.3.5, the use of the conventional input values (all set to 0.5) can be considered as adequate. But we can find problems where derivatives are close to 0 despite the presence of a causal link between the specific input and the specific output: we can look, as an example, at the effect of the presence of a trigonometric function in the data generating process where derivatives take any value larger than or smaller than 0 in the presence of a definite causal structure. In these cases it is possible that the derivative calculated around input values of 0.5 is correctly equal to 0, but also that if we used a value minimally displaced from 0.5 the derivative value could change.

To verify if such a problem is relevant, a good strategy is to examine the distribution of derivative values calculated for the inputs of each pattern.

Let us suppose that we have calculated the partial derivative of the n-th output of the network with respect to the m-th input with N different input values, where N is the number of patterns in the training set. We have a distribution of numerical values of the derivative, for which we can calculate the mean and the related standard deviation, both based upon the sample of derivative values. We can therefore see if the value zero belongs to the estimated distribution of the mean. If zero does not belong to the distribution, the result is a conclusive one; if it belongs to the distribution, we have to see how wide the distribution is. A wide distribution is, for example, compatible with a sin function (or others), with both zero and non-zero derivative values.

3.3.4 Weight elimination and minimal networks

A tool that may be used to facilitate understanding is limiting network complexity, which can be obtained by limiting the number of hidden nodes or by forcing some of the weights linking hidden nodes to other neurons to be equal to 0.

Several methods to automatize this process have been developed: Weigend *et al.* (1992), Nowlan and Hinton (1992) and MacKay (1992a, 1992b). We will refer here mainly to the work by Weigend *et al.*, known as 'weight elimination'. Such a method is obtained by introducing a complexity term into the objective function used to estimate the weights of the ANN, which becomes:

$$\sum_k (\text{target}_k - \text{output}_k)^2 + \theta \sum_i \frac{w_i^2/w_0^2}{1 + w_i^2/w_0^2}$$

where w_0 is the scale for the weights. The first term measures the performance of the network, while the second measures the size of the network; it acts in a direction opposite to the first, as a complexity term. To minimize the error, weights increase and so the complexity term increases. To reduce it, we allow the error measured by the first term to increase. θ represents the relative importance of the complexity term in the global error measurement.

The problem with this method lies in finding good values for w_0 and θ. For $|w_i| \gg |w_0|$ the cost of a weight approaches unity (times θ); for $|w_i| \ll |w_0|$, the cost is close to zero. θ may be dynamically adjusted during training, starting with $\theta = 0$ to allow the development of the network structure, and then increasing on the basis of factors like the previous errors, the average error and the desired error. (Public domain software, named RNA, running under DOS and written in C, is available from the authors.)

3.3.5 Discovering endogenous rules

Another possible approach to discovering rules is to consider robust rules, that is, rules that (1) minimize the number of variables included, (2) are valid, regardless of the values of the excluded variables, and (3) contain neither superfluous variables nor useless operators, either logic or arithmetic.

We look first at Gallant's (1993) work. In the direction of extracting rules from NESs, Gallant points out four issues:

1. the definition of a contributing variable, namely a variable moving the weighted sum of the inputs of a neuron in a direction consistent with a given interpretation;
2. the suggestion of accounting for the size of the contribution and for the absolute value of the weights;
3. the proposition of an additive searching strategy, adding clauses (variables) to a rule until it becomes valid;
4. the opposite proposition about a strategy of elimination, based upon a removal algorithm eliminating clauses (variables) until the rule is still valid.

Gallant's work is also concerned with the algorithms which are necessary to develop his suggestions, even though such algorithms are specifically related to binary multilayer perceptron models.

Here we propose some simple devices and heuristic techniques useful for applying Gallant's principles to our behavioural problems, on the basis of an example. We introduce an artificial sample of 100 patterns, with three inputs and three outputs, to experiment with the possibility of defining a heuristic method useful for extracting rules from an ANN, especially behavioural continuous ones. The artificial sample is generated in the following way.

Input variables I_1, I_2 and I_3 are uniformly distributed random variables in the range 0–1. Output variables O_A, O_B and O_C are generated with:

$$O_A = 2I_1 + I_2 - 3I_3 \tag{3.12}$$

$$O_B = -I_2 + I_3 \tag{3.13}$$

$$O_C = I_2 \, I_3 \tag{3.14}$$

Indexes in variables follow Chapter 1 notation; in this section, the indexes of the output variables should repeatedly change as we adopt different hidden node configurations; to avoid this problem we use letters here instead of numbers in the output layer.

We adopt the following evaluation criteria:

*   the back-propagation (BP) error (see section 1.2.2);
*   the percent (%) error, a rough estimate of the relative error of the estimates, obtained by dividing the sum of the absolute value of the differences between network outputs and targets by the sum of the targets (the division takes place between the two sums and not between each pair of error and target values);

- the coefficient of determination R^2, that is, the ratio between explained and total variance of the target values A, B and C. Note that if r is the linear correlation coefficient, R^2 is not equal to r^2 ($R^2 = r^2$ holds only if the model is a linear one, with intercept).

With two hidden nodes we obtain the following results, after a learning process of 200 epochs of 100 patterns, examined in random order in each epoch.

The output values O_A, O_B, O_C are guessed by the network, while the T are the targets contained in a sample of 100 patterns generated with random inputs I_1, I_2 and I_3, following (3.12), (3.13) and (3.14).

BP error 0.006141 % error 32.68

O_A vs T_A, r = 0.915 (R^2 = 0.803)

O_B vs T_B, r = 0.960 (R^2 = 0.868)

O_C vs T_C, r = 0.979 (R^2 = 0.897)

With two hidden nodes we have a large % error.

Now we introduce the numerical derivatives between outputs and inputs, based upon conventional 0.5 input values; derivatives are defined in section 3.3.3.

$\partial O/\partial I$	I_1	I_2	I_3
O_A	0.188	0.301	0.515
O_B	−0.212	−0.476	0.483
O_C	−0.026	0.658	0.594

The only clear meaning in these derivatives is the value of O_C upon I_1, which is close to 0, which we know to be correct. The other values are less meaningful and this is consistent with the poor result obtained in term of % error.

In order to interpret the results of the derivatives, remember that the input is scaled between 0 and 1 and the output between 0.1 and 0.9; the latter is a choice that facilitates the achievement of learning results, since otherwise it is highly difficult to obtain outputs of the logistic function near 0 or 1 (see section 3.3.3).

Introducing three hidden nodes we obtain the following results, always with 200 epochs of 100 patterns.

BP error 0.001061 % error 11.33

O_A vs T_A, r = 0.995 (R^2 = 0.939)

O_B vs T_B, r = 0.993 (R^2 = 0.940)

O_C vs T_C, r = 0.987 (R^2 = 0.876)

Now the percent error is small and R^2 is large.

The numerical derivatives between outputs and inputs are more meaningful, showing clearly the absence of links between I_1 and O_B and between I_1 and O_C.

$\partial O/\partial I$	I_1	I_2	I_3
O_A	0.465	0.214	−0.464
O_B	−0.031	−0.500	0.471
O_C	0.026	0.682	0.608

With four hidden nodes the results are very close to the previous ones. Error values and correlations are:

BP error 0.000968   % error 11.17

O_A vs T_A, $r = 0.997$ ($R^2 = 0.944$)

O_B vs T_B, $r = 0.997$ ($R^2 = 0.944$)

O_C vs T_C, $r = 0.991$ ($R^2 = 0.868$)

Numerical derivatives between outputs and inputs are:

$\partial O/\partial I$	I_1	I_2	I_3
O_A	0.437	0.203	−0.455
O_B	0.015	−0.489	0.517
O_C	0.015	0.613	0.699

With five hidden nodes results are nearly unchanged; error measures diminish, but without significant changes in correlations and derivatives. Error values and correlations are:

BP error 0.000216   % error 4.87

O_A vs T_A, $r = 0.997$ ($R^2 = 0.953$)

O_B vs T_B, $r = 0.999$ ($R^2 = 0.959$)

O_C vs T_C, $r = 0.997$ ($R^2 = 0.910$)

Numerical derivatives between outputs and inputs are:

$\partial O/\partial I$	I_1	I_2	I_3
O_A	0.460	0.165	−0.402
O_B	0.001	−0.447	0.432
O_C	0.009	0.637	0.557

Therefore the example shows that if we increase the number of hidden nodes, network outputs become strictly related to examples (with errors approximating zero) and derivatives become meaningful. Here the 'best' hidden node number seems to be 3, as a compromise between complexity and clarity of derivative meanings.

We have not been looking for the distributions of the values of the derivatives upon each pattern, with the aim of simplifying our presentation. Doing it in the case of three hidden nodes, we obtain:

$\partial O/\partial I$	I_1	I_2	I_3
O_A	0.357	0.161	−0.374
	(0.079)	(0.057)	(0.077)
O_B	−0.020	−0.394	0.389
	(0.024)	(0.106)	(0.119)
O_C	0.017	0.426	0.453
	(0.028)	(0.263)	(0.229)

where the values are the empirical means of pattern derivatives; in parenthesis we have the standard deviations of the distributions; the empirical means can be compared with the conventional values of the preceding tables, verifying that our interpretation is also confirmed by looking at the distributions and considering their standard deviations.

Proceeding now to examining the weights directly, in the next two matrices and in Figure 3.4 we can observe that with three hidden nodes the weight structure is quite complex to understand, even in a simplified presentation obtained by changing to 0 the weights not exceeding ±0.3, which is the range of the initial randomly set weights in this case. In the next matrices the first row is devoted to the weights linking the bias node, always set to 1, to the hidden (or output) nodes.

From inputs (bias plus three input nodes, on the rows) to hidden nodes (three, on the columns), we have:

	H_4	H_5	H_6
I_0	0	0	0.8
I_1	−0.6	1.7	−0.3
I_2	1.3	0	−3.1
I_3	−2.7	−1.5	0.6

From hidden nodes (bias plus three hidden nodes, on the rows) to outputs (three, on the columns), we have:

	O_A	O_B	O_C
I_0	−1.7	0.4	3.7
H_4	0	−2.8	−5.1
H_5	4.2	−0.6	−2
H_6	−1.5	2	−5.5

It is hard to understand the meaning of the weights by direct inspection; also, in a simple case like that treated here, it is very difficult to look for the presence or absence of links between inputs and outputs in a systematic way.

From Figure 3.4 it is easy to understand why: the structure of links is almost inextricable. For example, it is easy to find a connection between I_1 and O_A, following the path I_1 [→] H_5 [→] O_A; on the contrary it is impossible to find a path, defined through relevant weights with the correct sign, linking I_2 to O_A, although we are aware that the link exists and the ANN behaviour reproduces it.

To overcome these difficulties, we can now introduce the direct calculus of the product of two matrices: (1) the matrix A of the weights between the input layer (inputs are on the rows, as before) and the hidden layer (hidden nodes are on the columns, as before); (our goal is accounting for

Input layer   Hidden layer   Output layer

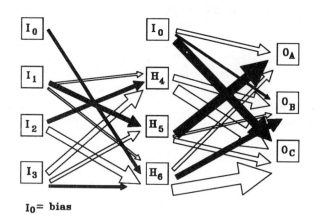

I_0= bias

**The size of the arrows is related to the
absolute values of the weights**

(empty arrows = negative weights)

Figure 3.4 *The simplified structure of the ANN.*

the rough links between inputs and outputs, and therefore we eliminate here the row related to the bias); (2) the matrix B of the weights between the hidden layer (on the rows) and the output layer (on the columns), again eliminating the row related to the bias. The matrix C is obtained by the product C = A B, and has the inputs on the rows and the outputs on the columns. Dimensions:

(input #, hidden #) × (hidden #, output #)

gives (input #, output #).

This kind of matrix, which we call a global weight matrix (GWM), has no quantitative meaning, but gives us qualitative information about true links and their signs. Proposing this new tool, we simply want to introduce an instrument that may be useful for discovering the hidden links between input and output variables; the matrix does not replace the ANN structure in any way.

We will review here the four cases introduced before, with the different hidden node schemes.

With two hidden nodes (inputs on the rows; outputs on the columns), we have:

	O_A	O_B	O_C
I_1	3.3	-3.7	-0.5
I_2	5.4	-8.4	13.2
I_3	-9.1	8.4	11.6

With three hidden nodes, we have:

	O_A	O_B	O_C
I_1	7.5	-0.1	1.4
I_2	3.9	-9.6	11.0
I_3	-7.6	9.8	13.7

With four hidden nodes, we obtain:

	O_A	O_B	O_C
I_1	7.1	0.3	0.1
I_2	3.8	-8.9	17.3
I_3	-7.8	9.0	5.4

And with five hidden nodes:

	O_A	O_B	O_C
I_1	7.6	−0.2	−0.1
I_2	8.8	−16.7	7.9
I_3	−14.3	18.1	16.2

By adding hidden nodes, the scheme becomes easier to understand with the same effect seen in section 3.2.2, showing that I_1 influences O_A, but it does not act upon O_B and O_C; that I_2 is positively linked with O_A and O_C and negatively with O_B; that I_3 is negatively linked with O_A and positively with O_B and O_C. In our simulation exercise these are only verifications of our prior knowledge; in an application in the field, these would have been 'discoveries'. The results show that here it is reasonable to work with a 3 hidden nodes network.

Following Gallant's scheme, we have therefore found the contributing variables of (1) and examined the size of contributions, as suggested in (2). We now introduce the remaining two steps, that is, (3) the additive searching strategy and (4) the opposite strategy of elimination.

To develop the two strategies, we shall use the GWM shown before, in the 3 hidden nodes case. We observe that the order in which input variables are introduced is very close to that followed by applying derivatives.

For example, to explain the output variable O_A in an additive way, we can feed our network (founded upon the weights obtained by the preceding learning) in an ordered way with the inputs I_3, I_1 and I_2. The order is built upon the importance of the absolute values of the weights appearing in the first column of the GWM, always in the 3 hidden nodes case. When we enter I_3, the inputs I_1 and I_2 are set at a value equal to the simple mean between minimum and maximum values and the outputs of the network are calculated; then we introduce I_1 also, keeping I_2 to the mean value etc. To adopt the elimination strategy we will proceed in the opposite direction. Remember that we use the ANN after the learning. The computation is made upon all patterns.

The results are (in parentheses we have R^2):

O_A additively explained with

I_3	r = 0.701	(0.434)
I_3, I_1	r = 0.949	(0.824)
I_3, I_1, I_2	r = 0.995	(0.939)

O_B additively explained with

I_3	r = 0.747	(0.492)
I_3, I_2	r = 0.994	(0.939)

Here, without introducing I_1, in terms of R^2 the result is very similar to the one obtained with three inputs.

O_C explained with I_3 r = 0.562   (0.094)

I_3, I_2 r = 0.989   (0.880)

Without introducing I_1, we have, in terms of R^2, a slightly better result than the one obtained with three inputs.

Adopting the strategy of elimination, which is useful with a small number of input nodes, we would obviously obtain the same results, in reverse order.

Finally, we have to look for mutual relations between the variables used to explain the outputs. We can easily do a check, for example for the last case, where by introducing I_2 in the explanation of O_C we obtain a huge increment in R^2: always with the fixed weights of the 3 hidden nodes case, we can calculate the O_C output with all the inputs set to their minimum values, obtaining 0; then we can increase I_3 to its maximum, obtaining a small increment (0.11 in our test case) in O_C; but with I_2 set to its maximum, the increment following the change in I_3 from minimum to maximum is large (the maximum O_C value is 0.72 in our case, due to the maximum pattern seen in the training set). The same phenomenon obviously does not occur when the effects are additive, as in the explanation of O_B, where the increment of I_3 always has a large effect, being independent of the I_2 value.

A very different approach is dealing with the rules in an explicit way. The work of Goodman *et al.* (1992) goes in the direction of considering large sets of rules: obviously not the set of all the rules hypothetically possible in relation to a specific input structure, but a choice made on the basis of some 'goodness' criterion. With a vector x representing the inputs and y representing the output, we would operate with rules like

$$\text{IF } (x_1 = x_1^{(i)}, \ldots, x_n = x_n^{(j)}) \text{ THEN } y = y^{(k)} \text{ with STRENGTH } w_{mn}$$

in which $x_1^a, \ldots, x_1^z$ and $x_n^a, \ldots, x_n^z$ are valid values of x_1 and x_n and $y^{(k)}$ is a valid output value.

The strength parameter is a weight linking the hidden nodes (representing rules) and the output nodes: specifically, w_{mn} is the weight linking rule n to output m.

In going from the input to the hidden layers we link, by a priori meanings, to each hidden node the set of inputs that are necessary to feed the rule represented by the node itself. Hidden nodes operate in a conjunctive way, like AND gates: each node outputs a value equal to 1 if all its inputs satisfy the rule wired into it. Learning takes place between the hidden and the output layers, modifying the w_{mn} strength values and so pruning the unnecessary or wrong rules by reducing the absolute value of the specific w parameter. In Goodman and Smyth (1993) we have an application of the preceding principles to rule extraction from a database of examples.

The method appears powerful but highly rigid from the perspective of our experiments, requiring the a priori definition of a set of rules. It can be considered closer to CSs than to ANNs.

3.3.6 Interpreting collective behaviour

In the preceding sections we have introduced several tools to study the implicit rules supporting the responses coming from an ANN. Those tools are not suited to understanding the outcomes collectively emerging from behaviour of many interacting units (e.g. AAAs). We must immediately say that we cannot offer tools that are as operative as the ones that we have just described in the case of interpreting collective behaviour, even though in future research it might be conceivable to explore the application of some of the previous techniques to a collective framework. For example, one could study clusters of agents, and see whether they can be interpreted in terms of behaviour. Or, to extend the idea of derivatives, one might think of 'social derivatives', where one analyses the reactions of the system as a whole to changes in the behaviour of some particular group, keeping constant the actions of other social groups, to see which group has more possibilities of affecting the aggregate outcome.

Here, however, we do not study such possible applications, but limit ourselves to a few general considerations.

The first consideration is about why understanding collective behaviour is more difficult than understanding individual behaviour. One can say that the problem is the 'classic' one of understanding links between genotype and phenotype. It may be impossible to forecast what kind of phenotype emerges from an engineered genotype, a subject that is central to the recent Artificial Life (AL) domain (Langton, 1989; Langton et al., 1992). Examples of this kind of model are Function-Object Gas (Fontana, 1992), Evolutionary Prisoner's Dilemma (Lindgren, 1992) and Tierra (Ray, 1992).

In this context the idea is to assume from the beginning that the behaviour of the individual agents is simple but adaptive, in order to explore the complexity of the aggregate behaviour. Clearly, from such a framework, unexpected results can easily arise in terms of the general characteristics of the system. Experience in many models of AWs shows, for example, the recurrent presence of a relatively short and almost unique period of great variance or turbulence, like the life explosion in the Cambrian period.

However, it is not easy to describe such structures in precise terms, even though such an operation would be useful to compare results of different models. If the adaptability allowed to the agents is only learning to forecast, as in case (1) of section 3.2.3, then the results follow directly from the behavioural rules and from the learning algorithms that have been wired into the model. All the collective emerging behaviour can therefore be understood as the result of alternative learning schemes that may be imputed to the agents.

The task is much more complicated in the context of models where agents not only learn to forecast, but also have to build up their own behaviour by themselves, as in case (2) of section 3.2.3. Here we must take separately into account both the variety of emerging behaviour of the agents and the aggregate effects of their different ways of acting. It is mainly in this context that we can discover the emergence of un-expected consequences of the initial choices that we have put into the model. The core explanation, and the related lesson useful to interpreting reality, is here the discovery of both the micro-mechanisms explaining individual behaviour and the way in which those mechanisms, even if very simple ones, can determine complex consequences, via the agents' interaction.

3.4 The behaviour of ANN-based economic models

This chapter has covered much ground, from the introduction of ANNs in the context of connectionist structures, to their use for simulating models with bounded rational agents, to the possibilities of interpreting individual and collective behaviour of systems formed by adaptive agents. Some of these aspects will be explored in the following chapters. At this stage it may be useful to use another quotation from an important piece of work by Holland and Miller (1991), which may now be more meaningful to the reader than if we had presented it at the beginning of the chapter: 'Economic analysis has largely avoided questions about the way in which economic agents make choices when confronted by a perpetually novel and evolving world. (. . .) This is so, despite the importance of the ques-tions, because standard tools and formal models are ill-tuned for answering such questions. However, recent advances in computer-based modelling techniques, and in the subdiscipline of artificial intelligence called machine learning, offer new possibilities. Artificial adaptive agents (AAA) can be defined and can be tested in a wide variety of artificial worlds that evolve over extended periods of time.'

This is the research programme that we explore in Chapters 4 to 7. We now give a short overview of the types of structures that will be explored there.

3.4.1 One-agent models

Here we do not have true interaction among agents: interaction is produced implicitly by environment responses. For example, assuming that single agent actions are relevant, we will be employing consequent rules in the determination of aggregate data.

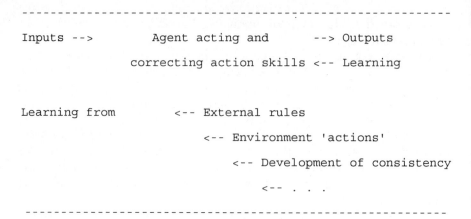

Figure 3.5 *One-agent model structure.*

Figure 3.5 shows the outline of a general one-agent model. In the figure, external rules and environment actions influence agents' learning, but this is not mandatory. In the training process, we can use data just produced by the network during the training itself. Data can also come from outputs of previous cycles or from the environment with which the network is supposed to interact; the last is, for example, the field of econets, see Parisi *et al.* (1990).

A special tool useful for specifying data upon which the agent learns is the development of consistency between two kinds of guesses made by the agents: guesses about actions to obtain given effects and guesses about effects achievable with given actions. Producing consistency between the two types of guesses is the internal goal of the cross-target technique described in Chapter 4. It is surprising that consistency is sufficient to develop or to explain either simple or sophisticated behaviour.

The cross-target technique is not introduced specifically for one-agent models, as it is relevant to all types of models listed here.

3.4.2 One-population and multi-population models

Figure 3.6 shows the outline of a general many-agent model, with all the agents belonging to the same population (that is, sharing the same characteristics, goals, knowledge, etc.) or belonging to several populations.

The agents are interacting, learning and adaptive ones. We shall examine the agents' capability in improving their behavioural skills and we monitor the global effects of their actions.

The role of rules, the environment and the development of consistency is the same here as in one of one-agent models. What makes things substantially different is the presence of interaction. The degree of unpredictability of model results is here at the maximum intensity. Interaction among agents

```
------------------------------------------------------------

Inputs -->          Agent acting and      --> Outputs
                 correcting action skills <-- Learning (*)

             .                     .
             .                     .
             interaction among agents
             .                     .
             .                     .

Inputs -->          Agent acting and      --> Outputs
                 correcting action skills <-- Learning (*)

             .                     .
             .                     .
             interaction among agents
             .                     .
             .                     .

Inputs -->          Agent acting and      --> Outputs
                 correcting action skills <-- Learning (*)



(*) Learning <-- External rules            | with data
    from     <-- Environment reactions     | generated by
             <-- Development of consistency | agents
             <-- . . .                      | interaction
             or
             <-- DIRECTLY from agents interaction

------------------------------------------------------------
```

Figure 3.6 *Many-agent model structure*

in the presence of nonlinearity gives the model the capability of producing very complex global outcomes. As a consequence of a minimal modification of the agents, the rules, the goals or the environment, the whole system can dramatically change, showing the enormous capability of these techniques to produce synthetic experiments in which unexpected phenomena can emerge.

Above all it is useful to develop models in which many different types of agents (populations) interact: this is crucial to improve the interpretative strength of our simulations vs real-world complexity.

Here we summarize a variety of situations, but others can appear. Populations can differ (1) with regard to the information set (the input structures, if we are working with ANNs) or (2) the outcomes representing the actions or the forecasts made by the agents. Also, they can differ from the point of view of (3) the rules applied to agents' expectations or from that of (4) the agents' structure used to develop endogenous rules.

Other differences are in the fields of (5) explicit goals, if wired into the agents' behaviour or (6) suggested as training elements. Finally, they can differ (7) as a consequence of external suggestions (such as imitation) made to the agents' actions.

From the point of view of the interaction among agents and between agents and the economic environment, we can construct models with increasing levels of complexity.

In the first step, we have models of agents (one-agent or one-population of agents) interacting with the economic world. In this kind of model we employ equations generating both input data and 'responses' to agents' actions. Input data can also come from historical time series, as in Chapter 5. The specification of the equations may (1) include the economic theory supposed to exist in the background of the economic system or (2) simply play an accounting role among the variables. Using the cross-target technique of Chapter 4, we limit our equations to be of the second type, with the purpose of building models without a priori economic theory.

In a second step, models include interacting agents generating aggregate results that endogenously influence the environment responses. An example: if we have agents buying or selling goods, prices can be established by a market model figuring out values consistent with the actions of those agents.

The third step is models of interacting agents, influencing each other directly by their actions: in such models, we can avoid the use of aggregate equations. This is the most complex and realistic of situations: in many real complex systems agents regulate their action by what they know about the behaviour of a small set of other agents, and the whole system runs. A good example is the 'New York city problem', where the question is: 'How is it possible for a group of independent companies to supply food for the millions of people in the city when most restaurants and supermarkets keep only a few days' worth of food in reserve? More generally, how is it possible for adaptive agents to find good solutions to complicated problems?' (*Scientific American*, January 1993). We underline that, in the last case, agents do not exchange information only by prices, but also learn continuously by observing other agents' behaviour, in an iterated trial and error process.

Another fundamental aspect of the role of the environment in models of AAAs is the co-evolution process, which we will describe in Chapter 7.

4
The cross-target method

Outline of the chapter

In this chapter we introduce an ANN technique developed to build AAAs without using a priori economic rules. Section 4.1 deals with the meaning of developing such models and introduces the structure of the method. The core of the technique is explained first and then some sophistications are introduced, the possibility of tuning AAAs' behaviour.

In section 4.2 the method is gradually applied, from simple to complex cases, also allowing interaction and imitation among agents. Experiments start, in section 4.2.1, with a simple analysis of motion behaviour, made by agents foraging for food, learning while acting and relearning from their experience. Learning by imitation is then introduced, developing agents able to do a specific task and studying their internal structures.

In sections 4.2.2 agents are supposed to behave in an economic context, starting with one-agent models describing a consumer reacting to price changes and a risk-averse stock market agent: the capabilities of the two agents come from micro-mechanisms developed by this method. The framework of the stock market model is described in section 4.2.3.

In section 4.2.4 we introduce external objectives in one-agent models; in sections 4.2.5 and 4.2.6 we use models of interacting agents, with two different populations and introducing both external objectives and external proposals: we will see high rationality behaviour emerging from randomness and imitation.

4.1 The cross-target method

We must, first of all, explain the name and the idea that exists behind the name. The name 'cross-targets' (CTs) comes from the technique used to figure out targets in a class of models founded upon artificial adaptive agents whose main characteristic is developing some kind of internal consistency. Our agents are developed by neural networks; we can specify two types of outputs of the ANN upon which we build each AAA: (1) actions to be performed and (2) evaluations of the effects of those actions. With our technique, both the targets necessary to train the network from the point of view of the actions, and those connected with the effects, are built in a crossed way. The former are built in a consistent way with the outputs of the network concerning the guesses of the effects, in order to develop the capability of deciding actions close to the expected results. The latter are similarly built in a consistent way with the outputs of the network concerning the guesses of the actions; here, we will improve the agent's capability to estimate the effects emerging from the actions that the agent itself is deciding.

What is the idea behind such a mechanism? Our hypothesis is that an agent acting in an economic environment must develop and adapt his or her capability to evaluate in a coherent way what he or she has to do in order to obtain a specific result or to appreciate the consequences of a specific action. The same is true if the agent is interacting with other agents of the same population or of other populations.

Beyond consistency, we can add other characteristics, mainly to obtain the possibility of tuning agents to make experiments.

4.1.1 Developing models without a priori rules

The CTs technique attributes a central role to learning mechanisms and can be applied without introducing, either explicitly or implicitly, economic rules in order to influence or to characterize agents' behaviour. The aim is to conduct economic experiments without the influence of any prior economic hypothesis (Terna, 1991, 1992a, 1992b, 1993a, 1993b).

We will see that CTs can reproduce economic subjects' behaviour, often in internal 'ingenuous' ways, but externally with apparently complex results. Mainly, economic behaviour, simple or complex, can appear directly as a by-product of developing consistency between (1) decisions about actions and (2) guesses about effects. For an external observer, this kind of AAA is apparently operating with goals and plans. Obviously, it has no such symbolic entities, which are inventions of the observer. The similarity that we recall here is that the observations and analyses about real-world agents' behaviour can suffer from the same bias.

Certainly, the CT algorithm introduced here is not the only way of dealing with AAAs, but it represents an interesting tool because it doesn't require injections of rules, optimizing behaviour or planning capabilities, but only a limited computational ability: that necessary to take simple decisions and to compare guesses with results.

4.1.2 The cross-target technique

Following other authors' work (Parisi *et al.*, 1990), we choose the neural approach to develop CTs mostly as a consequence of the intrinsic adaptive capabilities of neural functions. Here we will use feed-forward multilayer ones.

Targets in learning process are: (1) on one side, the actual effects of the actions made by the simulated subject; (2) on the other side, the actions needed to match guessed effects.

Figure 4.1 describes an AAA's learning and behaviour in a CT scheme. The AAA has to produce guesses about both its own actions and their effects, on the basis of an information set (the input elements are $I_1, \ldots, I_k$). Actual effects are estimated through the guessed actions, also taking into account the consequences from the interaction among agents, if any; the results are used to train the mechanism that guesses the effects. Actions that we measure to be necessary to match guessed effects are, on the contrary, employed to train the decision mechanism about actions. In the last case we have to use inverse rules, even though some problems arise when the inverse is indeterminate.

The CTs method, introduced to develop economic subjects' autonomous behaviour, can also be interpreted as a general algorithm useful for building behavioural models without using constrained or unconstrained optimization techniques. The kernel of the method, conveniently based upon ANNs (but it could also be conceivable with the aid of other mathematical tools), is learning by guessing and doing: the control capabilities of the subject can be developed without defining either goals or maximizing objectives.

The CT method can appear to be related to the Temporal Difference (TD) Learning of Barto and Sutton (Sutton, 1988; Tesauro, 1992), which learns from the differences between temporally successive predictions – or action outcomes – of the system, having a final target perfectly known at the end of the run. In the TD method we have a special and powerful case of true supervised learning, where an external teacher can suggest

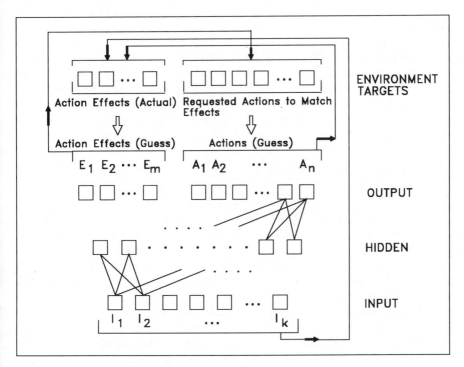

Figure 4.1 *The cross-target construction.*

correct target values. Also TD, like CT, addresses the issue of consistent learning, but with delayed feedback founded upon a true target value; CT uses immediate tentative targets, self-generated and never corrected by an external teacher. The aim of CT is in effect to generate time paths for relevant variables, without any final or intermediate externally known objective, operating only with simple rules to adapt both behaviour and predictions.

Now we may introduce some technical explanations of CTs, with the aid of the general scheme of Figure 4.1, observing that (1) the inputs of the model are mainly data coming from the environment or from other agents' behaviour, (2) they can be dependent on or independent of the previous actions of the simulated artificial subject, and (3) targets are known only when actions take place.

The CT algorithm is a learning and acting one: action is necessary to produce the information from which we can construct targets to train the ANN that simulates the subject. A training set cannot be constructed here in the usual way because the rules linking the inputs and outputs of the ANN have 'to be discovered' by the experiments led by AAAs. Learning and acting take place in four steps each 'day'; a day is the sum of the four steps required to perform a full cycle of estimation of outputs and of back-propagation of errors, correcting the neural network weights. Initial weights are randomized in a given range.

Looking at Figure 4.1, the four steps can be introduced in the following sequence.

1. Outputs of the ANN: The actions to be accomplished, reported on the right side of Figure 4.1, and the effects of these actions, reported on the left side of the same figure, are guessed following inputs and network weights.

2. Targets for the left side of the network: The targets for the effects supposed to arise from actions, as guessed in the left side of the output layer in Figure 4.1, are figured out by the independently guessed actions. In this way, guesses about effects become closer to the true consequences of actual actions.

3. Targets for the right side of the network: The differences measured in step 2 between targets and ANN outputs on the effect side can be inversely interpreted as starting points for action modifications, to match the guessed effects. So they are used to build the targets for the mechanism that guesses the actions. Since the inverses of the formulas shown below are often undefined, corrections are shared randomly among all the targets to be constructed; besides, when several corrections concern a target, only the one with the largest module is chosen. In this way, we would like to imitate the actual behaviour of a subject requested to obey several independent and inconsistent commands: probably the most imperative, here the largest value, will be followed.

4.   Back-propagation: Learning takes place, correcting weights in order to obtain guessed effects closer to the consequences of guessed actions, and guessed actions more consistent with guessed effects. Thus, we have two learning processes, both based upon the guesses of the elements of the opposite side of the network.

This double-sided process of adaptation, with interaction among agents and long-term learning introduced at the end of this section, ensures the emergence of non-trivial self-developed behaviour, from the point of view of the time paths of the values generated by the outcomes of the agents.

We can now explain in a formal way the acting and learning algorithm of CTs, introducing a generic effect E_1 arising from two actions, named A_1 and A_2. The target for the effect is:

$$E_1' = f(A_1, A_2) \tag{4.1}$$

where f is a definition, linking actions to effects on an accounting basis.

Our aim here is to obtain an output E_1 (the guess made by the network) closer to E_1', which is the correct measure of the effect of actions A_1 and A_2. The error related to E_1 is:

$$e = E_1' - E_1$$

or, by convention in ANN development, one half of the square of $E_1' - E_1$. To minimize the error, we back-propagate it through network weights.

Our aim now is to find actions, as outputs of our network, more consistent with the outputs produced by the effect side. So we have to correct A_1 and A_2 to make them closer to A_1' and A_2', which are actions consistent with the output E_1. We cannot figure out the targets for A_1 and A_2 separately. From equation 4.1 we have:

$$A_1 = g_1(E_1', A_2) \tag{4.2}$$

$$A_2 = g_2(E_1', A_1) \tag{4.3}$$

Choosing a random value τ_1 from a random uniform distribution whose support is the closed interval [0, 1] and setting $\tau_2 = 1 - \tau_1$, from equations 4.2 and 4.3 we obtain:

$$A_1' = g_1(E_1' - e{\cdot}\tau_1, A_2) \tag{4.4}$$

$$A_2' = g_2(E_1' - e\tau_2, A_1) \tag{4.5}$$

Functions g_1 and g_2, being obtained from definitions that link actions to effects mainly on an accounting basis, usually have linear specifications; so equations 4.4 and 4.5 generally give solutions that are globally consistent. The errors to be minimized are:

$$a_1 = A_1' - A_1$$

$$a_2 = A_2' - A_2$$

Equations 4.4 and 4.5 would be unacceptable as inversions of true dynamic functions, but they are used here as a simplifying tool (mainly for the presence of random separation obtained by τ_1 and τ_2 values), always to generate time paths for variables, without a priori or external suggestions.

When the actions determine multiple effects, they are included in multiple definitions of effects. So, those actions will be affected by several corrections; as reported in 3 above, only the largest absolute value is chosen.

Input and target variability, generated in both deterministic and random ways, is required to ensure the economic plausibility of the experiments, but is also necessary to ensure that the outputs and the targets of the ANN change. Lacking such variability, on the basis of the initial random weights of the network and following CTs, in most cases all outputs would be frozen at about 0.5, with perfect but merely apparent learning results.

With the proper variability, we repeat for a given number of cycles (days) the four steps introduced to describe Figure 4.1. The learning following the fourth step of each day gives a sort of local adaptation to the changes of the environment.

Analysing the changes in the weights during the process we can show that the matrix of weights linking input to hidden elements has little or no changes, while the matrix of weights from hidden to output layer changes in a relevant way. Only hidden-output weight changes determine the continuous adaptations of ANN responses to the environment modifications, as the output values of hidden layer elements stay almost constant.

This situation is not caused by linear separability of the problem (see section 3.3.1 where the XOR function represents a classic case of a linear inseparable problem), as we can verify by applying the long-term learning explained above, but it is the consequence of very small changes in targets (generated by the CT method) and of a reduced number of learning cycles.

The resulting network is certainly under-trained (see also section 3.1.5). Consequently, the simulated economic agent develops a local ability to make decisions, but it has difficulties in coping with large environmental changes. This case resembles an actual consumer who is not able to determine his/her demand if prices change dramatically.

This is short-term learning as opposed to long-term learning, in analogy with the psychologists' distinction between short- and long-term memory: (1) the learning and acting phase produces neural agents continuously modifying their weights, in a local way, to adapt to environmental changes; (2) *ex post*, relearning the weights of the neural networks engaged in the experiment and using as data the historical records of the events that have occurred, we can obtain ANNs also able to react, without subsequent learning, to major changes in environmental conditions.

The second type of learning can also take place periodically upon a short segment of data (for example, every fifty days referring to the previous one hundred days – or upon a sample of the full historical data set, always with satisfying results).

We will introduce two examples of long-term learning: the first in section 4.2.1, related to a little experiment of motion, and the second at the end of section 4.2.6, to develop a long-term trained agent behaving in the stock market. From the structure of such an agent we will extract the rules implicitly developed, as in section 3.3.5.

4.1.3 Cross-targets, external goals and external proposals

With CTs we obtain agents that behave on the basis of the development of consistency among guesses about their actions and related effects. This sort of consistency is sufficient to obtain self-developed micro-mechanisms, as reported in the connectionist robot literature (Connell, 1990), which are very simple, but sufficient to characterize realistic economic behaviour.

To improve the capabilities of CTs in the development of economic experiments and to offer to the experimenter useful tools directed to the tuning of the agents' behaviour, some improvements on the method can be introduced: (1) the use of external objectives (EOs), to direct the guesses of the effects, and (2) the use of external proposals (EPs) to influence the guesses about actions. EPs and EOs are external targets: the EO replaces the cross-target to train the specific output processing element, but the original CT target survives for the crossed training of the actions; any EP represents one of the multiple targets – from which only the largest is chosen – used to train the side of the model that guesses the actions.

Simple examples of EOs are the following: for a household, obtaining a good match between food purchase and food requirement, increasing money at a constant rate or not working more than a maximum, etc.; for an entrepreneur, maintaining a constant difference between costs and benefits, etc.

EPs suggest actions: the source of the suggestions can also be randomness, which is for example sufficient in section 4.2.6 to explain in a radical way what apparently could be the effects of reason. Another kind of EP is imitation, which is a powerful means of exchanging information among agents; imitation is well known to sociologists, but it is almost unknown in economic models, where agents exchange information mainly by prices.

In conclusion, EOs are targets used to train the side of the ANN that guesses the effects, while EPs represent one of the multiple targets used to train the side of the model that guesses the actions.

4.2 Experiments with cross-targets

We now introduce several experiments developed with the CT method, mainly in the field of economics. Before doing so, however, we will present two analyses of artificial behaviour: (1) subjects foraging for food on a plane, with imitation of other subjects' actions; (2) subjects learning to solve a problem by imitation. The role of these experiments is to introduce some technique capabilities in our work, such as learning repetition and imitation, starting with very simple situations in a stylized environment.

In the examples, we will look both for emerging aggregate behaviour and try to discover the internal mechanisms, often micro-mechanisms, generating the behaviour of each agent. Some very interesting results in the connectionist literature about robots (e.g. Beer, 1990; Connell, 1990; Mel, 1990) stress the importance of uncorrelated mechanisms governing independent single minimal aspects of the apparent global action of a connectionist robot, whose complexity is the consequence of those independent functions.

With Connell (1990), we have: 'Like Simon's metaphorical ant (Simon, 1969) the complexity of a creature's action is not necessarily due to deep cognitive introspection, but rather to the complexity of the environment it lives in.' R.A. Brooks, introducing Connell's book (Connell, 1990): '... has shown how a robot can appear to an observer to be successfully carrying out high level tasks, seemingly with goals and motivations, persistence and plans. In fact, as we read his description we find that the robot has no such entities. They are inventions of the observer.'

For an observer, the behaviour produced by the AAAs of our models also seems to match the actions of realistic economic actors, appearing to be rational, as if they operated with goals and plans. Obviously, our agents have no such symbolic entities, which exist only in the observer's mind. The assumption is that the observations of economists about real-world agents' behaviour could suffer from the same bias.

Finally, we stress the following aspect: operating only on the basis of the development of agents' consistency, CTs develop behaviour without optimization, always explaining actions and their effects in a simple and 'parsimonious' way.

4.2.1 Simple preliminary experiments

We now introduce the two preliminary experiments proposed in section 4.2, which are useful both for explaining the role of the repeated *ex-post* learning proposed at the end of sections 3.1.5 and 4.1.2, and for presenting the capabilities of random or imitative behaviour in explaining complex situations.

(a) Agents foraging for food

The experiment on the motion of agents foraging for food is built upon the following scheme.

On a plane with (x, y) coordinates, the subject is initially in (10, 10) while the food is fixed in (0, 0). The ANN simulating the subject has as inputs (which are the targets founded in the previous cycle):

X(t–1),   the position in the x direction at time t–1;
Y(t–1),   the position in the y direction at time t–1;
dX(t–1),   the step in the directions x, at time t–1 (bounded in the range ±1);
dY(t–1),   the step in the directions y, at time t–1 (bounded in the range ±1).

Using CT terminology, the same ANN produces as outputs two guesses about effects and two guesses about actions.
    Guesses about effects are:

X(t), Y(t)

Guesses about actions are dX(t) and dY(t), all with the same meaning of the input values.
    Targets are:

$X'(t)$ = $X(t–1) + dX(t)$;
$Y'(t)$ = $Y(t–1) + dY(t)$;
$dX'(t)$ = $dX(t) + X(t) – X'(t)$, which is the correct action to match $X(t)$, increasing $dX(t)$ if $X(t) – X'(t) > 0$ and decreasing it in the opposite case;
$dY'(t)$ = $dY(t) + Y(t) – Y'(t)$, as before.

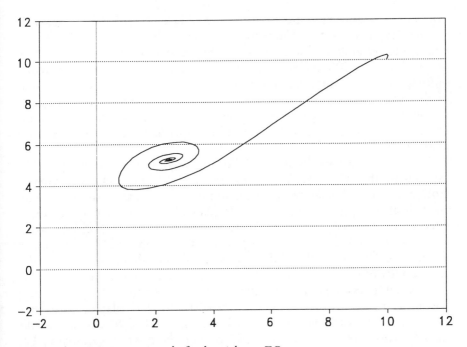

Figure 4.2 *Moving towards food, without EO.*

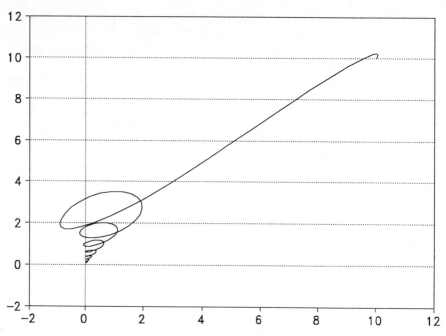

Figure 4.3 *Moving towards food, with EO.*

Positions X(t) and Y(t) also have the meaning of measuring the distance of the artificial subject from the food (the distance is evaluated by employing rectangular coordinates). In Figure 4.2 we report the position of the agent in 200 cycles of acting and learning; in each cycle, representing one day or step, the movement is determined by the action outputs of the ANN. Each position is linked with the succeeding one, plotting a continuous line. The agent goes towards the food on the basis of a simple implicit mechanism, which also explains the locking situation in the middle of the path.

The mechanism works in the following way: at the beginning of the experiment the ANN produces random outputs, but in a small interval around the central value between the minimum and maximum ones. This effect is always present and is easily explained by considering the consequence of the initial random choice of the weights, which gives on average a null sum of the inputs of the sigmoidal transformation. In the case of the logistic functions, that input gives an output about 0.5, which also corresponds to the simple mean between minimum and maximum values. The initial guesses about the effects of the movement give estimated positions around the point (0, 0), where the food is placed, with large variability; this result emerges from the range [−20, 20] assigned to the spatial coordinates. CTs immediately correct these wrong estimates, but they also correct the guesses about actions (the movements), to develop

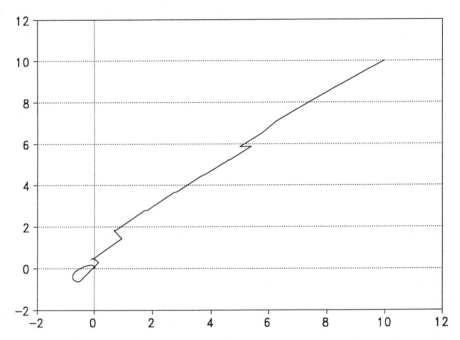

Figure 4.4 *Moving towards food, following an ANN with weight coming from repeated learning.*

their consistency with the guesses of effects. So, the artificial agent moves in the correct direction, but the process rapidly goes into a locking situation, with mutual consistency between effects and actions.

If we now impose an EO on the side of the effects, namely the target of reducing the distance from the food, in each cycle, to 75% of the distance in the previous cycle (the measure of the distance from the current position to the point $(0, 0)$ is directly obtained by the rectangular coordinates of the position), the food is easily gained, as reported in Figure 4.3. We underline that no suggestion is introduced about the direction of the movement.

In Figure 4.4 we present the case of Figure 4.3 again, but with an ANN whose weights come from a repeated learning process of 200 000 cycles. The learning process is applied upon the full 200 cycles of historical data of a single acting and learning run, in sequential order, with a 0.9 momentum coefficient.

The simulated agent reaches the food in a few steps (fewer than one hundred), going directly towards it, despite some uncertainty.

We can now produce two GWMs (see section 3.3.5), the first related to the agent described in Figure 4.3, representing the effect of short-term learning (see section 4.1.2), the second related to the agent of Figure 4.4, with the effects of long-term learning.

The GWM of the agent of Figure 4.3 is the following; the rows represent the input values, that is, the targets of the previous cycle, while the columns contain the output values.

Outputs Inputs	X(t)	Y(t)	dX(t)	dY(t)
X'(t–1)	–0.1035	–0.0171	0.0330	0.0017
Y'(t–1)	–0.0406	–0.0308	–0.0449	–0.0213
dX'(t–1)	0.0381	0.0245	0.0144	–0.0125
dY'(t–1)	–0.0140	–0.0227	0.1088	0.0290

Clearly, with short-term learning, we have a limited amount of weight correction, here only 200, determining soft links between each input and each output; our ANN rapidly reacts in each cycle or day to the targets coming from the CT mechanism mainly because, by construction, they are never very different from the output values; so the adaptation is obtained by changing the weights slightly, mainly those from the hidden layer and the output layer. We can observe this kind of soft ANN structure in the GWM matrix.

We can also observe that other adaptive functions or algorithms could be used, such as classifier systems, but with a lack of generality and without the simple passage from short-to-long term learning that we are considering here.

Going to the long term, with the agent of Figure 4.4, we have the following GWM, showing hard input–output links.

Outputs Inputs	X(t)	Y(t)	dX(t)	dY(t)
X'(t–1)	– 16.9111	– 5.7756	7.2730	40.0658
Y'(t–1)	–8.3577	–1.6650	6.1658	20.0175
dX'(t–1)	–75.9463	–46.7457	182.9647	81.7869
dY'(t–1)	–71.1736	–46.5281	99.4387	42.3390

To interpret this second GWM matrix, we will extract the implicit rules developed by long-term learning. However, first of all we observe its values: guesses about the position on the plane, evaluating the effect of the actions, are influenced mainly by the action inputs. The reasons for this result, which seems to be counter-intuitive, come from the strong links joining input and output values about actions. The actions are strongly influenced by the previous ones and so guesses about the position on the plane can be founded upon previous actions, while actually they depend on the current ones. As an interpretation we can suggest that the subject has memorized completely the sequence of steps necessary to reach the food and acts to reproduce that sequence, regardless of the position in each day or after each step. Is this global interpretation confirmed by a technical analysis?

Considering the ANN weights after the relearning process, that is, the ANN upon which the agent of Figure 4.4 is founded, we analyse the derivatives between each output and all the inputs. For each output variable we consider: (1) derivatives calculated for a hypothetical mean point of input, where all variables assume their mean value (in the ANN metrics, all the values are 0.5). These derivatives are called Mean Point Derivatives (MPDs); (2) derivatives calculated for each pattern. In order to facilitate the analysis of these results, we calculate the mean and the standard deviation of the derivatives of each pattern. These derivatives are called Mean Derivatives (MDs).

Output variable X(t)

inputs	X′(t–1)	Y′(t–1)	dX′(t–1)	dY′(t–1)
MPD	0.024	0.008	0.009	0.028
MD mean	–0.016	–0.009	–0.144	–0.127
MD stdv	0.146	0.063	0.530	0.558

Output variable Y(t)

inputs	X′(t–1)	Y′(t–1)	dX′(t–1)	dY′(t–1)
MPD	0.009	0.003	0.003	0.010
MD mean	–0.014	–0.004	–0.128	–0.127
MD stdv	0.088	0.027	0.461	0.494

Output variable dX(t)

inputs	X′(t–1)	Y′(t–1)	dX′(t–1)	dY′(t–1)
MPD	–0.071	–0.014	0.064	–0.127
MD mean	–0.033	0.000	0.315	0.092
MD stdv	0.190	0.060	0.831	0.842

Output variable dY(t)

inputs	X′(t–1)	Y′(t–1)	dX′(t–1)	dY′(t–1)
MPD	0.036	0.019	0.088	0.003
MD mean	0.080	0.040	0.140	0.041
MD stdv	0.176	0.081	0.202	0.184

To read these data we observe both the value of the derivative at the average point and the standard deviation of the average of pattern derivatives: a large standard deviation can signal the existence of situations where a modification of the input value has an important role, even if the mean does not appear to be relevant. We confirm here the previous interpretation: all the output variables are mainly affected by the third and fourth input values; we can see however that a location coordinate, that is, $X'(t-1)$, also has a role. The sequence of steps is self-determined, but also controlled by a spatial coordinate. We can also investigate the implicit rules developed by the training process, following the method proposed in section 3.3.5.

In a CT exercise, the values of R^2 are not interesting, since the targets can be interpreted as values suggesting corrections to develop consistency, and not values to be approximated. To apply that method here, we have to define the maximum R^2 result artificially, in order to get the R^2 values obtained by introducing only subsets of the input values into the ANN; as in section 3.3.5, the excluded inputs are set to their intermediate value between minimum and maximum. The artificial R^2 is set to $R^2 = 1$, corresponding to the result that we obtain by applying the ANN to a set of data in which the targets are exactly the output values of the ANN after the relearning process. (Alternatively, we could use the outputs vs the targets of the relearning task, in which case $R^2 < 1$.)

From the GWM values and MD analysis we can adopt the following sequence in the additive rule construction, for all output variables: $dX(t-1)$, $dY(t-1)$, $X(t-1)$, $Y(t-1)$.

The $X(t)$ reconstruction with limited input gives the following R^2 results:

Variables in input	R^2
$dX'(t-1)$	−0.357
$dX'(t-1)$, $dY'(t-1)$	0.121
$dX'(t-1)$, $dY'(t-1)$, $X'(t-1)$	0.940

The $Y(t)$ reconstruction gives:

Variables in input	R^2
$dX'(t-1)$	−0.304
$dX'(t-1)$, $dY'(t-1)$	0.588
$dX'(t-1)$, $dY'(t-1)$, $X'(t-1)$	0.980

The results show that data related to the previous movements are essential in explaining guesses about the agent's current position, but only if they are jointly considered. Furthermore, we have a near perfect ANN performance when we introduce a spatial coordinate (the X).

The $dX(t)$ reconstruction gives:

Variables in input	R^2
$dX'(t-1)$	0.758
$dX'(t-1)$, $dY'(t-1)$	0.849
$dX'(t-1)$, $dY'(t-1)$, $X'(t-1)$	0.985

The $dY(t)$ reconstruction gives:

Variables in input	R^2
$dX'(t-1)$	0.915
$dX'(t-1)$, $dY'(t-1)$	0.696
$dX'(t-1)$, $dY'(t-1)$, $X'(t-1)$	0.959

These results point to the specific importance of the previous steps and, in the case of $dY(t)$, of $dX'(t-1)$. Therefore the movement in the x direction is the key in interpreting the behaviour of our AAA.

Certainly, we are discovering here a sophisticated agent structure with interesting characteristics, reliable, but not easy to foresee before the experiment. This result underlines the importance of the experimental approach: we see complex results emerging from simple structures, built in a parsimonious way, without optimization capabilities. We are developing simple

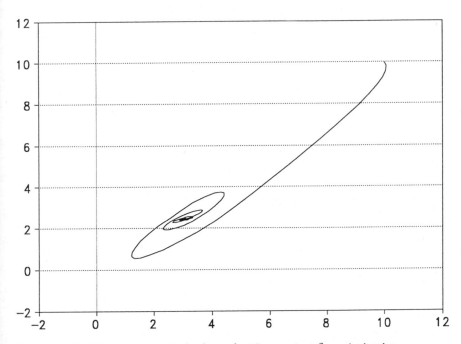

Figure 4.5 *Moving towards food, with EPs coming from imitation.*

agents, or mechanisms, that are capable of achieving a goal. Again, is that also the explanation of the behaviour of real agents? To understand more about this issue, consider what happens if we introduce an imitative habit in the model of the agent foraging for food.

The last analysis of this model is developing a population of similar agents, all acting without an EO, like the one in Figure 4.2, but with an EP (see section 4.1.3). In Figure 4.5 we have the itinerary towards the food of an agent which has as an EP the instruction to imitate the current movement, that is, the step in the x and y directions, of the other agents.

The imitative mechanism works as follows: the agent whose action is to be imitated is chosen randomly; the imitation occurs only if the action of that agent is greater in absolute value than that of the imitating agent. In the case of imitation, a random factor in the range [0,2] amplifies or mitigates the two measures of the action (which is a step defined in the x and y directions).

The artificial agents, without an EO, come close to the food. The reason is that the choice of imitating another agent reproduces a situation of inconsistency among CTs, from which – as seen before – the implicit simple mechanism driving the agent restarts, avoiding locking situations. Also note that if the imitated action is directed towards the food, the consequence is immediately convenient; if the imitated action goes in the opposite direction, the process corrects the error rapidly, always strength-

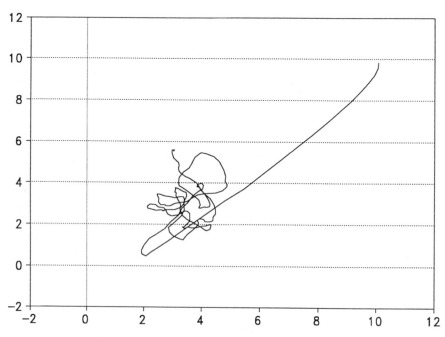

Figure 4.6 *Moving towards food, with random EPs.*

ening the global convergence process. In addition, when all agents are close to the food, all act with small steps and the imitative process loses importance.

If the EP is randomly generated, as in the case of Figure 4.6, the effect of avoiding locking situations is replicated, but the random behaviour prevails: it is more difficult to recognize a plan in this kind of artificial crazy agent, which is in any case capable of going close to the food.

Finally, note that in these experiments imitation and chance seem to have the same effect, but imitation can develop more subtle situations, as one might expect.

Learning to solve problems by imitation

The second experiment with imitation involves agents learning to solve a problem. Here we have several ANNs doing numerical products of their two inputs, which belong to a given range and are equal for all the ANNs. Some of them receive correct teaching, with a target obtained by multiplying the two inputs; the others carry out their imitative behaviour, using as their target the output of an ANN chosen randomly. The imitated ANN can be one with correct teaching or one that imitates others.

Here the meaning of imitation is more relevant than that implicit in the previous experiment, where imitation is mainly a source of noise. Surprisingly, apparent rationality emerges from noise: this is the power of experimental techniques. In this second case, the surprises are the capabilities emerging in the imitative ANNs and of the strong similarities that we can measure in the GWM of the imitating ANNs.

In a first run we have ten ANNs, one with the correct target (this ANN is named T) and the other nine ANNs (named I) imitating randomly. In a second run, there are ten T ANNs and 90 I ones .

In the first run, the GWM of the one ANN of type T (i1 and i2 are the input values, o1 the output one) is:

	o1
i1	18.45
i2	19.83

The GWMs of the nine ANNs of type I are presented as mean values, with standard deviations in brackets; the matrices composing the GWMs are different for each ANN, while GWMs (as a phenotype) are strongly similar:

	o1	
i1	10.78	(0.32)
i2	10.68	(0.30)

In the second run, the GWMs of the ten ANNs of type T show high variability; we summarize them in the following data:

ol

i1   17.05   (2.89)

i2   18.31   (2.22)

The 90 ANNs of type I are again very similar in terms of GWMs:

ol

i1   10.99   (0.42)

i2   10.90   (0.39)

The result in terms of similarity can be explained on the basis of the following consideration: the I ANNs evolve towards a 'mean' of the different existing structures, while the T ANNs maintain their structural differences untouched, producing analogous results. We therefore discover the influence of the environment in the development of both agents' capabilities and their structures.

4.2.2 Economic regularities in one-agent models

Now we introduce the theme of the economic regularities arising from CT models, when used in an economic situation. Starting with the agent's actions in one-agent models, the following examples of simple mechanisms directly developed by CTs will be introduced: (1) the capability of reacting to price changes; (2) a characterization of portfolio decisions.

Reacting to price changes

The first simulated agent is making two independent guesses on the basis of a single input, the price p_a, which changes exogenously by means of a sin function plus a random noise. Guesses are: the quantity q_a of the good C_a to be acquired; the expenditure x. Cross-targets are easily established here with:

$$x' = p_a \cdot q_a$$
$$q_a' = q_a + (x - x')/p_a = x/p_a$$

where, on the one hand, x' is the true expenditure consistent with the decision q_a; on the other hand, q_a' is the correct decision necessary to acquire the quantity of A consistent with the guess x. If $x' > x$, the guess of qa must be increased by the amount $(x - x')/p$ and vice versa.

In Figure 4.7 we have prices and guessed quantities (qa_g) for a thousand days of learning and acting; in the figure, we have chosen a sample of one day every ten days. The simulated subject has self-developed its

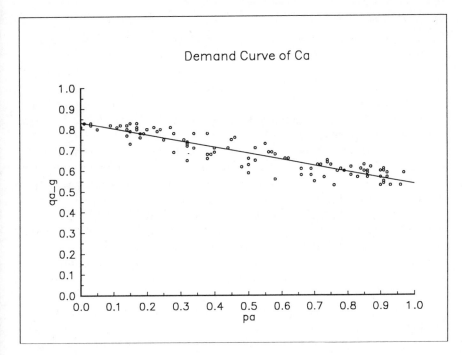

Figure 4.7 *Experimental reactions to different price levels.*

capability of reacting to price changes, smoothing the effects on its level of expense by quantity adjustment: what is emerging is a kind of demand curve without optimization. What is surprising is that the mechanism, albeit very simple, is autonomously and endogenously developed by the model.

Things go as follows: when the price changes, the cross-target mechanism determines two symmetrical corrections. Let us suppose that the price is augmented. The neural network outcomes, at the beginning of the learning process, are very conservative. Consequently, in short-term runs (see section 4.1.2 for details of short-vs long-term learning), the guesses about the expenditure (the effect) and the quantity (the action) adapt themselves very slowly to the changing input. The expenditure evaluation will therefore be underestimated and corrected by increasing it; vice versa, the quantity, which has to be consistent with the guess about the expense, which is underestimated, has to be corrected by decreasing it. We thus have two symmetrical corrections, less relevant than those that we could obtain separately by acting upon only one of them, keeping the price or the quantity constant. Realistically, the results are neither strictly exact nor deterministic. Is this a demand curve? In a strict sense it is not, but it describes common behaviour very well!

Agents in a stock market

We introduce an agent behaving in a stock market, starting with neither EO nor EP. The general framework of the model is described in section 4.2.3.

Here we summarize the model structure, emphasizing the rules related to the behaviour of a single agent model. Rules related to the interaction between populations of agents will be introduced in section 4.2.5, which also describes the market structure.

The AAA decides actions, as guesses about actions that it will make: there are two decisions, both related to the quantities of shares to buy A_t and to sell V_t (the double contract could be simplified considering only the net amount of the two transactions, but by considering them independently we can better investigate the rationality of the AAA). The AAA also makes guesses about the effects of its actions, first of all the actual contracts Ac_t and Vc_t that it will stipulate with another subject (in a one-agent model, the hypothesis is that the AAA always finds its counterpart, so $Ac_t = A_t$ and $Vc_t = V_c$). Exchanges are regulated at the opening price of the day, equal to the closing one of the previous day, p_{t-1}. Other guesses about effects are: M_t, the quantity of money after buying and selling; S_t, the quantity of shares, always after buying and selling; W_t, wealth valued as the sum of M_t and S_t, pricing shares at the closing price of the day, p_t. This difference in prices is the key to interpreting our AAA behaviour, both in this case without EO and in section 4.2.4. The inputs of the ANN emulating the AAA are: M_{t-1}, the quantity of money owned at time $t-1$; S_{t-1}, the quantity of shares at the same time; W_{t-1}, global wealth (money and shares); A_{t-1}, V_{t-1}, A_{t-2}, V_{t-2}, the quantities of shares owned bought (A as acquisition) and sold (V as vendor) at time $t-1$ or $t-2$; p_{t-3}, p_{t-2}, p_{t-1}, exogenous prices at the specified time.

We refer here to equations 4.1 to 4.7 in section 4.2.3. Due to the independence of the agents, we replace (4.1) and (4.2) with:

$$^*Ac_t = A_t$$
$$^*Vc_t = V_t$$

(For practical reasons, in this case the computer model is over-simplified, eliminating the Ac and Vc variables.)

Only the graph of one agent per experiment is shown: all values other than p_t are denoted by _gm where g means guess and m is the number identifying the agent (an interacting one or behaving independently in a population of independent agents). In Figures 4.8 to 4.13, we will mainly look at $M_{\_g}$ and $S_{\_g}$, to discover their positive or negative relations with the price cycle.

In Figure 4.8, without EO and without EP, we have an agent acting as if it were trying to avoid risk: it sells all the shares and keeps the money. This result arises because of the CT mechanism; in our model, share prices change continuously and those changes determine errors among the guesses

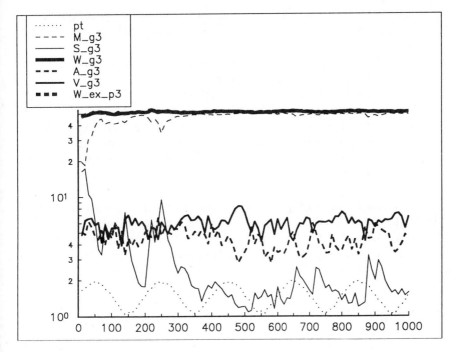

Figure 4.8 *Agent trying to avoid risk, without EO.*

and the targets related to the effects of the actions. Without external suggestions, the agent chooses to hold only money, greatly simplifying the task of developing consistency between the guesses of the actions and those of their effects. Again, we have the emergence of sophisticated behaviour from a simple self-developed micro-mechanism.

4.2.3 The general framework of the stock market model

We now introduce, following the first quick explanation of the previous section, the general framework of the stock market model used until the end of the chapter. However, the reading of this section can be skipped, coming back to it after sections 4.2.4 to 4.2.6 which present the results from the experiments.

The model shown here follows Terna (1993b); globally we have 10 inputs, 13 hidden elements and 7 outputs, as described in section 4.2.2 (b).

We adopt the following operators:

- $H[x_1, x_2, \ldots x_n] = x_i$, where x_i is the largest absolute value;
- C_i, i-th random value uniformly distributed in the $[0, 1]$ range; we operate here with 20 agents; the C operators (such as C_{61} in equation

4.1; or C_{31}, C_{32} and C_{33} of equations 4.9 and 4.10; or C_{81} in the EPZ definitions of section 4.2.6) are numbered taking into account the presence of the other agents;

- $\{i \ n \ s_1 \ s_2 \ ... \ s_n\}$ list operator number i, which chooses randomly among n agents, avoiding the choice of the agent itself; the complete list is shown only in the first declaration; in subsequent uses the operator is written in the short form $\{i\}$; so $V_t\{i \ n \ s_1 \ s_2 \ ... \ s_n\}$, or $V_t\{i\}$, means the value V_t of one of the n agents, randomly chosen. Several list operators can appear in a model, with different numbers. In each simulation period, or 'day', the value of each list operator is kept constant.

The equations describing the targets are reported below; variables with a little star on the left are targets; they will have eventually have EO or EP on the left. In the following experiments we have 20 agents. The complex notation adopted here is strictly related to the necessity of writing rules for CT determination.

$$*Ac_t =$$

$$(V_t\{1 \ 20 \ 1 \ 2 \ 3 \ 4 \ 5 \ 6 \ 7 \ 8 \ 9 \ 10 \ 11 \ 12 \ 13 \ 14 \ 15 \ 16 \ 17 \ 18 \ 19 \ 20\}$$
$$- A_t) \cdot C_{61} + A_t \qquad (4.1)$$

$$*Vc_t = (A_t\{ \ 1 \ \} - V_t) \cdot (1 - C_{61}) + V_t \qquad (4.2)$$

$$*M_t = *M_{t-1} + (*Vc_t - *Ac_t) \cdot p_{t-1} \qquad (4.3)$$

$$*S_t = *S_{t-1} + *Ac_t - *Vc_t \qquad (4.4)$$

$$*W_t = *M_t + *S_t \cdot p_t \qquad (4.5)$$

$$*A_t = H[(Ac_t - *Ac_t), \ - C_1 \cdot (M_t - *M_t)/p_{t-1}, \ C_2 \cdot (S_t - *S_t), \ -$$
$$C_3 \cdot (W_t - *W_t)/(p_{t-1} - p_t)] + A_t \qquad (4.6)$$

$$*V_t = H[(Vc_t - *Vc_t), \ (1 - C_1) \cdot (M_t - *M_t)/p_{t-1}, \ -$$
$$(1 - C_2) \cdot (S_t - *S_t), \ (1 - C_3) \cdot (W_t - *W_t)/(p_{t-1} - p_t)] + V_t \qquad (4.7)$$

This is the general framework of our agents, with neither EO nor EP. The implicit goal of this cross-target neural model is the development of coherence between the effect and the action of the outputs. Everybody acts (buying or selling) at the price p_{t-1}, which is the closing price of the previous day, known by all agents; after the action – at the end of the day – the agents know the closing price of the day (p_t); we remember that all prices are exogenous. The goal of equations 4.1 and 4.2 is stating a random matching between the demand and the supply of any pair of exchanging subjects; other solutions (the min value, the arithmetic mean) do not give significant differences.

Subdividing agents into two populations, we can introduce for the first one an external objective (EO) like the one expressed in equation 4.8, with the obvious meaning of improving wealth at a daily fixed rate:

$$_{EO}{}^*W_t = {}_{EO}{}^*W_{t-1} \cdot 1.0005 \qquad (4.8)$$

The cross-targets original equation 4.5 always runs to determine $^*W_t$ which is employed in equations 4.6 and 4.7. EO agents (first population) adjust the weights with which they guess their actions to take advantage of the difference between p_{t-1} and p_t.

The experiments are conducted on the basis of an exogenous price, generated by a sinusoidal function with min 1.05, amplitude 0.9 and a random perturbation of ±0.05, giving a complete range [1, 2]; the starting price is about 1.5. In equations 4.6 and 4.7 the corrections are made to A_t and V_t values which influence the proper Ac_t and Vc_t values, that is, the effects upon which the determination of all the other effects is founded.

Finally, to run the experiments of section 4.2.6, and only for the agents of the second population of those cases, equations 4.6 and 4.7 must be replaced with:

$$^*A_t = H[(Ac_t - {}^*Ac_t), - C_{31} \cdot (M_t - {}^*M_t)/p_{t-1},$$

$$C_{32} \cdot (S_t - {}^*S_t), -C_{33} \cdot (W_t - {}^*W_t)/(p_{t-1} - p_t), {}_{EP}z] + A_t \qquad (4.9)$$

$$^*V_t = H[(Vc_t - {}^*Vc_t), (1 - C_{31}) \cdot (M_t - {}^*M_t)/p_{t-1},$$

$$-(1 - C_{32}) \cdot (S_t - {}^*S_t),$$

$$(1 - C_{33}) \cdot (W_t - {}^*W_t)/(p_{t-1} - p_t), {}_{EP}z] + V_t \qquad (4.10)$$

to account for EP, as defined in section 4.2.6 itself.

4.2.4 External goals in one-agent models

Until this section, the role of the experimenter in designing models was limited to the definition of the input and output variables and of the accounting rules linking actions and effects. Economic theory and behavioural prescriptions were unnecessary in this first phase. Some theoretical hypotheses have however been introduced in the definition of variables, such as the choice in section 4.2.3 of using the p_{t-1} price in accounting for the effect of share bargaining and the price p_t in the evaluation of wealth, so introducing a lag of length 1 in the strategy of the agent.

We now look for the effect of a simple external goal. Always using the model of section 4.2.3 and with equations 4.1 and 4.2 modified as in section 4.2.2, we adopt the target W definition of equation 4.8, imposing

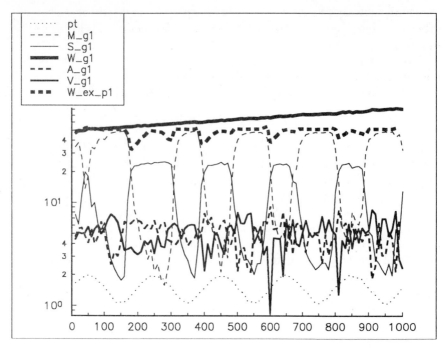

Figure 4.9 *Cyclical behaviour induced by EO.*

an increase of the variable in each cycle. Our stock market agent now has the goal of increasing its wealth.

The introduction of the goal modifies the agent's portfolio decisions, developing a short-term strategy. The CT mechanism smoothly propagates external correction applied to the effects of actions, to action guesses. The interest of this approach is to evaluate the cognitive consequences of simple objectives, such as improving wealth.

It is meaningful to compare results obtained both with and without external goals. With EO the agent is compelled to augment W and so it acts in the short term, as in Figure 4.9, selling when the price diminishes and vice versa. This strategy is incorrect in a long-term view, but it is very frequent in small investor decisions. Again, it is completely self-developed, as a consequence of CT consistency and of an EO which corrects only guesses about effects.

4.2.5 Interacting cross-target agents

Here we use CT agents interacting with or without external goals, in many-agent and many-population models. In the next section we will show in one table the results of all the experiments with interacting agents: the experiment of this section is labelled Exp. A. Equations 4.1 and 4.2 are

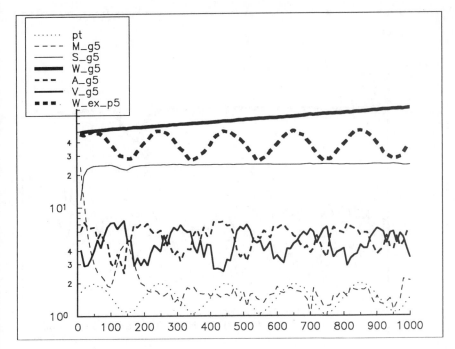

Figure 4.10 *Interacting agent with EO, without counterpart.*

used as specified in section 4.2.3, eliminating the corrections of sections 4.2.2(b) and 4.2.4.

In Exp. A we have 20 interacting AAAs of two types: one population of ten agents acting with the EO of equation 4.8 and the other, also of ten agents, without an EO. In the first case all the agents are similar to the one described in section 4.2.4; in the second case, all the agents are similar to the one described in section 4.2.2(b).

Always relating to the complete presentation of section 4.2.3, we have to introduce here the market rule and the conditions of the exchange among AAAs. Our attempt is to reproduce a market in which each AAA has to find another AAA in order to have a counterpart to bargain with. The counterpart, the same for both selling and buying, is chosen randomly each day; the differences between the quantities A_t and V_t or V_t and A_t of the two AAAs is randomly divided among them. Other criteria, such as the min value or the average value, do not give significant differences.

The agents of the first population cannot easily find a counterpart for their exchanges, either among themselves because of the analogies in their actions, or in the second population, whose objective is keeping only money. So they are compelled to keep shares in an attempt to augment W, as in Figure 4.10. Those of the second population are risk-averse, but as they have no EO, they are more oscillating in their erratic behaviour,

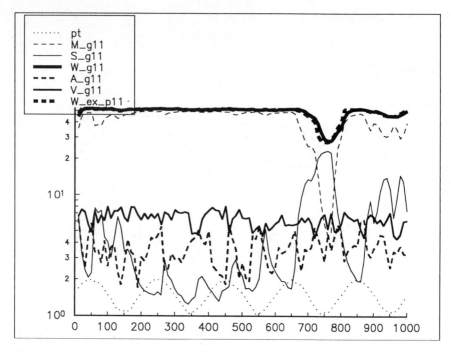

Figure 4.11 *Erratic behaviour of an interacting agent without EO.*

with spurious effects of constant, limited cyclical or limited anti-cyclical behaviour. In Figure 4.11 we have an example of constant behaviour, with two episodes of anti-cyclical acting.

The whole effect of our simple rules is somewhat surprising; the appearance of sophisticated behaviour, such as the anti-cyclical behaviour, will be explained in the following section.

4.2.6 External proposals in agents' interaction

Always using 20 agents in two populations, we develop four experiments (from B to E). As in section 4.2.5 the first population receives an EO from equation 4.8. Targets related to the A_t and V_t values of the agents of the second population are influenced by four types of EP. Equations 4.6 and 4.7 are replaced by equations 4.9 and 4.10 to account for EP in the targets of the agents of the second population.

EP influences learning on the side of action determinations: we use imitation and random hints here, with a high degree of similarity to the experiments involving agents foraging for food in section 4.2.1(a).

Imitation is introduced as a means to explain behaviour complexity and to obtain results which resemble a reasoning process.

As well as using imitation, we carry out experiments on the effects of random hints, clearly representing a source of noise. In these experiments, imitation is also a source of noise, as in section 4.2.1(a); however, the use of imitation and randomness together seems to be very powerful.

We now define the term $_{EP}z$ of equations 4.9 and 4.10, in four different ways.

- Exp. B: First population with the EO of equation 4.8. Second population with the following EP, showing the consequence of randomness in action determination:

$$_{EP}z = C_{81}\cdot 2\cdot K$$

  K represents the maximum amount of shares that can be bought or sold daily and 2 is an amplifying coefficient; see section 4.2.3 for the meaning of C and its index.

- Exp. C: First population with the EO of equation 4.8. Second population with the following EP, showing the consequences of generic imitation, with the agents of the second population imitating all agents. The list operator { } is explained in section 4.2.3.

$$_{EP}z =$$

$$A_t\{2\ 20\ 1\ 2\ 3\ 4\ 5\ 6\ 7\ 8\ 9\ 10\ 11\ 12\ 13\ 14\ 15\ 16\ 17\ 18\ 19\ 20\ \}$$

in equation 4.9

$$_{EP}z = V_t\{2\} \text{ in equation } 4.10$$

- Exp. D: First population with the EO of equation 4.8. Second population with the following EP, showing the consequences of specific imitation, with agents belonging to the second population imitating agents of the first population.

$$_{EP}z = A_t\{2\ 10\ 1\ 2\ 3\ 4\ 5\ 6\ 7\ 8\ 9\ 10\} \text{ in equation } 4.9$$

$$_{EP}z = V_t\{2\} \text{ in equation } 4.10$$

- Exp. E: First population with the EO of equation 4.8. Second population with the following EP, showing the consequences of generic imitation plus randomness. The H operator is introduced in section 4.2.3.

$$_{EP}z =$$

$$H[A_t\{2\ 20\ 1\ 2\ 3\ 4\ 5\ 6\ 7\ 8\ 9\ 10\ 11\ 12\ 13\ 14\ 15\ 16\ 17\ 18\ 19\ 20\},$$
$$C_{81}\cdot 2\cdot K]$$

in equation 4.9

$$_{EP}z = H[\ V_t\{2\}, C_{81}\cdot 2\cdot K] \text{ in equation } 4.10$$

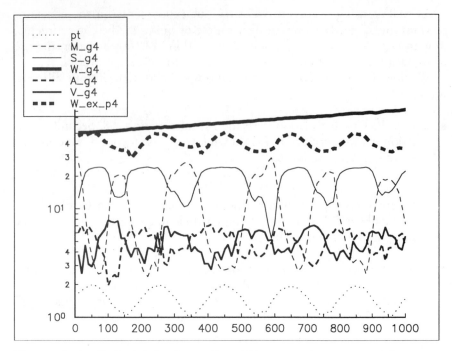

Figure 4.12 *Cyclical behaviour of an EO interacting agent, with counterpart.*

By introducing randomness (Exp. B), generic imitation with the second population imitating all the agents (Exp. C), specific imitation, with the second population imitating the first one (Exp. D) and finally imitation plus randomness, we allow the agents of the first population to find a counterpart for their exchanges, again showing the behaviour of section 4.2.4; the agents of the second population imitate or accept random suggestion and buy or sell against their natural inclination to avoid risk; then actions to avoid risk prevail again, thus producing anti-cyclical behaviour. We show here two representative cases of Exp. E, with an agent of the first population in Figure 4.12 and an agent of the second population in Figure 4.13.

Summarizing, agents 1–10 of the first population and agents 11–20 of the second population show opposite behaviour in almost all the experiments (Table 4.1).

We have to consider the importance of both imitation and randomness in the emergence of 'rational' behaviour, and to notice that the global effect is not simply the sum of the two individual effects. We stress the importance of these experiments, explaining what is apparently the consequence of reasoning as the result of random shocks and of imitation in a constrained environment.

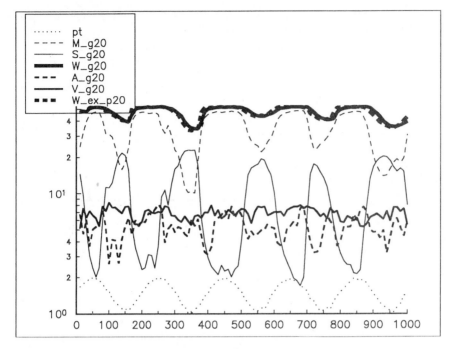

Figure 4.13 *Anti-cyclical behaviour of an interacting EP agent.*

To deeply analyse the behaviour of the agents of Exp. E, and especially of AAAs 4 and 20 shown in Figures 4.12 and 4.13, we adopt here the long-term learning strategy introduced in section 4.1.2. At the end of the experimental cycle of 1000 days, each AAA relearns from its own experience (emerging from the data that it has generated as a result of its behaviour), repeatedly adapting the weights of the ANN upon which it is founded.

Data used in the relearning task are the outputs of the ANN simulating the agent behaviour during short-term learning and acting; outputs are preferred to targets to refer to the actual agents' actions. The relearning is extended to 100 epochs, corresponding to 100 000 cycles of weight corrections.

After relearning, the ANNs simulating the AAAs produce outputs by applying the weights to the historical inputs, without the effects of CT rules. R^2 is determined from historical outputs (those of the learning and acting short-term phase) and actual outputs after relearning. In evaluating R^2 we have to remember that situations in which agent interaction produces unexpected results always exist: this kind of event reduces the capability of an ANN to measure the outcomes of a given input vector.

We will now evaluate the additive analysis of output values connected with M_t and S_t, following section 3.3.5. We adopt a simplified notation, with M instead of M_t, M_{-1} instead of M_{t-1}, etc.).

Table 4.1 *Mean correlation coefficients between p_t and M_g, S_g, first and second population (Exp. A from section 4.2.5)*

Ag. [#]	Exp. A		Exp. B		Exp. C		Exp. D		Exp. E	
	M_g	S_g	M_g	S_g	M_g	S_g	M_g	S_g	M_g	S_g
1÷10	0.101	–0.069	–0.316	0.401	0.030	0.034	0.140	–0.089	–0.622	0.634
11÷20	0.102	–0.164	0.422	–0.475	0.119	–0.185	–0.026	–0.057	0.619	–0.636

Table 4.2 *AAA number 4*

Output	Input									
	M_{-1}	S_{-1}	W_{-1}	A_{-1}	V_{-1}	A_{-2}	V_{-2}	p_{-3}	p_{-2}	p_{-1}
GWM										
M	15.0	–2.1	–4.4	4.7	–5.2	5.3	–5.3	–6.9	–2.9	7.2
S	–14.8	7.1	2.1	–5.9	6.8	–5.1	6.0	7.3	2.6	–6.4
MPD										
M	0.836	–0.168	–0.318	0.269	–0.305	0.310	–0.311	–0.378	–0.135	0.456
S	–0.835	0.356	0.148	–0.323	0.374	–0.346	0.339	0.429	0.142	–0.450
MD										
M	0.434	–0.053	–0.116	0.138	–0.156	0.155	–0.154	–0.233	–0.105	0.209
S	–0.433	0.191	0.002	–0.176	0.201	–0.180	0.176	0.250	0.094	–0.216
MD (sqm)										
M	0.194	0.046	0.106	0.066	0.079	0.079	0.082	0.101	0.047	0.129
S	0.210	0.092	0.084	0.080	0.102	0.088	0.093	0.111	0.040	0.112

Table 4.3 *AAA number 20*

Output	Input									
	M_{-1}	S_{-1}	W_{-1}	A_{-1}	V_{-1}	A_{-2}	V_{-2}	p_{-3}	p_{-2}	p_{-1}
GWM										
M	18.8	4.9	13.0	4.0	–2.0	4.4	–2.4	4.6	1.0	–2.2
S	–14.3	5.3	–7.4	–4.5	3.8	–4.0	3.3	–4.2	–1.6	0.9
MPD										
M	0.869	0.221	0.612	0.204	–0.141	0.221	–0.155	0.215	0.048	–0.113
S	–0.578	0.140	–0.357	–0.261	0.172	–0.236	0.152	–0.198	–0.083	0.041
MD										
M	0.647	0.163	0.448	0.143	–0.100	0.156	–0.109	0.161	0.037	–0.083
S	–0.418	0.120	–0.243	–0.173	0.117	–0.156	0.101	–0.138	–0.056	0.034
MD (sqm)										
M	0.170	0.037	0.129	0.063	0.039	0.065	0.043	0.047	0.013	0.020
S	0.123	0.035	0.091	0.073	0.032	0.074	0.033	0.047	0.025	0.009

Referring to agents 4 and 20 of Figures 4.12 and 4.13, the additive searching strategy is applied by introducing clauses (variables) to the rules until they become valid in explaining the AAA's behaviour about M and S, namely the quantity of money and shares that the subject is holding. Rule building is founded upon the data of Tables 4.2 and 4.3, reporting: the GWM matrix defined in section 3.3.5; the Mean Point Derivatives (MPDs), introduced in section 4.2.1(a), and the Mean Derivatives (MDs) also introduced in section 4.2.1(a) calculated for each pattern; to simplify the analysis of these results, we calculate the mean and the standard deviation of the derivatives of each pattern.

The following results explain the determination of M and S, with the R^2 value obtained by introducing only the included variables in the ANN input and keeping the other one constant, as in sections 3.3.5 and 4.2.1(a).

- Agent 4, rule explaining M:

Variables included in input	R^2 (with full input: 0.873)
M_{-1}	0.724
M_{-1}, p_{-3}	0.457
M_{-1}, p_{-3}, p_{-1}	0.730
M_{-1}, p_{-3}, p_{-1}, W_{-1}	0.769
M_{-1}, p_{-3}, p_{-1}, W_{-1}, A_{-2}	0.761
M_{-1}, p_{-3}, p_{-1}, W_{-1}, A_{-2}, V_{-2}	0.776

- Agent 4, rule explaining S:

Variables included in input	R^2 (with full input: 0.866)
M_{-1}	0.701
M_{-1}, p_{-3}	0.611
M_{-1}, p_{-3}, p_{-1}	0.709
M_{-1}, p_{-3}, p_{-1}, S_{-1}	0.810
M_{-1}, p_{-3}, p_{-1}, S_{-1}, V_{-1}	0.816

- Agent 20, rule explaining M:

Variables included in input	R^2 (with full input: 0.945)
M_{-1}	0.781
M_{-1}, W_{-1}	0.832

M_{-1}, W_{-1}, S_{-1}	0.888
M_{-1}, W_{-1}, S_{-1}, p_{-3}	0.923
M_{-1}, W_{-1}, S_{-1}, p_{-3}, A_{-2}	0.925

- Agent 20, rule explaining S:

Variables included in input	R^2 (with full input: 0.945)
M_{-1}	0.756
M_{-1}, W_{-1}	0.812
M_{-1}, W_{-1}, A_{-1}	0.821
M_{-1}, W_{-1}, A_{-1}, A_{-2}	0.816
M_{-1}, W_{-1}, A_{-1}, A_{-2}, p_{-3}	0.908

Note that agent 4, which behaves according the EO applied to W and develops unproductive cyclical behaviour, assesses M on the basis of M_{-1}, two prices and W. Notice that if we consider the two prices separately, R^2 diminishes: clearly those variables interact in a nonlinear way. Agent 4 assesses S on the basis of the same variables, plus S_{-1}. Therefore, both variables are explained by their preceding value, with a relevant effect from M_{-1} and prices.

Agent 20, influenced by the EP and developing anti-cyclical behaviour, in an apparently rational way, chooses M mainly on the basis of M_{-1}, W_{-1}, S_{-1}, with a small effect on prices. The same agent establishes S by M_{-1} and W_{-1}, taking into account the quantities of shares bought in the previous days. We underline the interesting presence of W_{-1} in this scheme: a link to wealth in a context in which the previous EO does not operate upon W; this is a case of apparent rationality, emerging from randomness and imitation. Links emerging from input to output variables in our learning and adapting agents have the main characteristic of being totally self-developed, without using learning strategies such as least squares with a priori functions or complex credit assignment techniques as found in CSs. As a conclusion, from the models presented in this chapter we learn that simple micro-mechanisms are sufficient to develop complex behaviour and that the CT structure is sufficient to develop those mechanisms autonomously. These are only demonstrations of the plausibility of some intuitions and absolutely not proofs or verifications of those intuitions. However, this is a possible way to conduct artificial experiments, also useful for investigating and understanding the reasons for and the consequences of the actions of real economic subjects.

Part Three

Models of Artificial Markets

5
One-agent models

Outline of the chapter

The chapter considers situations where a single agent acts in an exogenous environment by using ANNs of the type described in Chapter 1. The environment is exogenous in the sense that the agent takes all relevant variables as given and does not affect the environmental situation with his or her actions. One might take as an example the case of a financial trader who may buy or sell shares at a market price that is not affected by the trader's operations. We study both simple forecasting problems, where the neural network is used for forecasting the values of certain important variables, and more complicated decision problems, where the neural network is used as an expert suggesting the action to perform, for example buying or selling. In complicated problems it often happens that the action cannot be evaluated in terms of simple targets which signal the error connected with the action. We therefore apply unsupervised learning techniques as genetic algorithms for analysing those cases in which targets are impossible to define.

Finally, we also discuss the important issues of the evaluation and interpretation of the rules which are discovered by neural networks in decision problems.

Section 5.1 presents the framework of one-agent models and their characteristics. We then describe the global decision process of the agent by discussing the following topics: forecasting problems are addressed in section 5.2, and decision problems in section 5.3, while criteria for strategy evaluation are discussed in section 5.4. Section 5.5 presents a genetics-based model of a financial trader. Finally the problem of interpreting the rules is addressed in section 5.6.

5.1 The definition of one-agent models

5.1.1 One-agent models

All the models we consider in this book are based upon agents (one or many) acting in a given environment; they receive information, process it to generate some output and finally take a decision based on this output. The resources available to each agent change as a consequence of their actions. Agents are adaptive in the sense that they possess learning abilities: they learn and adapt their structure and their reactions according to their understanding of the evolving environment. Models differ in the number and type of agents, the structure of the environment and the relations among agents and between the agents and the environment. In this and the following chapters we use a particular taxonomy which distinguishes between one-agent, one-population and multi-population models. This taxonomy relates to other attempts to classify environments (Emery, 1967) but differs in some aspects. While Emery defines four types of environmental complexity related to simple social systems, the classification we propose is more oriented towards high-level social systems. One-agent models correspond to Type 2 of Emery's classification, while one- and multi-population models correspond to Type 4 (Turbulent Fields in the Emery's terminology).

One-agent models (Figure 5.1) are the first step in complexity. While highly simplified, they represent a good tool for decision-makers because of their adaptability to situations encountered in real markets. Our definition is the following:

A one-agent model considers a single agent acting in an exogenous context. Such a context is represented by an external environment that provides information to the agent and/or other agents living in this same environment. It is essential that the actions of the agent who is studied in the model do not in any way affect the behaviour of the environment or the behaviour of the other agents, but only the resources with which the agent is endowed.

We comment on four important aspects of this definition:

1. Exogeneity of the context: The environment is not affected in any way by the actions of the agent. This is the situation encountered by a small agent trading in a large financial market who, given the agent's relative size, cannot affect the market price. Such a hypothesis is not always valid: for example, in thin markets small changes in demand may produce significant effects on the price. Thin markets are markets where, at every time, there are few buyers and few sellers, and where the frequency of transactions is low. Transaction prices in very thin markets exhibit strong discontinuities (Garbade, 1982).
2. Other agents: Even when other agents are present, the single agent we consider does not influence their behaviour. Moreover, other agents are treated as a whole, and not individually, as if they were a subset of the environment.
3. Unidirectionality of the information flow: Information flows only from the environment to the agent. The latter takes information as given and processes it to determine his or her action.
4. Actions and forecasts: The actions may or may not be based on a previous forecast of the relevant variables. In some cases the forecast supports the subsequent action while in others it is implicitly incorporated in the agent's decision support system.

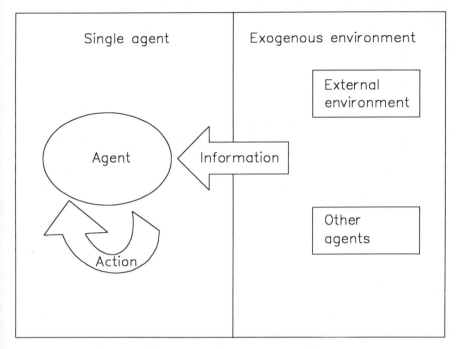

Figure 5.1 *The general structure of one-agent models.*

An agent acting in a system of this sort is successful, in terms of reaching the agent's own targets, if they can predict the consequences of his or her own actions with a good degree of confidence. This ability follows from the use of available information to understand the structure of the system. We describe seven steps in the agent's global decision process (Figure 5.2), the sequence that brings the agent from processing information to action and learning:

1. Some exogenous information about the environment becomes available to the agent.
2. The agent preprocesses information (see section 5.2).
3. The agent uses his or her neural network to process information.
4. Processing may yield a forecast or a decision.
5. The agent acts on the basis of the output of step 4 by using external or internal rules about which we will be more specific in section 5.3.
6. The agent updates his or her resources on the basis of the action (see section 5.4.1).
7. The agent evaluates the profitability of his or her action in order to learn and improve the outcome of future decisions.

These steps are repeated for all the periods of the simulation.

By following this behaviour the agent can take advantage of his or her

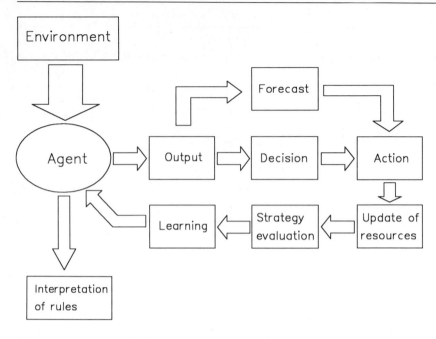

Figure 5.2 *The global decision process of the agent.*

experience in order to improve their fitness with respect to the environment. In economic systems and financial markets this may mean improving their market share, making a profit or increasing wealth. Many indexes can be built to measure economic performance, as we will discuss in section 5.4.

In this book we distinguish between forecasting and decision problems:

- A forecasting problem describes an agent who behaves in a way that is simply and directly related to the forecast of one or more variables; the forecast is built upon the evaluation of an information set, and the decision rule is exogenous to the agent.
- A decision problem describes an agent who behaves in a way that is not necessarily related in a simple way to the forecast of one or more variables; in some problems the forecasting aspect may even be non-existent. The decision rule is endogenously discovered by the agent as an efficient way of exploiting a mapping between the information set and his or her ultimate target.

In forecasting problems, therefore, the neural network is used as an efficient computational device on the part of an agent who wants to reach a target by forecasting a set of variables on the basis of an information set. In decision problems attention is not necessarily focused on forecasting, but on a mapping between information set and actions that is efficient with respect to the achievement of certain goals.

The examples contained in this and the following chapters will make the meaning of these definitions more transparent. Before coming to this, however, we need to clarify several other aspects of the structure of the problems, beginning with agent learning.

5.1.2 Individual learning

As mentioned in section 5.1.1, learning may be about forecasts or actions.

'Learning to forecast' problems correspond to practical situations where agents typically ignore many aspects of the environment, and act on the basis of a limited and partial knowledge. Suppose for example that the environment at time t generates the values of a set of variables y_t depending on a set of variables x_{t-1} according to some nonlinear function f, $y_t = f(a, x_{t-1}) + e_t$, where a is a vector of parameters and e_t a random disturbance. In general the decision-maker, who wants to act before the environment sets the value of y_t, will have to form an expectation of the variable. Apart from the intrinsic uncertainty due to the shock e_t, the decision-maker will know neither the values of the parameters a nor the shape of the function f, and will therefore look for methods that allow a forecast to be made with a good degree of accuracy. Such methods, of which linear econometric models or nonlinear models like artificial neural networks are examples, use past information on the realizations of the variables to make an inference about unknown parameters and functional forms. Note that this does not necessarily imply an effort to understand the mechanisms that have caused the patterns detected in the data, since for many purposes it is sufficient to recognize such patterns. In Chapters 6 and 7 we present a synthetic approach for understanding these mechanisms on the basis of interactions between many agents, dropping the hypothesis that the single trader's actions are irrelevant to the market.

In 'learning to act' problems the agent tries to choose an action directly, and the learning process acts on the mapping from inputs to a measure of the action's profitability: $p_t = g(a, x_{t-1}) + e_t$, where p is a measure of profitability. The type of mapping that one is trying to learn has changed with respect to simple forecasting problems, since the agent is now directly interested in the ultimate consequences of the market dynamics on his or her personal situation, but the techniques that may be used to implement learning remain the same.

Due to their statistical properties (White, 1991) and their learning-based approach, neural networks stand as valid forecasting instruments, which may well be more effective than simple linear forecasting tools. We do not explicitly consider the statistical problems related to forecasting with linear and nonlinear models.

Some aspects of learning in ANNs, as described in Chapter 1, must be considered: learning paradigms, supervised or unsupervised learning techniques and objects of learning.

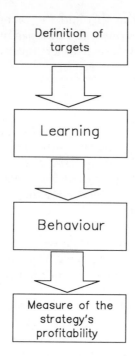

Figure 5.3 *Logical phases of supervised learning.*

(a) Learning paradigms

These are divided into individual and collective learning. An example of the latter is learning by imitation, in which agents observe the actions of the others. In one-agent models we are restricted to individual learning, since the agent is either alone in the environment, or facing other agents with whom there is no real interaction. Even in the case of genetic algorithms, as applied in section 5.5, one may say that the individual only learns from experience, for the population is a virtual one, a replication of similar non-interacting agents for the purpose of applying selection mechanisms.

(b) Supervised or unsupervised learning techniques

Chapter 1 described the difference between supervised and unsupervised learning techniques. We point out here that they have very different implications for the relationship between the intentions of the model-builder and the final model itself. In the case of supervised learning the model-builder decides the targets and therefore affects the learning and the emerging behaviour. This form of learning can be described by means of the flow chart of Figure 5.3.

Instead, with unsupervised learning, the model-builder only sets a general goal, for example maximization of wealth, and does not constrain

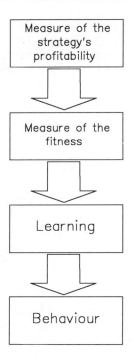

Figure 5.4 *Logical phases of unsupervised learning.*

the model to reach certain targets period by period. This allows the network to search in a much larger space, and as a result behaviour emerges in a more endogenous fashion. Figure 5.4 describes the logical steps of unsupervised learning.

(c) Objects of learning

In most applications the structure of the network is taken as exogenously given, and learning applies to the values of the weights. Sometimes learning can be performed over a larger space, including the number of layers, the number of neurons of the network or the way neurons are connected. An example of the determination of the number of hidden neurons is provided in section 5.5. The effectiveness of learning, an important measure, is checked in the validation process described in section 5.5.

5.2 Forecasting problems

Agents forecasting economic variables use both internal and external information. Internal information (past prices, spreads and volumes, for example) originates from within the market, while external information (the inflation rate, the interest rate, prices and returns of other assets) comes from the economic system surrounding the market. In the applications considered in this chapter we will limit ourselves to considering one-agent models in which agents analyse internal information in order to discover recurrent patterns in the relevant variables (external information could be easily included without substantial modification). The two important topics in this case are the information set and the method that is used to process that set.

(a) The information set

An important concern is careful tuning of the definition of the inputs in the information set. As in traditional models, forgetting important variables or taking into account useless variables may lead to mis-specified models with erratic behaviour and low significance. The tuning of the information set has two aspects to consider.

1. The choice of input and output variables to be included. Input and output variables must be causally related to confer plausibility and coherence on the model. The main issues are: the relevance of available information, the mix of internal and external information, time lags and causality from input to output variables, and the inclusion of previous actions in order to develop some coherence between actions and build a multi-period strategy.

    A very important issue is periodicity of the data; in this case the crucial problem is given by the possible heterogeneity in periodicity of the variables. This problem arises, for example, when one is trying to forecast variables that are collected daily by using variables that become known only once a week.

2. Preprocessing of variables: Once all the variables are identified, some preprocessing may be required to build new variables on the basis of others (such as calculating a moving average of past data, for example), and to transform variables into new ones that are more significant for learning. In economic and financial problems, the latter is an important point to deal with, especially in forecasting applications. For a variable such as the price of a share, we can consider its level (stock price), its level relative to some index, its absolute change (difference from price at time t and price at time t–1), its rate of change (absolute change divided by price at time t–1) or its change relative to some baseline (difference between price and moving average, for example). This process can make the learning task easier by eliminating trends and smoothing spikes in the time series.

In the specific case of artificial neural networks the preprocessing of the variables is even more important, as practitioners of this technique know. For example, it is useful to normalize the input variables to be between 0 and 1, in order to make them compatible with the output of the logistic function.

(b) The auto-regressive and the macroeconomic approaches

The auto-regressive approach tries to predict future values of a series on the basis of its past realizations, while the macroeconomic approach tries to build a model of this series based on external information that is supposed to be relevant.

In the auto-regressive approach (Figure 5.5), the steps one follows basically involve defining:

1. the input window size on the time series, that is, the number of past observations one wants to include in the input set;
2. any transformation of the original series into moving averages, trend indicators reversal signals. The total number of variables determines the number of input neurons in the network;
3. the output window size, that is, the number of future observations one wants to predict. The number of output neurons corresponds to the chosen size;
4. the forecasting time lag; predictions may refer to next day's price, next week's price or the price a month ahead;
5. the number of hidden neurons. Empirical results seem to recommend a low number of hidden neurons in time series forecasting, to confer good generalization (e.g. prediction) capabilities on the network (see section 3.3.4 on the weight elimination technique);
6. the training set, built by iterating a one-period shift on the time series of the input and output windows;
7. the features of learning over the entire training set. When targets are available, back-propagation may be used for training.

The macroeconomic approach (Figure 5.6) is based on a modification in the input set of the previous scheme. Step 1 now defines the variables

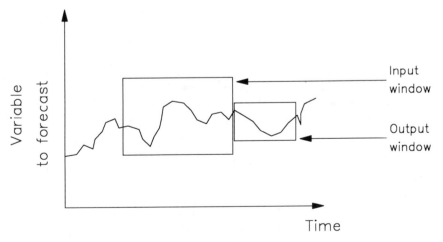

Figure 5.5 *The auto-regressive approach.*

included in the information set. For example, in forecasting the exchange rate between two currencies, it is customary to include as external variables the exchange rates between other currencies, and interest rates (Würtz *et al.*, 1993; Windsor and Harker, 1990). Variables that are likely to influence the output ought to be chosen, using suggestions from theoretical models or from a preliminary statistical analysis. It is difficult for the network to discover efficiently which variables are really useful out of a large set of variables.

The total number of variables corresponds to the number of input neurons in the network.

The macroeconomic approach is likely to require a mix of data with different periodicity, since most macroeconomic data are only available monthly or quarterly. To avoid learning problems that may arise when one follows the approach of inserting data into the training set when they become available (once a month) and otherwise inserting zero (or the

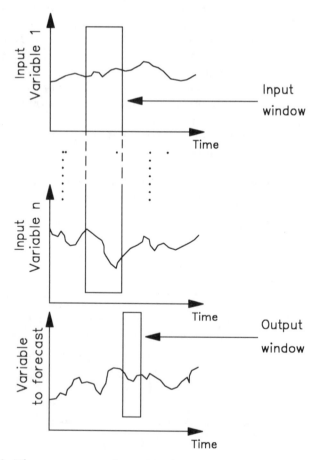

Figure 5.6 *The macroeconomic approach.*

mean), one may for example combine the forecasts of many networks trained by supervised learning, where each network takes care of a specific periodicity.

Mixed forms can obviously be implemented by inserting into the input set information that arises not only from past prices but also from external economic indicators.

In the next section we present some techniques for dealing with decision-making. Two main approaches are considered: (1) building decision rules, either internal or external, based on the output of the forecast process and (2) by-passing the forecast step with direct decision-making.

5.3 Decision problems

The aim of the forecasting step is to build a set of inputs upon which to base the subsequent decision. The crucial question is how one generates an action from such data. We can devise three solutions to this problem: external rules, internal rules and the non-forecasting approach.

5.3.1 From forecasts to decisions with external rules

The first possibility is to generate rules which are external to the neural network, and which define a decision on the basis of the forecasted values (Figure 5.7). These rules are generally supported by economic laws or by empirical market rules. For example, suppose that an agent acts in a stock market and forecasts the change in price from today to tomorrow to determine his or her action today. A possible rule set for choosing among three actions such as buy, sell or wait is:

Rule #	Condition	Action
1	IF absolute value of expected change is lower than a threshold	THEN Wait
2	IF expected change is positive	THEN Buy
3	IF expected change is negative	THEN Sell

In this example rules must be explored sequentially, in order to follow the one which is relevant to the particular set of circumstances. In the first rule, the threshold value depends on transaction costs: the aim of this rule is to avoid an action when expected profit is lower than transaction costs. Rules 2 and 3 state that the agent must buy (sell) if the expected change is an increase (decrease) in price. If the forecast is correct, the agent can make a profit by buying (selling) today and selling (buying) tomorrow, in accordance with this set of rules.

There are three main drawbacks to this first approach.

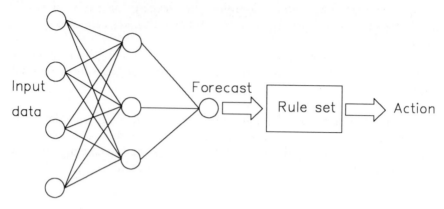

Figure 5.7 *From forecast to decision: External rules.*

1. External rules are arbitrary. The way external rules process the output of the network is decided by the researcher on the basis of expert advice. But experts themselves often disagree on the interpretation of data patterns and are not unanimous in the decision process, so external rules generally encapsulate the advice of only one expert.
2. It can induce undesirable behaviour. The three rules in the example above are simple and seem sensible, but they can induce complete inactivity if daily changes are always below the transaction cost threshold. A more complex set of rules should avoid this problem and take into account possible profits coming from a change in price over a longer time period.
3. Forecast, action and learning are difficult to integrate. The action depends on the rules rather than on the output of the network, so it may be difficult to relate the profitability of the action to the forecast: a bad action in terms of economic outcome may follow a good forecast and vice versa. In this approach, external rules cannot be subject to learning because, in most cases, there is no way to back-propagate a measure of the profitability of action to the forecast for learning purposes.

On the other hand, simplicity is a merit of this approach. It does not require complex forms of learning and may represent a first step in building financial models.

5.3.2 From forecasts to decisions with internal rules

In this approach rules are built internally instead of being set externally. This can be done by building a single network with one output as the forecast (forecasting neuron) and one (or more) outputs as the action (acting neuron), or by using two networks, where the first produces the

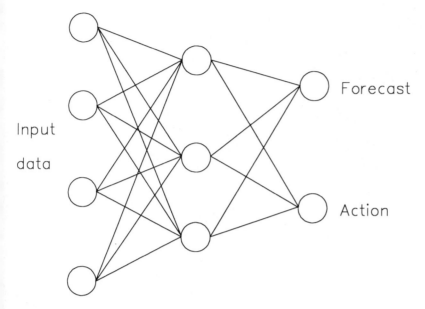

Figure 5.8 *From forecast to decision: Internal rules with a single network.*

forecast (forecasting network) while the second processes the forecast, and possibly other data, and produces the action (acting network).

(a) The single network

We consider a single network with one forecasting neuron and one (or more) acting neurons representing the action (Figure 5.8). The number of output neurons depends on the representation of the action: we can use one neuron for many actions by assigning a range of output values to each action (for example, output from 0.0 to 0.5 corresponds to Action 1, and 0.5 to 1.0 corresponds to Action 2) or, alternatively, use one neuron to code each action.

While learning in the forecasting neuron is typically based on back-propagation, learning in the acting neuron, for which a target is not available, can occur through a method such as indirect learning. If one is not willing to use an unsupervised learning technique such as genetic algorithms, one may use the changes in weights (from input to hidden) resulting from the back-propagation learning in the forecasting output neurons (which also influence the output of the acting neurons, due to the structure of the back-propagation algorithm). In this case, the network learns the mapping from the information set not only into a forecast but also, to a certain extent, into an action. Although this form of learning can be effective for simple problems, it is too 'soft' to be applied success-fully to economic and financial models.

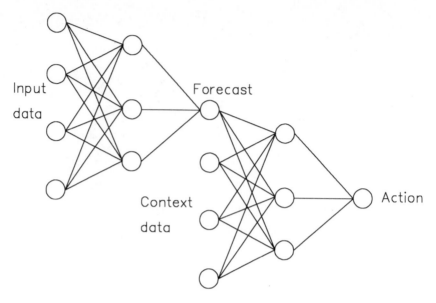

Figure 5.9 *From forecast to decision: Internal rules with a dual network.*

(b) The dual network

The dual network is composed of two linked neural networks. The forecasting network feeds into a second network which processes the forecast and outputs the action (Figure 5.9). This second network has an information set composed of the output of the forecasting network and possibly some other data, for example the same inputs as used by the forecasting network, in order to relate the forecast to the data upon which it is based.

Learning in the acting network can occur in a mixed form: the forecasting network learns the mapping from input to forecast, through back-propagation, while the acting network learns the mapping from the forecast and its context (the inputs) to action, remaining unsupervised because of the absence of a target. Genetic algorithms can be used to implement this unsupervised learning in a similar fashion to the application described in section 5.5.

(c) Non-forecasting approach

In the dual network approach just described, the mapping between forecast and action can be considered as a by-product of the architecture. Although in some situations knowledge of such a mapping is important – to gain some insight about the internal mapping rules of the network, for example – in others this information is useless. In this last case one can follow an approach based on acting without forecasting. The structure

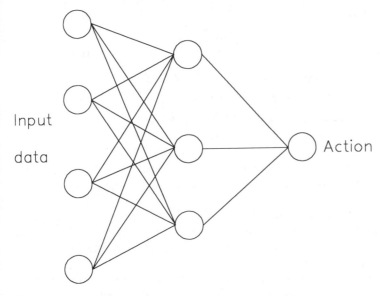

Figure 5.10 *The structure of an acting network.*

of the network reflects this change: a simplification eliminates from the network all the neurons previously devoted to the forecast (Figure 5.10).

While, in the two approaches we described above, learning takes place in a supervised form (back-propagation for external rules) or in a mixed form (supervised and unsupervised for internal rules), in the non-forecasting approach unsupervised learning is the most commonly applicable. Direct targets are not available, and supervised learning through back-propagation must be replaced with unsupervised learning techniques. Genetic algorithms are the main method of unsupervised learning in ANNs, particularly because of their ability to build internal rules and to cause spontaneous behaviour to arise.

5.3.3 Feasibility of an action

One final issue we want to mention relates to the actual feasibility of carrying out the action, given the constraints which have to be met by the agent (action feasibility). For example, in the case of a trader, the decision to buy shares depends on the availability of financial resources. When decision rules are external, action feasibility is easily guaranteed by the structure of the rules: the model builder must ensure the coherence of the rules and submission to possible constraints. For example the simple set of rules proposed in section 5.3.2 can be modified in the following way to take a budget constraint into account:

Rule #	Condition	Action
1	IF absolute value of expected change is lower than a threshold	THEN Wait
2	IF expected change is positive AND stock of money is adequate	THEN Buy
3	IF expected change is negative AND number of owned shares is adequate	THEN Sell

When decision rules are internal, with or without forecast, action feasibility can be guaranteed in two ways.

1. Externally: Network action is filtered by an external accounting system that checks the feasibility of the action and prevents it from being executed if constraints are violated. This solution is effective in practical decision-making models.
2. Internally: The network is taught to produce only feasible actions, for example by rewarding feasible actions and punishing impossible actions. While this approach is more elegant, and a good exercise when studying learning techniques and building theoretical models, there are some problems with applying it in practice: the model produces inadmissible actions until learning is fully performed, and learning becomes much more complex.

5.4 Strategy evaluation

5.4.1 Economic criteria for strategy evaluation

The action performed by the agent has economic consequences on resources. In a stock trader model, for example, changes occur in the amount of money and shares owned by the agent. In a model of firms evolving in a banking system, the value and the debt of the firms change depending on the banks' decisions (see the application in Chapter 7).

(a) Updating the agent's resources

After the action, an update of the agent's resources takes place. The mechanism for updating resources may be implemented in two ways: internally, by teaching the network to predict the consequences of its actions, or externally, through accounting rules which are not under the control of the network. The internal approach produces more complex and complete models (more input and output neurons, and a greater complexity in the learning process) with indirect effects on the structure of the agent, while external updates, used in the models of Chapters 6 and 7, allow one to build more specialized agents whose learning abilities focus on specific tasks.

(b) Evaluation of an action's profitability

An evaluation of the profitability of the action or of the strategy is the next logical step in the decision process. This evaluation is generally based on one or more indicators measuring the effectiveness of the strategy in economic terms. It is impossible to present general criteria for defining such indicators: they are, in fact, highly problem-dependent. We now discuss some of the most important economic indicators for financial models.

(c) Wealth and other related economic indicators

Wealth is the most immediate and intuitive indicator one can devise when dealing with economic applications: economic agents generally face decisions which influence their wealth, and act in order to preserve or increase it. Although wealth seems a natural measure, let us examine by means of an example certain difficulties that arise from its use. In the model of an artificial trader previously described, wealth is defined as the sum of money and of the value of shares. This definition is used to compute daily wealth, and of course on the last day of the simulation as a fitness indicator for the genetic algorithm: the higher the value of wealth on the last day, the better the strategy.

Note the following in this example.

- Final wealth is highly dependent on the final price: a low (high) price tends to penalize (reward) all strategies. The importance of this problem depends on the model: in most cases, the indicator must simply measure the relative effectiveness of one strategy with respect to the others, and not its absolute effectiveness with respect to the environment. In an exogenous environment, prices and price trends are given, while in endogenous models they depend on the strategies of the agents. Therefore in the former case, the overall measure of fitness of the strategy is largely affected by external factors, so that this measure can be used only relatively to other strategies. In the latter case (for example, in population-based models) there are no external influences and the measure can also be used in absolute terms, for example for comparing the performance of strategies across different environments.

  The importance of this measurement problem can be reduced by considering some transformations of wealth, such as the ratio or the difference between the value of wealth at the end and at the beginning of the whole time period. Such measures have the advantage of reducing the dependence on the final stock price, but may introduce some arbitrariness through the valuation of initial wealth.

- If we want to reduce the arbitrary influence of first day and last day prices, we can build an indicator that takes into account the evolution of wealth during the entire simulation, such as the average of wealth over time.

- Wealth is not the only target for economic agents. Other indicators can be chosen depending on the nature of the problem: in a bank decision problem (see section 7.4) we can choose the value of the bank or the number of customers (firms), in a dealer-traders stock market (see section 7.3), the number of stocks owned (exposure) or the imbalance between global supply and demand.

5.4.2 Evaluation criteria and learning

The performance of the model strictly depends on the evaluation criterion. This is very important, especially for practical applications of the technology. In fact the effectiveness of these computing technologies can be interpreted as implying that neural networks learn what the user wants them to learn; attention has therefore to be paid to teaching the models the right goals. From a theoretical point of view, the definition of a particular evaluation measure can implicitly and surreptitiously introduce some hypotheses in the model which are far from the intentions of the researcher. This can be avoided only if the description of the problem is complete, and if the decision-maker incorporates his or her preferences into the learning function in an appropriate way.

We discuss such general principles with three examples.

1.   Minimizing the sum of squared errors is a very specific criterion corresponding to the case of a quadratic utility function. A neural network that is trained with such a target will assign a great deal of weight to extreme outcomes and will therefore try to reduce these large errors in the learning process. Moreover, it will implicitly consider all the errors from a symmetric point of view. A decision-maker may or may not be satisfied with such a training process. Risk aversion would imply putting more effort into avoiding large losses, which is equivalent to pursuing an asymmetric target. A neural network trained under symmetry assumptions will tend to follow strategies that are too risky. In the case of unsupervised learning the problem is even more complicated, as shown by the next two examples.

2.   Evaluation of strategies by means of wealth ignores problems related to risk. If we start with K different strategies and evaluate their relative merits in terms of the simple accumulation of wealth, the algorithm will tend to choose the riskier strategies as candidates for reproduction. In fact the safer strategies are likely to put more wealth into assets with low return and low risk, and are unlikely to be the winners in terms of wealth. A risk-averse decision-maker may therefore want to evaluate fitness in terms of a composite index that takes into account both wealth (or change in wealth) and risk. Risk can be calculated through such measures as the sum of the absolute values of the exposure to risky assets, for example.

3. Ignoring transaction costs in the learning phase may favour those strategies requiring frequent trading, penalizing the more prudent strategies that act only when there is more confidence in the forecasts. This may have negative consequences when the strategies that come out of the maximization process are used for actual trading in environments characterized by transaction costs. In this case strategies may indeed be effective, but may incur large expenses by continuously buying and selling. In order to avoid these phenomena it is necessary to include transaction costs in the learning phase, either by adjusting prices or by defining a penalty based on the number of operations.

To illustrate more precisely some of the topics that we have discussed, we present an application based on genetic learning in the next section.

5.5 A model of a genetics-based learning trader

In this application, a single ANN-based trader acts in a stock market by selling and buying shares at a given exogenous price (Margarita, 1991, 1992a). The trader directly chooses the action, without attempting to forecast future prices. Referring to the different methods discussed in sections 5.3.1 and 5.3.2, this is equivalent to incorporating the mapping from forecasts to decisions in the internal rules of the system. The aim is to find the optimal strategy for reaching a target defined in terms of an economic outcome. The strategy is implicitly encoded in the network, so it is necessary to find the network's structure and the value of its weights.

5.5.1 The trader's network

The decision system of the stock trader is based on a feed-forward, three-layer, fully connected ANN. A recurrent connection from output to input is added in order to take into account the previous action (Figure 5.11).
The network receives the following information:

1. The prices of the last five days: P_{t-1}, P_{t-2}, P_{t-3}, P_{t-4}, P_{t-5};
2. The simple average of the prices of the last 30 days: P_{mt-30};
3. The action taken on the previous day: A_{t-1}.

The output is composed of only one neuron, A_t, encoding the three possible actions: buy, sell, or wait. These actions are taken according to the activation value of the output neuron:

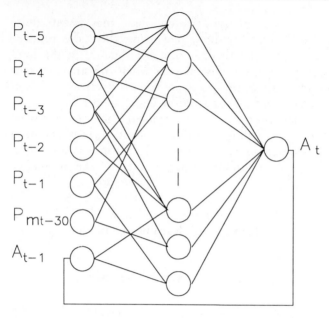

Figure 5.11 *The structure of the trader's network.*

Sell	If $0.00 \leq A_t \leq 0.33$
Wait	If $0.33 < A_t \leq 0.66$
Buy	If $0.66 < A_t \leq 1.00$

To complete the specification of this basic structure, one also needs to determine the number of hidden neurons, a problem that will be considered later on.

Wealth is the economic criterion chosen to evaluate the trader's performance; it is computed, in each time period, as the amount of money owned plus the number of shares owned times the stock price.

5.5.2 Learning

In this model the output of the network is the action at a given time, rather than a forecast of the price. For this reason, the target is not known and cannot be defined. The appropriateness of a strategy (that is, a sequence of actions) cannot be measured action by action, but only globally in terms of the wealth accumulated over the given time period. Learning is based on GAs, both because of their effectiveness in this kind of search problem, and because of their ability to orient the search process by means of a fitness function.

In the process of selecting a strategy, GAs act upon a population of individuals. Although this is a one-agent model, we have to consider what

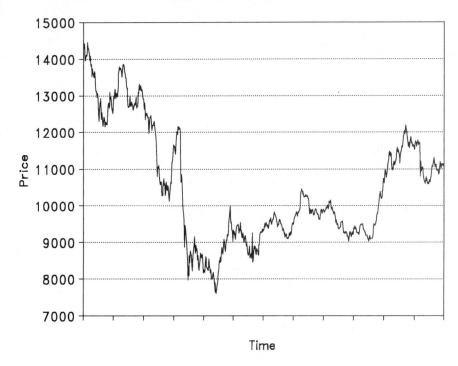

Figure 5.12 *The training set: Time series of Fiat stock prices (1987–89).*

we call the 'virtual population', a fictitious population, made up of non-interacting homogeneous agents, created only for the requirements of the GAs' selection process. It is important to distinguish between this kind of population, from which our aim is to select one individual among many, and true populations, where heterogeneous agents interact and contribute to create an aggregate outcome.

The virtual population is made up of 100 traders, all with the same structure but with different randomly generated weights. GAs use this population both for solving the hidden neurons problem and for finding the trader with the best performance.

5.5.3 The environment

The environment is based upon a stock price time series. For the numerical simulation, we used the daily prices of the Fiat share on the Milan Stock Exchange, from 1987 to 1989. A graphical representation of the training set is shown in Figure 5.12.

In one run using the whole time period (known as a generation, by analogy with GA terminology) traders act every day by selling, buying or waiting. The traders' performance is measured in terms of accumulated wealth at the end of the run.

Traders are subject to a set of market rules:

1. Traders are independent and do not interact.
2. Every day they receive the same public information about prices.
3. All the operations take place at the same price.
4. Each trader can sell or buy only one share per day.
5. Initially all the traders own the same number of shares and the same quantity of money.
6. Traders are subject to a budget constraint: they can act only if they own the money or the shares they want to trade.
7. Price is exogenous: the actions of traders do not influence it.
8. Transaction costs are not considered.
9. The traders' performance is evaluated in terms of final wealth.

5.5.4 The problem of hidden neurons

We start our search for the best trader by first choosing the number of hidden neurons and then tuning the weights. We search for the optimal number by using the following algorithm.

Step 1: The parameters of the model are initialized with averages. The main parameters are (1) the minimum and maximum value of weights for random initialization, (2) the starting conditions in terms of traders' assets, and (3) the parameters of GA (number of networks to reproduce, mutation rate).

Step 2: The number of hidden neurons is fixed at 3 and weights are randomly initialized.

Step 3: A complete run over 50 generations is made and the final wealth of the best network is measured and recorded.

Step 4: The number of hidden neurons is increased by one.

Step 5: The simulation is repeated from Step 3 until the number of hidden neurons equals 15.

Step 6: We choose the number of hidden neurons corresponding to the best performance over 10 iterations of steps 1 to 5.

The performance of the best network over 10 iterations by number of hidden neurons (from 3 to 14) is presented in Figure 5.13, as well as the number of actions (purchase or sale) taken by that network as a measure of the possible influence of transaction costs. The 10-hidden-neuron network (10-HNN) exhibits the best performance and is the one used in the next simulations, although a comparison will be done later on with 5-HNN and 15-HNN.

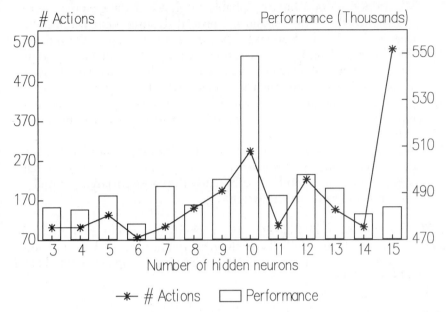

Figure 5.13 *Performance of the Stock Trader Network as a function of the number of hidden neurons.*

5.5.5 The genetic algorithm

After defining the structure, we have to tune the weights of the networks in order to select the best trader. For this training phase, we use a modified form of standard GA.

Step 1:   We randomly generate a population of 100 traders, all with the same structure.

Step 2:   Traders act in the environment for a generation that lasts three years.

Step 3:   Final wealth is computed for each network.

Step 4:   The best 10 traders reproduce 10 times each in order to create a population of the same size as the initial one.

Step 5:   Random mutation is applied to the new population.

Step 6:   The next generation begins with the new population evolving in the same fashion over the same data.

Step 7:   The different steps of this process (from Step 2) are repeated for 50 generations.

The GAs used in this application differ from standard GAs in the following aspects:

1. We do not adopt a binary alphabet to represent the genotype (set of weights) of the networks and use instead floating-point real numbers (see section 2.3.6). Standard GAs act on binary representation.
2. We choose a deterministic selection technique by exogenously setting the percentage of networks that will reproduce. Standard GAs use stochastic mechanisms such as roulette wheel selection.
3. We used only two out of three of the primary genetic operators: reproduction and mutation. The third, crossover, is not implemented here.
4. We implement a form of real-valued mutation, rather than a standard binary one. With a given probability, mutation changes weights by an amount randomly distributed within a given range centred on the previous value of the weight.

We are interested in following the performance of the best trader in each generation. Figure 5.14 shows the performance for the best individual during the genetic evolution over 50 generations, compared with that of 5-HNN and 15-HNN.

Two aspects are worth noting.

1. 10-HNN networks achieve by far the best results, which confirms the appropriateness of the chosen structure.

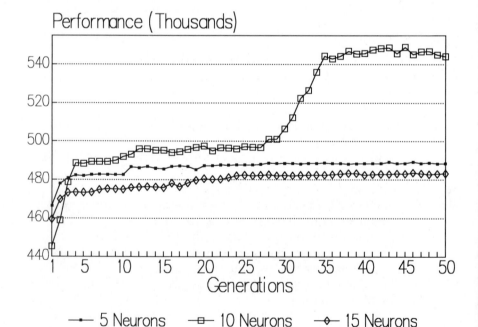

Figure 5.14 *Increase in performance for the best individual over 50 generations for three network architectures.*

2.   The 4-phase evolution of the best individual across generations: (i)
     An increase in wealth in the first 4 generations, (ii) from generation
     5 to 28, a period of stability, (iii) another improvement from 29 to
     35 and (iv) stability again from 36 to the end of the run in gener-
     ation 50.

Interpretations of this behaviour can follow two lines of thinking.

1.   Wealth assumes an arbitrary initial value and early generations are
     likely to increase it, although by limited amounts. In the second
     phase, small random changes introduced by mutation accumulate
     without noticeable effect until they reach a threshold. After this
     threshold is reached, in the third phase, the accumulated effects of
     mutations become evident. Finally, mutation loses its relevance and
     another phase of stability is encountered.
2.   In accordance with GA search capabilities, we can state that the appli-
     cation of genetic operators orients the exploration of the search space
     towards regions of high fitness. Once one of these regions is found,
     GA explores it, but at the same time it continues to explore other
     regions. In this way, contrarily to gradient-based algorithms, GAs can
     escape from local maxima. The dynamics of performance of the best
     trader can be explained in terms of local maxima in the fitness func-
     tion: while the GA is trapped at a local maximum, performance does
     not change substantially; when it escapes from it and reaches a new
     region, fitness measures show a substantial increase. Subsequent explo-
     ration of this new region leads to a period of stability.

Once the optimal trader is identified, we want to test his or her performance not only in the environment used for learning but also in a different
environment. In this way we can measure the trader's mapping and generalization capabilities. This is the aim of the validation process.

5.5.6 The validation process

The validation process is based on the out-of-sample comparison of the
performance, of the best trader with (1) the best possible performance (2)
the results obtained by a trader operating randomly or (3) a buy-and-hold
strategy where the trader buys shares at the beginning of the period and
holds them until the end of the period.

The validation set is made up of the daily prices of the Fiat share in
1990. A graphical representation of the validation set is shown in Figure
5.15.

The validation process has been carried out with the following initial
conditions: a sum of money equal to 100,000 Italian Lire and a number
of shares equal to 100. Table 5.1 summarizes the results of this process.
It is worth noting that the best genetic trader's performance is very close

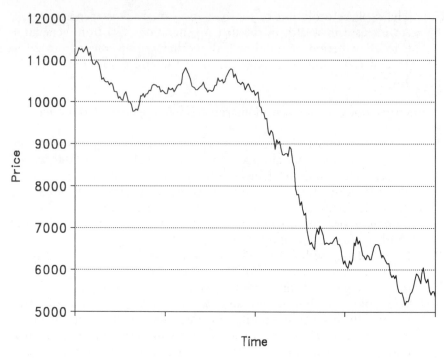

Figure 5.15 *The validation set: Time Series of Fiat Stock Prices (1990).*

to the best possible, while the two other strategies perform very poorly. Given the market rules described in section 5.5.3, the best possible performance corresponds to buying (selling) when the current price is higher (lower) than the final price.

Two features of the rules strongly influence the dynamics of the system and the performance of the trader:

1. the fixed number of shares that operators can trade in each period (one share in our simulations);
2. the traders' budget constraint, which restricts the number of actions by allowing only feasible actions.

It is possible to observe that the former rule induces an increased number of operations due to the day-by-day strategy, while the latter tends to make the performance dependent on initial conditions, namely the sum of money and number of shares. If the trader chooses a bad strategy, he or she is likely to be restricted in later operations by the limited availability of resources.

As a further step in the validation process, we attempt to analyse the sensitivity of the performance to changes in the initial conditions. We run a set of simulations with different initial conditions and with other parameters left unchanged. In Table 5.2 we report a performance index of the

Table 5.1 *Comparison among different strategies (W_0 = Initial wealth = 1209000, W_T = final wealth)*

Strategy	W_T	$W_T - W_0$	$(W_T - W_0)/W_0$
Genetic trader	1136460	− 75540	− 6%
Best possible	1144171	− 64829	− 5%
Random	628693	−580307	−48%
Buy and hold	584441	−624559	−52%

Table 5.2 *Performance index as a function of initial conditions*

Shares Money	0	25	50	75	100	125	150
0	0.00	0.93	0.92	0.93	0.93	0.92	0.84
50000	0.88	0.94	0.93	0.93	0.94	0.92	0.85
100000	0.89	0.95	0.94	0.94	0.94	0.92	0.85
200000	0.94	0.96	0.94	0.94	0.94	0.93	0.86
300000	0.96	0.97	0.95	0.95	0.95	0.93	0.87
400000	0.97	0.97	0.96	0.95	0.95	0.93	0.87
500000	0.98	0.97	0.96	0.96	0.95	0.94	0.88
600000	0.98	0.98	0.96	0.96	0.96	0.94	0.88
700000	0.98	0.98	0.97	0.96	0.96	0.94	0.89
800000	0.99	0.98	0.97	0.96	0.96	0.95	0.89
900000	0.99	0.98	0.97	0.97	0.96	0.95	0.90

best artificial operator as a function of the initial number of shares and the initial sum of money. This index is the ratio of the wealth at the end of the year and the wealth at the beginning of the year. Values less than 1, the only kind present in the table, indicate a loss.

Some aspects have to be pointed out in order to interpret these data.

1. Year 1990 represents a highly negative trend in Fiat stock value.
2. Data patterns in 1990 (validation set) seem to be quite different from those encountered in the years from 1987 to 1989 (training set).
3. During the validation process, we observe a high number of no-action periods, which denotes uncertainty in the operator's decision-making process. This can be partly explained by considering points 1 and 2.
4. The performance index is nearly proportional to the initial liquid assets and inversely proportional to the initial quantity of stocks; this is partly a consequence of the trend in year 1990.

The sensitivity of the performance to initial conditions is high: the performance index ranks from 0.84 to 0.99. The value 0.99 is quite satisfactory in terms of economic performance, especially if we consider the trend of the period and the fact that shares are initially valued at a high price.

5.5.7 Results

The results we obtain in this application of one-agent models allow us to point out some of the advantages and weaknesses of this approach.

1. One-agent models reflect the situation commonly encountered by decision-makers who act in stock markets. By building this kind of model, we can provide traders with an effective decision support system, able to help them in defining trading strategies.
2. By using ANNs, the model captures the regularities of the data belonging to the training set. The possible non-stationarity of the time series must be investigated and taken into account, because it can invalidate the generalizability of the model and its practical usefulness as a guide to trading. If there is non-stationarity, it may be necessary to build many sub-models to be used in different situations.
3. By coupling GAs with ANNs we obtain an effective method for solving problems which require an unsupervised learning technique (see Chapter 1).
4. The difficulty in interpreting the meaning of hidden neurons, an aspect that we discussed in Chapter 3, becomes critical when building decision support systems where the reasons for the decision are nearly as important as the decision itself. Discovering the links between data patterns and actions would help in interpreting the behaviour of the artificial trader and understanding the limitations of the models.
5. One aspect of the complexity of the problem lies in the number of parameters to tune. One of them, the length of the training set, is of primary importance. Generally, ANNs exhibit better results when trained with a large set of patterns to learn, if the environment is stationary.
6. An economic measure of the performance of the model has to be defined: wealth is only one of the criteria we can adopt.

Measuring model performance is a fundamental aspect of the problem, partly because performance can change when we change the way we measure it, and partly because in most cases, performance is the main source of information on which to base subsequent performance. The aim of the next section is to examine this problem.

5.6 Interpretation of decision rules

The final issue we face in this chapter (see also Chapter 3) is the interpretation of decision rules arising from a neural network. This is a very important practical problem, as the possibility of introducing these technologies to a wider public of practitioners depends to a large extent on the possibility of explaining the strategies that the models are following.

5.6.1 Problems of interpretation

The structure of a neural network is highly nonlinear, and this immediately explains the difficulties with understanding its solutions in terms of simple relationships between inputs and outputs. The weight that connects one specific input to one specific hidden neuron or a hidden to an output neuron generally depends on the global state of the network, so that it is in general impossible to assign a specific interpretation to the various weights. This issue is related to the concept of distributed representation of information at a subsymbolic level.

The basic impossibility of interpreting a given structure of even simple networks of course does not mean that such structures are black boxes, which must be used without any understanding of the decisions that are being made. The possibilities that have already been discussed in Chapter 3, for example the analysis of the relationships between inputs and output in terms of partial derivatives, are general and application-independent. We now discuss another approach that is more suited to decision-makers. This technique is closer in spirit to a classifier system interpretation of the neural network, as an algorithm reacting to certain patterns in the data. The problem of the exact equivalence between neural networks and classifier systems has been studied in the literature by Davis (1989) and by Belew and Gherrity (1989).

The technique that we propose begins with the configuration of the network after training and tries to evaluate it by analysing its reaction to patterns chosen so as to suggest simple interpretations to the user. For example, one may be interested to know what the network decides after certain specific sequences of data that may or may not have been observed in the learning process. Suppose that one trains a network to forecast the change in stock prices using as input data the 10 most recent lags of the changes in prices, the last available price and the average price of the last month. One may then apply the optimal weights to an imaginary case where the changes in prices in the last 10 days are always positive and the last price is below average, to see whether the suggestion of the network is to buy or to sell, and compare this with the suggestions given by experts in the field or by the decision-maker him or herself. This technique gives a qualitative and intuitive (although not a rigorous) insight about the rules built autonomously during learning by the network.

5.6.2 Complex behaviour and economic behaviour

The interpretation of the network is also very important from the point of view of more theoretically oriented applications. Indeed, one might say that the degree of freedom offered by neural networks contrasts sharply with the rigidity of neoclassical economic models as far as hypotheses about behaviour are concerned. In a typical microeconomic model the decision-maker always maximizes a utility function, independently of the environment and of any experience derived from past interactions with the environment. For example, a neoclassical investor maximizes a time-invariant expected utility function and behaves according to demand functions reflecting the shape of the utility function.

In the theoretical applications of this book we do not use such a rigid framework; the agent has more flexibility, and is more responsive towards the environment. The preference function is well defined, but the actions aimed at maximizing such a function are taken on the basis of continuous learning from the environment. In many cases the agent has to learn the consequences of his or her actions, taking into account the varying reactions of the environment. The dealer considered in Chapter 6 performs certain actions in order to maximize wealth, but does not know the consequences of these particular actions in terms of wealth, since these depend on unknowable actions from the other agents in the system. The behaviour emerging from such a maximization procedure is typically difficult to interpret, but is endogenously developed as a reaction to the main features of the environment.

To some, the difficulty in interpreting decision rules in terms of simple demand functions relating price and quantity may seem a drawback. We believe instead that the impossibility of interpreting the decision rules of networks in simple ways reflects the complexity of the environment. There are examples showing that economic agents do not behave in ways that are similar to those implied by economic models. For example, Shiller (1989) found that the actions of traders, in the days of the stock market crash of 1987, looked at what others were doing, and traded on the basis of very short horizons. This certainly does not come out of any stable demand function, but may be in part rationalized as the reactions of agents to a multi-dimensional unknown environment that is not even easy to describe with standard economic models.

While one-agent models reflect situations encountered in real markets, they are based upon some restrictive hypotheses limiting their applicability. In fact they leave out the whole class of problems where collective learning and interactions among agents contribute substantially to determining the aggregate outcome of the system. Models corresponding to this class of problems are presented in the next chapter.

6
One-population models

Outline of the chapter

The chapter is concerned with the analysis of one-population models, where we study interactions among agents who belong to a unique population but at the same time retain important sorts of heterogeneity with respect to various dimensions that are relevant to their ability to reach their goals. Such models are also important as a preparation for the more complex multi-population models that are described in the next chapter. After a general introduction, the chapter discusses two one-population models of financial markets in detail. The common features of the basic framework around which the first model is built will be fully described, since many of its elements reappear in the subsequent models. This same structure will also be echoed in the structure of the multi-population models of Chapter 7, and this will facilitate comparisons between one-population and multi-population models.

It is useful to clarify the difference between the two models considered in this chapter, as far as the use of neural networks is concerned. In the first model, neural networks are essentially used as forecasting devices in the context of a standard model with wealth-maximizing agents. These agents make decisions according to well-defined rules derived from utility maximization, and use nonlinear models to forecast the future values of the relevant variables. In the second model, agents do not follow pre-specified rules, but create their own behavioural rules as experience about the structure of the market accumulates over time. Neural networks are no longer simple forecasting devices, but are used as instruments for finding new rules of adaptation to a partially observable environment.

6.1 One-population models

6.1.1 Basic definition

One-population models represent situations with interactions among agents who differ as far as some characteristics are concerned, but who are fundamentally similar in terms of strategies and goals. To further clarify the concepts we propose the following definition:

> One-population models consider agents interacting in an environment that they themselves contribute to determine. They all try to achieve

the same goals with the same decision rules implemented with different instruments, and this, together with possibly different learning abilities, creates heterogeneity among the various agents.

We underline some important aspects of this definition.

1. The environment is not exogenous: Agents contribute to determining the variables characterizing the environment. In the case of a financial market, for example, one-population models explain the endogenous formation of the market price on the basis of the interactions among the agents.

2. Other agents: Interactions among agents are essential in determining the aggregate dynamics, as interactions determine the evolution of the agents' endowments, and contribute to learning and to the evolution of the aggregate variables.

3. Bidirectionality of the information flow: By determining the aggregate outcome, the actions of the agents are recorded in the market variables, which are then used by all the agents during learning as a part of their information set.

4. Decision rules: The decision process is based on decision rules that may be external or internal. This goes back to the definition of forecasting and acting agents given in section 5.1.1: the former use their information set to forecast a variable which is then processed by exogenous rules, while the latter decide the action directly from their information set. A classification of the different models described in the book is presented in Figure 6.1.

5. Instruments: To use an ANN terminology, instruments include both the structure of the network and the values of the weights. As we will see in section 6.2.7, the complexity of the agents' structure is one of the parameters influencing the dynamics of the system. In one-population models the structure is the same for all the agents, but the set of weights differs from one agent to another from two points of view.

    (a) Initial assignment: Agents are initially created with independently generated random weights corresponding to different initial endowments.

    (b) Evolution of the values: Initial values are modified during the learning process, which can differ from one agent to the other.

    Consequently, when the networks autonomously build behavioural rules, the different sets of weights must be interpreted not only from a numerical point of view, but also as devices which encode different sets of rules. This encoding possesses the same characteristics as described in section 5.3: the weights represent the parameters of the mapping between the information set and the forecast, in the case of external rules, or between the information set and the action, in the case of internal rules.

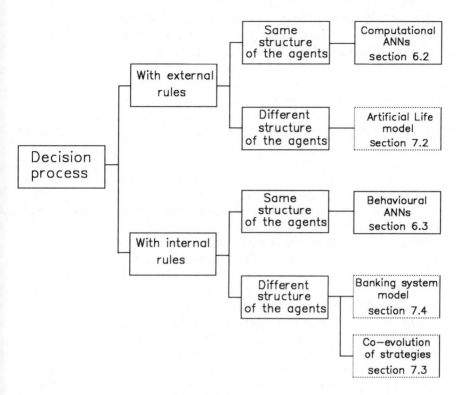

Figure 6.1 *Classification of models based on the rules and structure of the agents (dotted lines refer to multi-population models).*

6.   Learning: Even in one-population models agents may differ in learning ability. In addition to the different learning schemes that may be assigned to the agents, learning abilities, specifically the speed of learning, depend mainly on the different initial endowments. Section 6.2.5 considers this aspect.

6.1.2 Economics and heterogeneity

In Chapter 2 we described the representative agent model. From a scientific point of view this is certainly one of the possible approaches to the analysis of a system that is very complicated and impossible to describe in detail. This reaction is similar in spirit to the approach that led to the laws of thermodynamics, which in some sense allow one to predict the statistical behaviour of a system composed of identical parts with weak interactions. This approach turned out to be useful in physics in those cases where the systems are composed of units which are heterogeneous and/or interact in a very significant and strong way.

Physics and biology have therefore tackled the analysis of complex systems in different ways, looking for a theory of complexity. According to Weisbuch's definition (1991) 'a complex system is a system composed of a large number of different interacting elements'. This definition of course includes social and economic systems, where the single units are heterogeneous, and the interactions may certainly be strong in some contexts, at least locally. Therefore it is an open question whether one can analyse a complex economic and social system with tools which are better suited to the analysis of systems that are not complex. The fact that scientists coming from many diverse fields are trying to develop a unified theory of complexity that uses new tools is certainly a strong motive for applying some of these tools to the study of economic systems.

Of course diverse problems require the use of diverse tools. Heterogeneity is more important in some contexts than in others. For this reason we have decided to organize our artificial models of economic heterogeneity into two different classes, which we call one-population and multi-population respectively. In both cases the basic principle is that of heterogeneity, in the sense that the individual agents composing these populations differ in at least one characteristic.

However, it is useful to introduce a distinction between the instruments, decision rules and goals that place us in different classes of population heterogeneity. Such a distinction is clearly relevant for economic and social systems, where the agents may differ in one or more of these basic features. After a brief discussion of the relation between one-agent and one-population models we devote the rest of this chapter to one-population models, and the following chapter to multi-population models.

6.1.3 From one-agent to one-population models

The distinction between one-agent and one-population models is even more important conceptually than the distinction between one-population and multi-population models. In building one-population models it is possible to explain the equilibrium situation of the market endogenously, an achievement that is impossible with one-agent models where all the characteristics of the environment are taken as given and beyond the control of the single agent.

In the one-agent model of a trader in a stock market considered in Chapter 5, for example, the agent reacted to the information set coming from the market, and was supposed to buy and sell at the exogenously given market prices. This simplification is very convenient from an analytical point of view, since it makes all the simulations of the various trading strategies very easy. There is no need to understand where the market price is coming from; one may simply use the historical evidence, and assume that the trader may buy or sell any quantity at the prevailing price. This may be useful for analysing the performance of a small agent in a large market, but is less useful in two other cases, for example when one is trying to understand the aggregate market dynamics, and in situations characterized by thin markets and/or just a few classes of agents.

In the former case, in order to understand market dynamics one has to build a structural model of the market. In the case of market prices one needs to specify the mechanisms according to which prices are formed, and therefore also to explain the impact of every single agent on the price. Whereas in one-agent models prices are exogenous to the agent, in one-population models prices emerge as a consequence of the interactions between the different agents.

In the latter case, actions have some influence on the market price; the agent is no longer free to take any decision about quantity at the given market prices. The agent's decision to buy or sell creates some pressure on the price. This situation, already encountered in situations with thin markets (see Chapter 5), is also present in markets populated by just a few classes of agents. Think for example of one agent choosing among a restricted number of trading strategies which are also being considered by many other agents in the market.

Suppose for example that at night all the agents decide on the strategy that should be used the following day, choosing from a menu of potential strategies. It is then likely that most of the agents will choose similar strategies, and the assets being evaluated according to the same methodology by many agents will have large effects on the market price, much larger than those that one would have in the case in which only one trader chooses that evaluation over the others, everything else being equal. The forecast that one agent makes assuming that the others are not echoing his or her choices might be wrong. Note that here there is no interaction in the sense defined in game theory, but there is a strong complementarity among trading strategies just because many agents choose independently from a finite set of alternatives, evaluating the various options with a similar methodology. One existing example of this fact is provided in Kephart *et al.* (1990), where the authors show that prediction strategies based upon technical analysis which appear to be reasonable from the perspective of a single agent can be disastrous when adopted by a substantial fraction of the agents. The example shows that the forecast error is minimized when the trader assumes that the price will react to the trading. Since in most cases forecast errors are synonymous with losses, there are strong reasons for suggesting a more complete analysis that does not take the market as exogenous and immutable.

In the rest of the chapter we consider two one-population models: in section 6.2 agents adopt external decision rules using past prices for forecasting future price, while in section 6.3 agents build and use internal decision rules in choosing the quantity to be traded.

6.2 A financial market model with computational ANNs

This section presents a revised and extended version of the model described in Beltratti and Margarita (1994).

We consider a financial market populated by agents who are heterogeneous with respect to some characteristics, but similar with respect to two fundamental dimensions, namely the goals and the decision rules used to operate in the market. The difference with respect to one-agent models lies in the endogenous formation of market prices on the basis of agents' choices. We now clarify these issues, discussing in turn the dimensions of heterogeneity, and the mechanics that ensure the endogeneity of the market price.

6.2.1 Heterogeneity and endogeneity

(a) Homogeneity

The relevant dimension of homogeneity is given by uniformity of the goals and of the decision rules used by the agents. Everybody behaves similarly: an expectation of an increase (decrease) in the price generates purchases (sales). This strategy is implemented for the purpose of maximizing the expected increase in wealth, with no concern for risk.

(b) Heterogeneity

The strong assumptions shared by representative agent models contrast deeply with our intuition and our informal knowledge of the way markets work in practice; see for example the surveys contained in Shiller (1987), showing that agents differ in a number of factors, including the information set, the interpretation of the public information set, and personal characteristics such as wealth and risk aversion. In our model agents use different instruments to put into practice different decision rules used to achieve the same goal. Agents differ in their information sets, and in the way in which such information sets are interpreted. Moreover, agents learn in heterogeneous ways, even though they all use the same learning technique. These differences lead to agents whose total wealth evolves heterogeneously over time.

(c) Endogeneity

One very important characteristic of our model is the endogenous formation of the price. Interaction between demand and supply determines the market price, and this in turn helps agents to evaluate the efficiency of a forecasting rule. Each agent helps to determine the aggregate outcome, and therefore interacts fully with the environment. It is noteworthy that the learning process in turn generates new rules and induces new behaviour.

6.2.2 The behaviour of the agents

Agent i enters the early morning of day t with a given amount of money $M_{i,t}$, a stock of shares $S_{i,t}$ and an information set $I_{i,t}$. The content of the latter will be described later on. The agent has two options for carrying his or her wealth over to the following morning: money and shares, about which the agent will have to make a decision at noon of day t. Each day, shares can be bought or sold against money in a stock market opening at noon, at a price $P_{ij,t}$ which depends on the value assigned to shares by the agent j who will be randomly met in the marketplace. We also assume the following.

- Agents are risk-neutral (see definition in Chapter 2).
- Each transaction involves buying or selling a fixed quantity of shares.
- Actions on day t are based on expectations formed in the morning of time t before the market opens.
- Transaction costs are not taken into account.

Given these hypotheses, the agent is indifferent to any transaction costs or risk involved in buying or selling, and the action at t depends only on the comparison between the actual price and the expected price. The relevant forecast for agent i is the price at which the share may be sold in period t+1. We denote this expectation with $E_{i,t}P_{t+1}$, a general symbol to underscore that agent i does not know the identity of agent j with whom agent i will transact. Given these assumptions (in particular that of risk neutrality) the optimal action is the following:

buy shares at any $P_{ij,t}$ such that $(E_{i,t}P_{t+1} - P_{ij,t}) > 0$

sell shares at any $P_{ij,t}$ such that $(E_{i,t}P_{t+1} - P_{ij,t}) < 0$

buy or sell at any $P_{ij,t}$ such that $(E_{i,t}P_{t+1} - P_{ij,t}) = 0$

where $E_{i,t}P_{t+1} - P_{ij,t}$ is the expectation of agent i about the change in stock prices between the morning of day t and the morning of day t+1. The expected price is therefore also a reservation price, which is the maximum (minimum) the agent is willing to pay (receive) in order to buy (sell) the share on day t.

We make the following four remarks before describing the marketplace.

- Behaviour is simple to interpret: the anticipation of an increase in prices induces the agent to demand shares, since this is more attractive than holding money.
- Imposing a fixed ceiling on shares in any transaction is always binding, since risk-neutral agents would not diversify and would tend to keep their wealth either in the form of money or in the form of shares. From now on we set the ceiling to 1 share, without loss of generality.

- Each agent always takes a position: everybody wants to either sell or buy, since the alternative is money. We impose no constraint on buying or selling, in that an agent can go short in either money or shares, i.e. can freely borrow funds from an external source or sell shares without owning them.
- The transaction takes place because agents have different opinions about the value of the asset (for the way these opinions are formed and updated, see the next section).

6.2.3 The marketplace

After forming their reservation prices, agents meet at random in a decentralized marketplace deprived of any auctioneer. From the sample of N agents we randomly select two agents and allow them to trade. Given the assumptions we have made about the demand schedule, a transaction always occurs in our model, unless the two reservation prices are the same, in which case agents are indifferent (we assume that they always transact). The actual transaction takes place at a price equal to the simple average of the two expectations, with a rule similar to the one used by Albin and Foley (1992):

$$P_{ij,t} = 0.5 \ (E_{i,t}P_{t+1} + E_{j,t}P_{t+1}) \tag{6.1}$$

if $E_{i,t}P_{t+1} < E_{j,t}P_{t+1}$, j buys 1 share from i at $P_{ij,t}$

if $E_{i,t}P_{t+1} > E_{j,t}P_{t+1}$, i buys 1 share from j at $P_{ij,t}$

Expression 6.1 can also be justified as the focal point of a non-cooperative bargaining game between two players who have to split a pie (Rasmusen, 1989). In our example the size of the pie is given by the difference between the two reservation prices, and a transaction price that averages the two reservation prices divides expected gains equally between the two traders.

After the transaction is completed, we exclude agents i and j and sample from the remaining agents, obtaining another transaction and another price. When all the agents have been selected and all the transactions have been performed we have N/2 prices, whose simple average is taken as determining the market price at time t, π_t. Given the fact that each transaction price is the simple average of the two expectations, we have:

$$\pi_t = N^{-1} \sum_{j=1}^{N} E_{j,t}P_{t+1} \tag{6.2}$$

The market price π_t is not directly relevant to any transaction taking place during day t, but it is a useful signal of the average opinion. It can also be used by agents to calculate the market value of their wealth at the end of day t. For an agent i who bought during the day, the value of wealth at the end of the day is equal to $W_{i,t+1} = (M_{i,t} - P_{ij,t}) + \pi_t(S_{i,t} + 1)$, while for a seller $W_{i,t+1} = (M_{i,t} + P_{ij,t}) + \pi_t(S_{i,t} - 1)$. The next sections describe the expectations formation mechanism and the updating of that mechanism.

6.2.4 Neural networks for artificial agents

In order to close the model we need to specify a rule for forming expectations about the future exchange price. In the literature on financial markets with imperfect information, a rational expectations equilibrium implies that each trader forms expectations on the basis of both his or her own private information and the market price, which aggregates the heterogeneous information sets of the agents. Grossman and Stiglitz (1980), for example, derive an equilibrium where informed traders condition their forecasts on a private signal, while uninformed traders condition their forecasts on the market price. The equilibrium price is a function of the stochastic shocks, and takes into account the fact that uninformed traders are learning from the price itself. This equilibrium distribution is seen as the outcome of an unspecified process on the part of agents learning the correlation between dividends and market prices. In our model it is not possible to apply such a rational expectations equilibrium, for the simple reason that we do not assume the existence of an auctioneer who can compute the equilibrium price. Each agent has to form an expectation before observing the market price, and therefore cannot use the latter for inferring the valuations of the other agents. A 'rational' expectation model could in principle be based on the true structure of the economy as described in equations 6.1 and 6.2 in the text. Each agent would need to know the information sets of all the other agents, and the parameters of the models that are used to process such information. This also requires an incredible computational ability that we are reluctant to assume in our model.

We therefore choose to explicitly model the process of expectations formation of each agent, by considering a nonlinear algorithm based on ANNs (Arthur, 1991). Such an algorithm implies that learning takes place in every period as agents compare the forecasts made in the past with the actual realizations. Extensions of the literature on nonlinear regressions have shown the general applicability of neural networks to the learning of complicated nonlinear mappings, and their superiority with respect to simple linear rules (White, 1991). Our model therefore does not attribute to the agents any knowledge of the true model of the economy, but at the same time does not restrict them to forecasting with an inefficient model such as a linear one. Agents form their expectations on the basis of the available information, and we model this mechanism by means of a three-layer, fully interconnected, feed-forward neural network such as the one described in Figure 6.2.

We restrict the information set available at the beginning of t to the vector $I_{i,t} = [\pi_{t-1}, \pi_{t-2}, P_{ij,t-1}, P_{ij,t-2}]$, containing variables known at the beginning of day t, before markets open. The analytical expression for

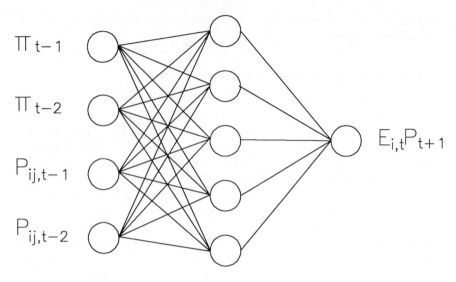

Figure 6.2 *The structure of the artificial agent.*

the formation of expectations corresponds to the structure described in Figure 6.2:

$$E_{i,t}P_{t+1} = g_{i,t}(\pi_{t-1}, \pi_{t-2}, P_{ij,t-1}, P_{ij,t-2}) = \qquad (6.3)$$

$$= f(f(I_{i,t}\,A_{i,t})\,B_{i,t})$$

where the functional form $g_{i,t}$ is a result of applying the function f and the various linear combinations described in expression 6.3 to the matrices $A_{i,t}$ and $B_{i,t}$. These matrices contain the value of the weights from the input to the hidden layer and from the hidden to the output layer, respectively, for the i-th agent at time t.

At the beginning of history networks are equal in terms of their structures (architecture, number of layers and number of nodes) but differ in the set of weights. Therefore an agent is not concerned with the possibility that others possess greatly superior computational abilities, and are therefore more likely to profit from a given trade. The expectational rule described in expression 6.3 is certainly not 'rational' in a strict sense; rather it is a time-varying nonlinear rule that becomes more and more efficient when it is coupled with a proper learning algorithm. Such learning will be considered in the next section.

6.2.5 Learning in artificial agents

The mechanism that produces the forecast is the nonlinear function $g_{i,t}$ specified in expression 6.3. This function varies over time because the parameters of the matrices $A_{i,t}$ and $B_{i,t}$ change over time, in such a way as to improve the precision of the forecasts. To understand how agents learn, note that the forecast made at the beginning of day t cannot be corrected on the basis of the information known at the end of day t, since the former is about variables which will be known during period t+1. What the network can do at the end of day t is to compare the forecast made at time t−1 with the new information available on day t.

In order to find the proper target, note that the transaction at time t was executed at a price given by equation 6.1, and this price was exactly what the network was trying to forecast at t−1. Therefore, conditional on dealing with agent j, the forecasted price of network i at t−1 is the simple average between the forecast of the output of the same network i at t and the forecast of the output of network j at t. Moreover, there is uncertainty due to the fact that no network knows which agent will be met in the marketplace at t. Given our random matching procedure, it is equally likely that any of the remaining N − 1 agents will be met, so the network should assign equal probability to meeting any of them. Therefore we can write:

$$E_{i,t-1}P_t = 0.5[E_{i,t}P_{t+1} + (N - 1)^{-1} \sum_{\substack{j=1 \\ j \neq i}}^{N} E_{j,t}P_{t+1}] \tag{6.4}$$

which can be rewritten in a more interpretable way by using equation 6.2 to rewrite the second term on the right-hand side of equation 6.4 as:

$$(N - 1)^{-1} \left(\sum_{\substack{j=1 \\ j \neq i}}^{N} E_{j,t}P_{t+1} + E_{i,t}P_{t+1} - E_{i,t}P_{t+1} \right) = \tag{6.5}$$

$$(N - 1)^{-1} (N\pi_t - E_{i,t}P_{t+1})$$

Substituting equation 6.5 in equation 6.4 we have:

$$E_{i,t-1}P_t = 0.5 [E_{i,t}P_{t+1} + (N - 1)^{-1}(N\pi_t - E_{i,t}P_{t+1})] =$$

$$= 0.5 (N - 1)^{-1}[(N - 2)E_{i,t}P_{t+1} + N\pi_t] \tag{6.6}$$

This shows that at t, network i modifies its weights by comparing its output at t−1 with a weighted average of its output at t and the market price at t. Given the previous parameters, the learning process allows agents to enter the morning of day t+1 with a new way of interpreting the new information set and of using it to predict the price at time t+2.

In this application we want to consider agents with different learning abilities in order to study the influence of learning on the behaviour of the system. We choose to tune the learning ability of agents by varying the slope of the logistic function. We adopt a form of the logistic function $y = [1 + \exp(-Gx)]^{-1}$ whose slope depends on parameter G. The larger the value of G, the steeper is the logistic over the relevant space, and the less willing the agent to learn from his or her past experience. On the contrary, a low value of G implies more willingness to learn from the environment. Note that in accordance with the definition of one-population models, the learning ability of the agents differs from one simulation to another. Within one simulation all agents are given the same learning possibilities (the same value of parameter G); actual learning ability may differ from one agent to another because of the initialization of the weights, as described below.

More precisely, consider the rule for modifying the weights given above, and note that the derivative of the logistic function is present in the multiplicative form $x_j (1 - x_j)$, where x_j is the activation level of the j-th neuron, varying from 0 to 1. We have

$$\lim_{x_{ti} \to 0} \Delta_t w_{ij} = \lim_{x_{ti} \to 1} \Delta_t w_{ij} = 0$$

So while this activation function implements a form of automatic gain control (small signals correspond to high gain and large signals produce a gain decrease), it is worth noting that in the case of a low number of learning cycles, this characteristic leads to forms of non-learning: the change in the weights is so small that it has no practical effect and the initial assignment of weights remains essentially unchanged. This learning problem is not peculiar to our application but depends intrinsically on the structure of the back-propagation algorithm and on the choice of the activation function. There are some well-known solutions in the literature for minimizing the impact of this problem: Rigler *et al.* (1991) propose a compensatory rescaling of the variables in the different layers; van Ooyen and Nienhuis (1992) resolve this shortcoming by modifying the error function that is to be minimized by the algorithm. We nevertheless continue to vary the slope of the logistic function because we need to be able to fine-tune the learning ability of agents.

How does this aspect influence our model of stock traders? Some networks, due to a particular initial configuration of weights, tend to exhibit a binary behaviour, that is, they tend to produce output values very close to either 0 or 1. Although the forecasting error is high, the term $\Delta_t w_{ij}$ tends to 0 and learning does not occur significantly during the limited number of cycles; therefore those agents do not learn from the environment in any significant way. This is equivalent to saying that the value of parameter G determines the proportion of agents who do not learn. Given an initial distribution of weights, the lower (larger) G is, the larger (lower) the proportion of agents who learn effectively. In order to characterize the learning ability of the population we define as 'dumb' those networks whose output is larger than 0.95 or lower than 0.05 in the first time period, since these are the networks which learn very slowly. The others are defined as smart agents. In Figure 6.3 we show a plot of the average proportion of dumb agents, as previously defined, as a function of the G parameter. The average is based on 100 random generations of the population for each value of G. In our simulations we use G = 1 as a situation

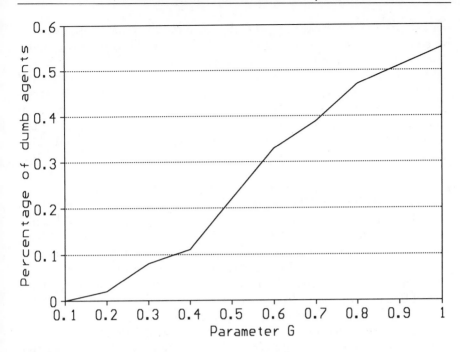

Figure 6.3 *Proportion of dumb agents as a function of the parameter G.*

with a high number of non-learning agents, and G = 0.3 to consider cases where most of the agents learn quickly.

6.2.6 The dynamics of the system

Finally we consider the implications in terms of market price dynamics. To forecast the long-run evolution of the market, for given initial conditions, one needs to study the laws of motion of the system:

$$E_{i,t}P_{t+1} = g_{i,t}(\pi_{t-1}, \pi_{t-2}, P_{ij,t-1}, P_{ij,t-2})$$
$$P_{ij,t} = 0.5 (E_{i,t}P_{t+1} + E_{j,t}P_{t+1})$$

$$\pi_t = N^{-1} \sum_{j=1}^{N} E_{j,t}P_{t+1}$$

$$E_{i,0}P_1 \text{ is given for each } i$$

These equations show how the information at the beginning of day t is processed into a market price, and how this then becomes a new input for future evaluations. The nonlinear structure of the difference equations and the randomness in the formation of bilateral prices make it impossible to solve such a system explicitly. It is certainly possible to characterize a steady state of the system in the following way: in a steady state the market price is a constant, π, and this requires all the forecast prices to be constant across both time and agents, $P_{ij,t} = P$. This in turn requires that all the expectations are constant and equal, so that $E_{j,t}P_{t+1} = E_{i,t}P_{t+1} = EP$. This is compatible with no learning on the part of the agents and an information set $I_{i,t} = [\pi, \pi, P, P] = I$. Equality of expectations across agents implies in turn that their average is equal to the market price, so that $\pi = P$, which is moreover compatible with the learning mechanism described in equations 6.5 and 6.6. We make two remarks about those dynamics.

- All transactions take place because agents differ in their expectations about the future. The interest of this simple model lies precisely in the fact that we can analyse a complex environment where each agent is trying to 'forecast the forecasts of others', as in Townsend (1983). The dynamics stop when all the agents have reached a consensus on the value, and are therefore able to forecast the forecasts of others. There is no 'objective' basin of attraction in this system, since the different evaluations depend on differences in the information set and on different ways of interpreting a given set of signals. It is interesting to see that this sort of aggregate behaviour, which is also similar to the Keynesian 'beauty contest' interpretation of the stock market, can be obtained from the simple microfoundations we are describing in this model.

- We have shown that, provided the system is in a steady state, there is nothing moving the economy from such a steady state. The only random component is the matching of the agents, but this becomes irrelevant when all the agents are forecasting the same value; the system is originally stochastic but becomes deterministic in the steady state. The relationship between the set of initial conditions and the long-run market price is stochastic since it is affected by the history of trades among the agents. Even starting the economy twice from the same set of initial conditions will not lead the market price to the same value, because of the two different histories of interactions among the agents. It is in principle possible to define a complicated joint distribution function defined over all possible meetings of the agents to describe the probability that the long-run price stabilizes at some specific range of values. However, this distribution is so complicated as to be useless. But a knowledge of the long-run behaviour of the system is important for evaluating the results of the simulations. In order to characterize the solutions provided by the laws of motion, we perform some simulations by calculating an empirical asymptotic distribution of the market price, as described in the next section.

6.2.7 Results

The population of traders is composed of 100 networks with five hidden neurons. The starting values of the weights are generated by drawing from a uniform distribution whose range is from −5 to +5 unless otherwise specified. The learning rate is 0.6 and the momentum is 0.9. Share prices are normalized between 0 and 1. We consider two different proportions of dumb agents: 10% of the population (G = 0.3) and 50% of the population (G = 1).

We discuss the results in different areas:

(a) Heterogeneity of the agents
(b) Asymptotic distribution of the market price
(c) Performance of the best and worst agents
(d) Agent complexity and market complexity
(e) Implications of the model.

(a) Heterogeneity of the agents

We start by studying the importance of heterogeneity in agents' models on the dynamics of market prices. More precisely, we consider the effects of different interpretations of the information sets on the part of the agents. Figure 6.4 shows the evolution of the market price and of the dispersion of forecasts of the various agents (standard deviation of the forecasts of the agents at each time t) when the initial values of the weights are uniformly randomly distributed between −0.5 and 0.5 and G = 1. The figure shows that the variability of the market price is low, and that the standard deviation of the forecasts quickly tends to 0. We interpret these results as saying that the market converges to an equilibrium fairly quickly when the agents are very similar in the first place.

Then we increase the heterogeneity of the agents (initial weights go from −5 to 5, but G is still equal to 1), and obtain larger volatility in the market price; the standard deviation decreases from 0.4 to about 0.2 by the end of the run, but is still considerable (Figure 6.5). Even when considering a longer period of time (Figure 6.6, where T = 2000), divergences of opinions do not disappear. Especially at the beginning the market price shows some quite interesting dynamics, with sudden booms and collapses.

How much of the dynamics of the market is affected by the agents' speed of learning? In order to answer this important question we now perform a simulation with G = 0.3, therefore reducing the initial number of dumb agents to about 10% of the population. This affects the initial conditions of the system: Figures 6.7 and 6.8 show frequency distributions of initial forecasts of the market price, that is, the first output of each network, for a given initial random configuration of weights and for a homogeneous information set across agents given by $\pi_{t-1} = 0.5$, $\pi_{t-2} = 0.5$, $P_{ij,t-1} = 0.5$, $P_{ij,t} = 0.5$. When G = 0.3 there are very few dumb agents, in the sense that only a small percentage forecasts values equal to either 0

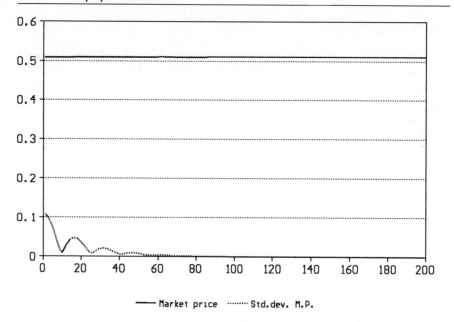

Figure 6.4 *Market price evolution and dispersion of forecasts (weights between –0.5 and 0.5, 50% dumb agents, 200 periods).*

Figure 6.5 *Market price evolution and dispersion of forecasts (weights between –5 and 5, 50% dumb agents, 200 periods).*

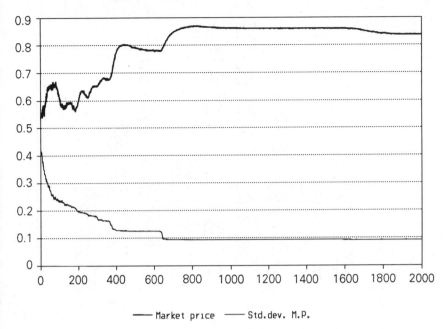

Figure 6.6 *Market price evolution and dispersion of forecasts (weights between –5 and 5, 50% dumb agents, 2000 periods).*

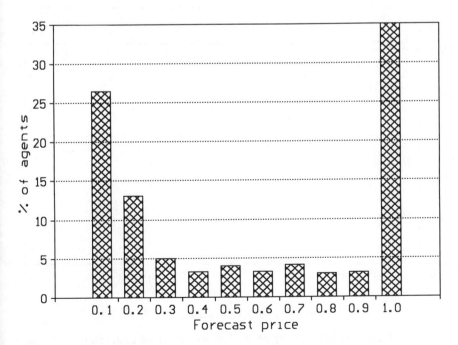

Figure 6.7 *Distribution of initial forecasts (50% dumb agents).*

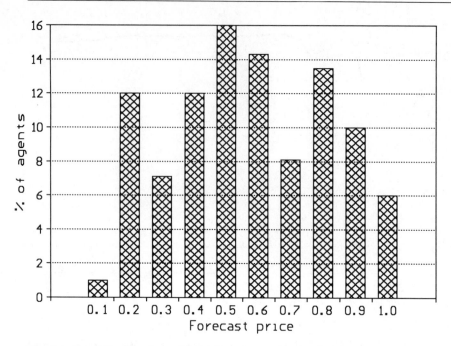

Figure 6.8 *Distribution of initial forecasts (10% dumb agents).*

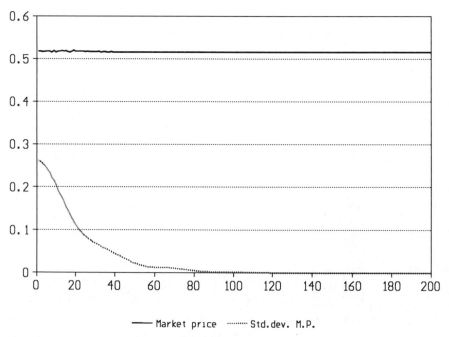

Figure 6.9 *Market price evolution and dispersion of forecasts (weights between −5 and 5, 10% dumb agents, 200 periods).*

or 1. When G = 1 instead, a significant proportion of agents forecasts values close to the extremes. In both cases the average, and therefore the market price at time 1, is about 0.5. At the end of day 1 there is still no learning, as it starts at the end of day 2. Dumb agents' mistakes will not make any difference to the structure of their future forecasts; new information set does not even affect the direction of the new forecast; if the forecast was 1 or 0, it will tend to maintain the same value.

As a consequence, price paths of markets with a low percentage of dumb agents converge rather quickly. Figure 6.9 shows that the price is more stable and the standard deviation decreases substantially. More speed in learning eliminates stubborn agents and makes forecasting the forecasts of others an easier task.

(b) Asymptotic distribution of the market price

To analyse the long-run evolution of the system we compute the asymptotic distribution in the following way.

- We consider three time horizons: T = 200, T = 1000 and T = 2000. We let the model run until T is reached, and record the market price at T.
- We repeat the exercise 100 times (from different initial conditions) to get a frequency distribution which can be used to evaluate the statistical 'significance' of our results.

In Figures 6.10 to 6.15 we present the histograms of the frequency distributions for G = 1 and G = 0.3. Figure 6.10 (T = 200), for example, shows that the histogram of the frequency distribution for G = 1 is wildly dispersed; the average and the standard deviation across simulations are respectively 0.49 and 0.33. This shows that the system does not converge to a definite equilibrium, at least within the time period of 200 epochs that we consider. We repeated the exercise with G = 0.3, and obtained a distribution which is less dispersed than before (Figure 6.11). When T = 1000 (Figures 6.12 and 6.13) and T = 2000 (Figures 6.14 and 6.15) these features are even clearer.

This shows the permanent and important effects of the presence of dumb agents on the evolution of the price. When their proportion is high enough, dumb agents drive the long-run evolution of the market price, since the smart agents learn that a large number of traders keep believing that the market price will go up or down, regardless of their own experience. The final outcome depends therefore on the proportion of dumb agents forecasting 0 or 1, and on the history of meetings among traders. If for example smart agents repeatedly meet people that forecast 1, while those forecasting 0 repeatedly meet themselves, the smart will move their beliefs towards 1, creating a tendency for the market price to rise. These results are similar to those obtained in another context by Haltiwanger and Waldman (1985), who showed that in situations characterized by

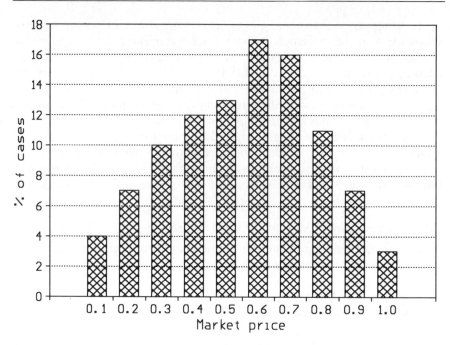

Figure 6.10 *Asymptotic distribution of market price (50% dumb agents, 200 periods).*

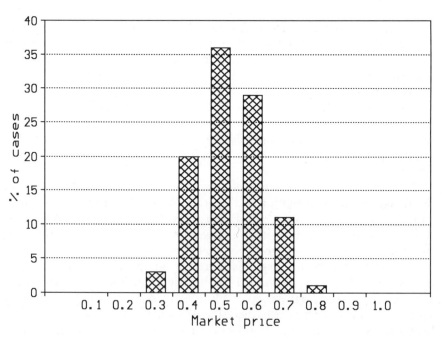

Figure 6.11 *Asymptotic distribution of market price (10% dumb agents, 200 periods).*

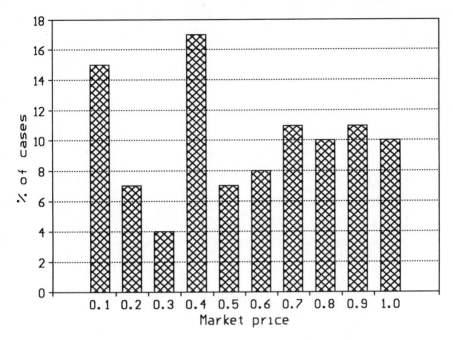

Figure 6.12 *Asymptotic distribution of market price (50% dumb agents, 1000 periods).*

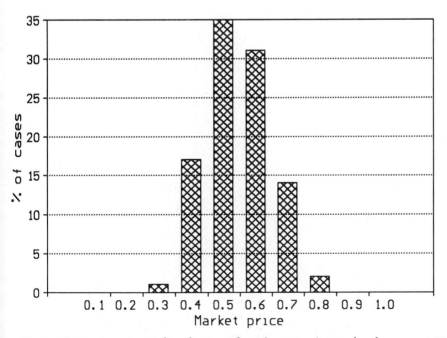

Figure 6.13 *Asymptotic distribution of market price (10% dumb agents, 1000 periods).*

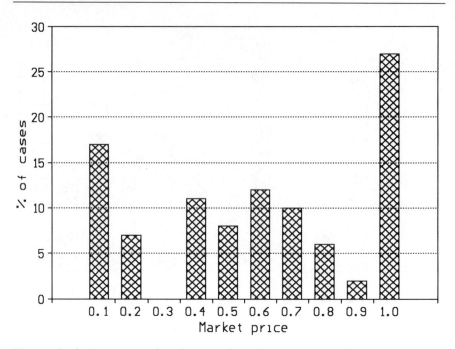

Figure 6.14 *Asymptotic distribution of market price (50% dumb agents, 2000 periods).*

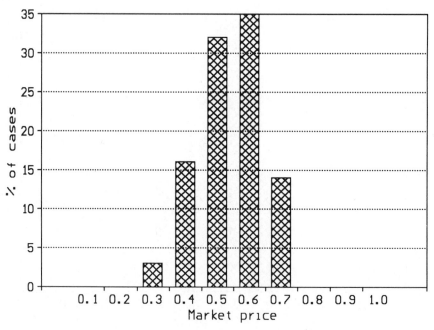

Figure 6.15 *Asymptotic distribution of market price (10% dumb agents, 2000 periods).*

synergistic effects, dumb (which they called naive) agents have a dispro-
portionately large effect on equilibrium, due to the rational anticipations
of smart agents. In our model we obtain the same result, though for a
different reason: it is not synergistic effects that push the smart to forecast the value forecasted by the dumb agents, but their ability and
willingness to learn, as opposed to the dumb agents' inability to learn.

Asymptotic distribution of market price
(50% dumb agents, 200 periods and 10%, 200 periods)
See Figures 6.10 and 6.11.

Asymptotic distribution of market price
(50% dumb agents, 1,000 periods and 10%, 1,000 periods)
See Figure 6.12 and 6.13.

Asymptotic distribution of market price
(50% dumb agents, 2,000 periods and 10%, 2,000 periods)
See Figures 6.14 and 6.15.

(c) Performance of the best and worst agents
What do these features convey in terms of forecasts, forecast errors and
the wealth of the agents? We consider the history of these variables for
the best and the worst performers (in terms of the market value of wealth
at the final date) in a given simulation. Figure 6.16 shows the forecast
error of the best agent; the forecasting performance is good, especially
when compared to that of the worst, who always forecasts 0 and makes a
permanent mistake.

These varying forecasting abilities have consequences in terms of wealth
accumulation. The smart get richer and some of the dumb agents get
poorer (Figures 6.17 and 6.18). Dumb agents on the 'wrong side of the
forecast' lose their wealth, while smart agents accumulate the wealth lost
by the dumb agents.

Being a dumb agent, however, is not necessarily bad for wealth, as long
as one is following the direction taken by the majority of the dumb agents.
When the price starts rising towards 1, the dumb agents who are forecasting 1 increase their wealth at the expense of those who, because of
their forecasting 0, keep selling in the expectation of a decrease in price.
However, it is likely that at the end of the story the wealthiest agent is a
smart one, who can profit not only from the general trend of the price,
but also from the various shorter cycles which take place. For example, a
dumb agent who always forecasts 1 will keep choosing stocks even when
the downward movement in the price would make cash a more attractive
asset, whereas a smart trader would move to the right asset at the right
time, thereby increasing wealth at a faster rate.

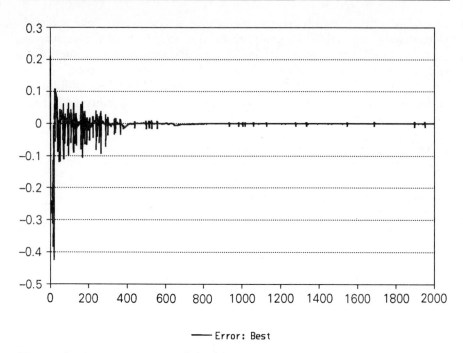

Figure 6.16 *Forecast error of the best agent.*

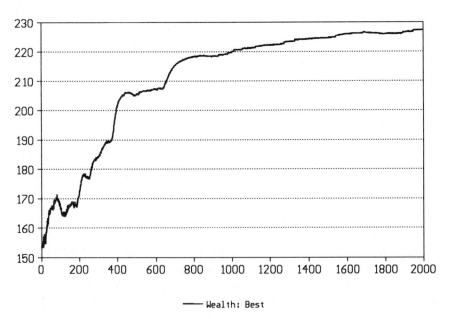

Figure 6.17 *Wealth of the best agent.*

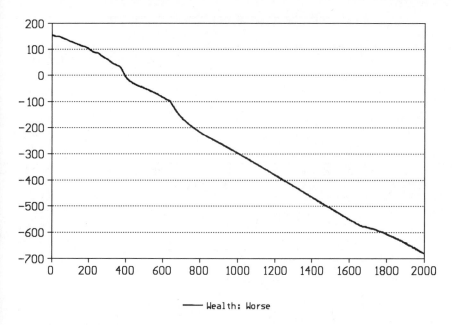

Figure 6.18 *Wealth of the worst agent.*

(d) Agents' complexity and market complexity

We now examine the importance of the computational abilities of agents. We analyse the relationship between the complexity of the structure of the individual agent and the complexity of market dynamics. We do this by varying the number of hidden neurons in each network, since the computational ability and complexity of each agent depends on the number of hidden neurons. Figures 6.19 to 6.22 show that a more sophisticated data processing methodology leads to a more complicated market price dynamic. The standard deviation of the opinions of the agents also rises as a result. It is interesting to note that the forecast errors of the best agent increases in size with increased complexity. Sophistication of the agents may therefore be an inefficient equilibrium, in the sense that everybody has to spend more time processing the information, but is less able to forecast the future as a result of the sophistication of the other agents.

(e) Implications of the model

We have shown that a market populated by agents acting according to some simple rules, and forecasting according to specific models, can generate rich dynamics. The final outcome of the market depends on the characteristics of the agents and on the history of the market, thus displaying a type of path-dependency that has also been discussed by Arthur (1989). Agents earn or lose money according to their forecasting ability. The system is stochastic as long as the evaluations of agents are heterogeneous,

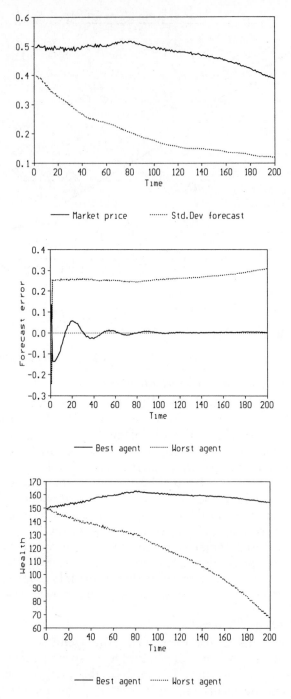

Figure 6.19 *The one hidden neuron case.*

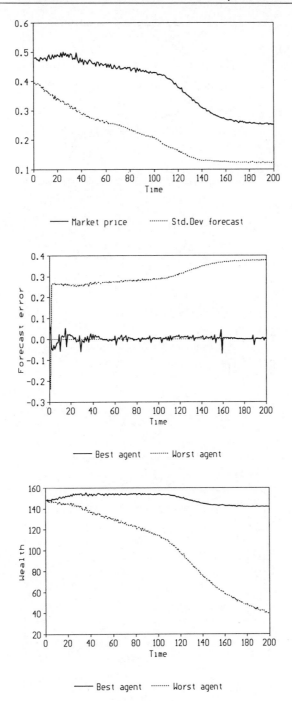

Figure 6.20 *The two hidden neurons case.*

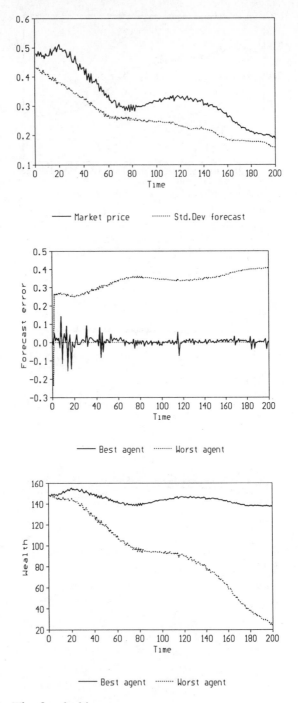

Figure 6.21 *The five hidden neurons case.*

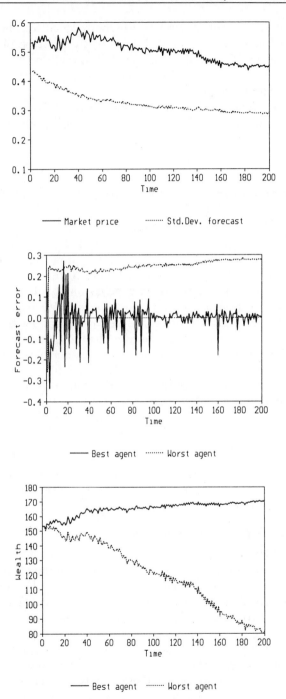

Figure 6.22 *The ten hidden neurons case.*

but becomes deterministic as soon as everybody agrees on the price of the asset. The level at which the market converges cannot be predetermined, but depends on the history of the trades. It is noticeable how much variation in prices and how much disagreement among the traders can occur even in such a simple model.

In the next section we introduce a second model, which considers agents who not only forecast the future price but also decide the quantity to be traded.

6.3 A financial market model with behavioural ANNs

The model considered in the previous section only used neural networks as efficient forecasting devices. This is not the only possible use of neural networks in economic and financial modelling, however. There are other more interesting possibilities, such as assigning to the instrument the role of a mechanism that may learn its own behavioural rules, on the basis of targets that need to be reached and on the basis of the learning that takes place from repeated interactions with other agents and with the environment. The second model considered in this chapter in fact shows a different use of neural networks, in the context of a model otherwise nearly the same as the one described in section 6.2. The only difference is that traders may now decide both the price that they are willing to pay or receive and the quantity that they want to trade.

6.3.1 Characteristics of the model

The seemingly minor modification consisting of adding a decision about the quantity on the part of the single agent has major consequences on the structure of the model.

(a) Coexistence of forecasting and decision

Agents forecast the change in price and also decide whether they want to buy or sell and the quantity to trade. This has important consequences in terms of the actual trade that occurs between agents: in the previous model, traders did not decide whether they wanted to be buyers or sellers, whereas now this decision is taken before meeting any other agent.

(b) Frequency of trading

In the previous model a trade always occurred between two agents, but now this is no longer true, since there can be a meeting between two agents who are on the same side of the market or who disagree about prices.

(c) Volume

While in the previous model the volume of shares traded each day in the market was a constant, in the present one it varies according to the decision of each agent and to the frequency of trading. Volume becomes an indicator of the market activity and is taken into account by the agents as public information.

(d) Learning

Learning is about both prices and quantities. While the former is simple enough and may follow the lines that were set up in the previous model, the latter is difficult in a supervised learning context: the way targets are defined is relevant for the learning process, and affects the behaviour of agents in a number of ways.

(e) Complexity

As a result of the previous elements, complexity increases dramatically both at the market and at the individual agent level. In general it becomes more difficult to understand and explain the behaviour emerging from agents who act and learn in this market.

(f) Budget constraint

In this model we also explicitly consider the existence of a budget constraint and at the same time we do not allow the agents to sell short or to borrow. This modification with respect to the previous model is not necessarily implied by the modification to the structure of the agents; however, we think it is interesting to study this aspect of the economic problem of portfolio choice.

(g) Economic interpretation

Agents do not behave in order to maximize a well-specified time-invariant utility function, as is typically assumed in the finance literature. Our agents learn to decide the valuation of the share, the quantity and the direction (purchase or sale) desired in a transaction with the purpose of increasing their wealth over time. They do that by learning which mapping between their information set and their actions allows them to improve their wealth over time. This is not done according to some demand function coming from utility maximization, but by learning to optimize with respect to the relationship between incoming signals and wealth. Neural networks now have three outputs, instead of just one. The first output determines a price, the second the quantity that the agent is willing to transact, and the third the sign of the transaction, indicating a sale or a purchase. If the third output is positive there is a buy signal, and the price is to be interpreted as the maximum amount of cash which the agent is willing to pay for a share. If the third output is negative there is a sell signal, and the price is to be interpreted as the minimum value which the agent is willing to receive.

This modification might be interpreted by an economist as an attempt to introduce some kind of risk aversion among the decision-makers, since, from the point of view of expected utility models, risk aversion is the reason why agents would refrain from moving all the shares in their portfolio from one asset to another when expected returns vary from one period to another. One can of course ignore this explanation if one does not want to use the framework of expected utility maximization, and interpret the decision rules that are learnt from the agents as those wealth-maximizing behavioural rules that might plausibly be learnt by humans. In this sense our model has some behavioural features of the bounded rationality hypothesis of Simon (1979), Nelson and Winter (1982) and others.

6.3.2 The behaviour of the agents

Behaviour is similar to what was assumed before, except that now at the beginning of day t all the agents determine whether they want to be buyers or sellers, of what quantity, and the maximum (minimum) price at which they are willing to buy (sell). Such a decision is made on the basis on the information available at the beginning of day t before the market opens. As in the previous model, agents compare the expected rate of return on

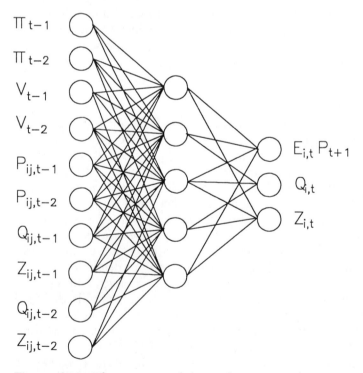

Figure 6.23 *The structure of the traders.*

stocks and money at each moment of time, the former depending on the difference in the price at which one sells and buys, and the latter being equal to 0. While risk-neutral agents would like to convert all their wealth into one of the two assets, risk-averse agents do not behave in such a simple way; it therefore makes sense to let the agents be free to choose the quantity of shares they would like to trade in the market.

In order to form an expectation about the rate of return on stocks, trader i forms an expectation about the price at which the share may be sold in period t+1. Such expectations are formed on the basis of an information set containing the previous history of market prices and volumes, and the price and the quantity of the trade made in the two previous periods (Figure 6.23).

The first output of the network is the expected price. A risk-neutral agent would buy at any price lower than the expected future price; with risk aversion this is no longer true, and in general the agent decides to allocate his or her wealth between both assets. This is exactly the decision made by the network in the hope of maximizing the agent's wealth, as we will discuss more thoroughly in the next sections.

6.3.3 A neural network representation of an agent

The network has three outputs, a price, a quantity and a sign. We can therefore write:

$$I_{i,t} = (\pi_{t-1}, \pi_{t-2}, V_{t-1}, V_{t-2}, p_{ij,t-1}, p_{ij,t-2}, Q_{ij,t-1}, Z_{ij,t-1}, Q_{ij,t-2}, Z_{ij,t-2})$$

$$E_{i,t}P_{t+1} = g^1_{it}(I_{i,t})$$

$$Q_{i,t} = g^2_{it}(I_{i,t})$$

$$Z_{it} = g^3_{it}((I_{i,t})$$

where t is the time index, and variables are defined as follows.

$I_{i,t}$ is the information set.
π_t is the market price.
V_t is the market volume.
$p_{ij,t}$ is the price in the transaction between agents i and j.
$Q_{ij,t}$ is the absolute value of quantity in the transaction between agents i and j.
$Z_{ij,t}$ is the sign of the transaction between agents i and j (+1 = i buys, −1 = i sells).
$E_{i,t}P_{t+1}$ is the expectation about price of agent i.
$Q_{i,t}$ is the quantity in absolute value that agent i wants to trade.
Z_{it} is the sign of the operation (+1 = i buys, −1 = i sells).

For example, $Z_{it} = 1$, $Q_{i,t} = 3$ and $E_{i,t}P_{t+1} = 100$ means that agent i wants to buy 3 shares at a price equal to or lower than 100. $Z_{it} = -1$, $Q_{i,t} = 3$, $E_{i,t}P_{t+1} = 100$ means that agent i wants to sell 3 shares at a price equal to or greater than 100. The three functional forms (g^1, g^2, g^3) are the same for each network, but the weights vary from one network to another. Note that the network only considers information, part of which is public, that is known in the early morning of day t.

Agents face a budget constraint; they can go into the market only after making sure that their desired position (selling or buying up to a certain price) is not incompatible with available wealth. We impose the constraints that in order to buy shares the agent needs to have money (a cash-in-advance constraint), and that in order to sell shares the agent needs to have the shares in his or her portfolio (no short-selling constraint). To take into account the budget constraint we do the following.

If an agent wants to buy ($Z_{it} = +1$) we check whether:

$$Q_{i,t} \leq (M_{i,t} / E_{i,t}P_{t+1})$$

because otherwise the agent would go to the market planning to spend more than his or her money would allow. The actual quantity which we impute to the agent is:

$$Q^*_{i,t} = \min\{Q_{i,t}, (M_{i,t} / E_{i,t}P_{t+1})\}$$

which means that if the agent is planning to buy too much, we force him or her to request to buy the maximum amount which is allowed by his or her money.

If an agent wants to sell ($Z_{it} = -1$) things are easier, since we only have to check that the agent does not want to sell more shares than he or she owns:

$$Q^*_{i,t} = \min\{Q_{i,t}, S_{i,t}\}$$

6.3.4 The marketplace

After forming their reservation prices agents meet randomly in a decentralized marketplace with no auctioneer. From the sample of N agents we randomly select two agents and match them. Given the assumptions we have made about the demand schedule, a transaction may or may not occur in this model. There is no transaction, for example, if the two agents are both sellers or both buyers; in this case we just put them back in the sample of potential traders and extract another two. If a trading possibility exists we organize a transaction which is dominated by the short side of the market. The best way to describe the transaction technology of the model is by example. If two traders with the following outputs meet in the marketplace:

Agent i $E_{i,t}P_{t+1} = 97$ $Q^*_{i,t} = 10$ $Z_{it} = +1$
Agent j $E_{j,t}P_{t+1} = 92$ $Q^*_{j,t} = 5$ $Z_{jt} = -1$

then the actual transaction is $Q_{ij,t} = 5$ at a price:

$$p_{ij,t} = \frac{Q^*_{i,t} E_{i,t}P_{t+1} + Q^*_{j,t} E_{j,t}P_{t+1}}{Q^*_{i,t} + Q^*_{j,t}}$$

equal to a weighted average of the expected prices of the two agents. Note that the weights are such as to push the price in the direction of excess demand. In our example the price is 95.33, larger than the simple average 94.5, to take into account the fact that for these two particular traders i and j the demand of i is larger than the supply of j. Once the transaction is completed we exclude agents i and j from the sample.

A given maximum number of attempted matchings is allowed; we define N_t, the number of successful matchings, or transactions that have been performed. As a result of these N_t transactions we have N_t prices, whose simple average is taken as the market price at time t, π_t. Note that the market price is now a weighted average of the expected prices of the individual traders since each individual trade is regulated at a price that is a weighted average of the expected prices of the two traders. We can also compute the market volume by summing the quantities that are actually traded in the various exchanges:

$$ V_t = 0.5 \sum_{i=1}^{N_t} \sum_{j=1}^{N_t} Q_{ij,t} $$

Note that the market price π_t is not directly relevant to any transaction which took place during day t; the market price is used, however, both to evaluate the stock of shares owned by the agent when markets are closed and to convey information about the average opinion of the traders.

6.3.5 Learning in artificial agents

At the end of the day agents know the market price π_t, and can therefore calculate the value of their wealth and update their view of the world. If agent i transacted with agent j during day t, agent i's wealth at the end of the day is:

$$ W_{i,t+1} = (M_{i,t} - Z_{it}\, Q_{ij,t}\, p_{ij,t}) + \pi_t(S_{i,t} + Z_{it}\, Q_{ij,t}) $$

Agents can also update their 'view of the world' (the weights of the network). The updating of the price, quantity and sign gives rise to two sets of problems, and will be discussed separately.

(a) Learning of prices
The learning of prices is similar to that in the previous model: the forecast of the price made at the beginning of day t by traders cannot be compared to anything known at the end of period t, since the forecast is about variables which will be known during period t+1. What the network can do at the end of day t is to compare the forecast made at time t−1 with the new information available on day t. We compare the forecast of the agent at time t−1 with the actual transaction price.

(b) Learning of quantity

In order to understand how the agent learns we need to know what the agent would like to have done at t–1 if he or she had known the actual price at t. From the point of view of agent i we can say that if $p_{ij,t} > p_{il,t-1}$ then i would have liked to buy more shares at t–1 (the notation involving j and l underscores that the transaction at t was performed with trader j and not necessarily with the same trader l who was met at time t–1). On the contrary, if $p_{ij,t} < p_{il,t-1}$ then agent i would have liked to sell more shares at t–1, and regrets not keeping all his/her wealth in the form of money.

This leads us to examine three alternative possibilities in computing the target.

- We first set the target equal to the quantity the agent could have bought had all his or her money been spent on shares, that is, $M_{i,t-1} / p_{ij,t-1}$. As a consequence the error is measured by comparing the quantity output at t–1, $Q_{i,t-1}$ with $M_{i,t-1} / p_{ij,t-1}$. If one wanted to interpret the decision rules that are learnt by the agent in this market as demand functions coming out of utility maximization then one might say that our training procedure amounts to teaching agents to become risk neutral. In the case of a decrease in price the agent compares $Q_{i,t-1}$ with $S_{i,t-1}$, the maximum quantity he or she could have sold at t, given the no-short-sale constraint.

- We then decrease the importance of the comparison between the act-ual quantity and the risk-neutrality benchmark defined in the previous experiment, by comparing the output of the network with the simple average between the quantity transacted in the last period and $M_{i,t-1} / p_{ij,t-1}$. Now the agent does not go to corner solutions where all wealth is allocated to either money or shares, but maintains some proportion of his or her wealth in money and some in shares.

- Finally we use a third method, which we call qualitative learning, that modifies only the sign of the transaction and not the amount. In this case the trader learns to increase wealth over time, without allocating all of it to either money or shares. Wealth maximization is pursued with a more balanced portfolio.

6.3.6 Results

The values of parameters are the same as in the previous model. For easier reference we report them here. The population is made up of 100 networks with five hidden neurons. The initial range of the weights is from –5 to +5 unless otherwise specified. The learning rate is 0.6 and the momentum is 0.9. Share prices are normalized between 0 and 1. We consider two different proportions of dumb agents: 10% of the population (G = 0.3) and 50% of the population (G = 1).

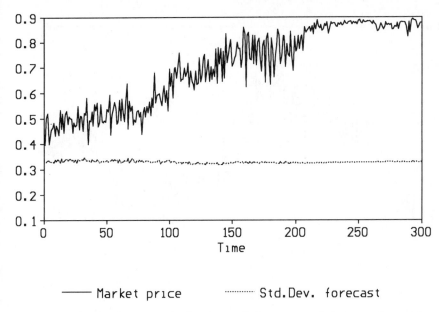

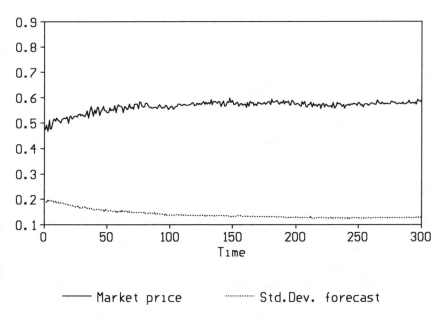

Figure 6.24 *Market price evolution and dispersion of forecasts (50% dumb agents).*

Figure 6.25 *Market price evolution and dispersion of forecasts (10% dumb agents).*

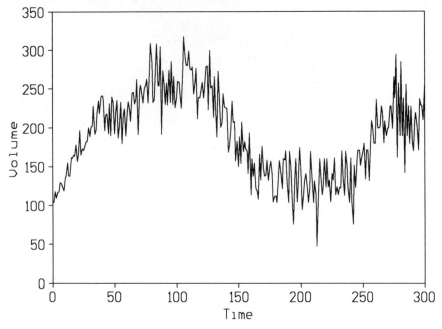

Figure 6.26 *Volume of transactions.*

We discuss the results in different areas:

(a) Heterogeneity of learning abilities
(b) Performance of the best and worst agents
(c) Agent complexity and market complexity
(d) Learning rules
(e) Implications of the model

(a) Heterogeneity of learning abilities

To analyse the importance of heterogeneity in learning abilities, which was such a significant factor in determining prices in the previous model, we compare two simulations, one where the proportion of dumb agents is 50% (Figure 6.24) and one where the proportion is 10% (Figure 6.25). As before, the volatility of price and dispersion of the forecasts are directly proportional to the number of dumb agents in the population. The resulting volume of trade (Figure 6.26) varies over the periods, without an upward or downward trend. It is interesting to observe that such variations in volume are of a completely endogenous nature, and result from the simple rules that we assign to the agents.

(b) Performance of the best and worst agents

We again consider the issue of forecast errors and wealth of the agents in

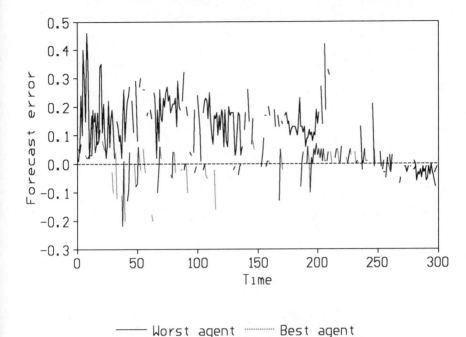

—— Worst agent ········· Best agent

Figure 6.27 *Forecast error of best and worst agents.*

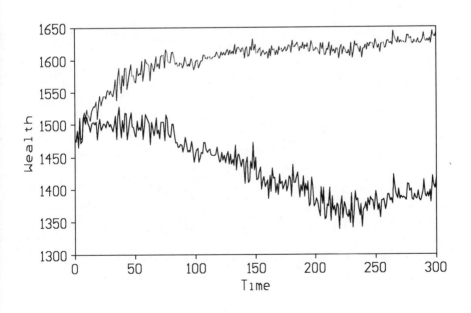

—— Worst agent ········· Best agent

Figure 6.28 *Wealth of best and worst agents.*

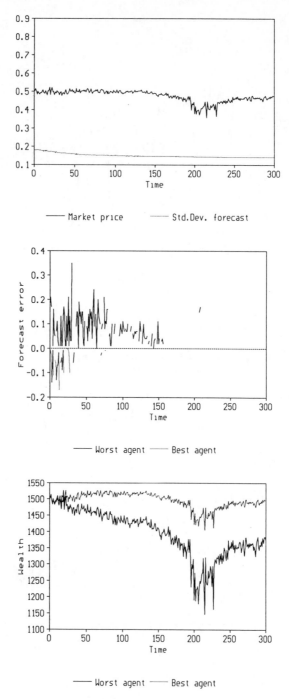

Figure 6.29 *The two hidden neurons case.*

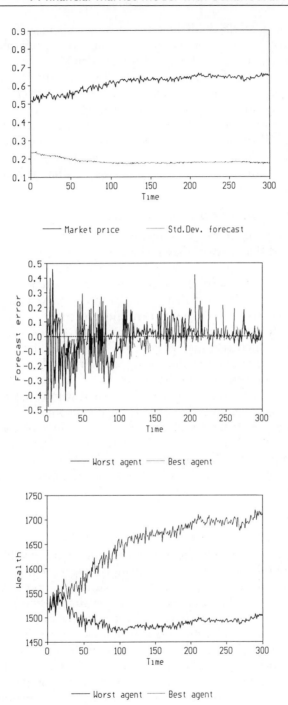

Figure 6.30 *The ten hidden neurons case.*

the context of a model with just a few dumb agents. We consider the history of these variables for the best and the worst performers (in terms of the market value of wealth on the final date) in a given simulation. Figure 6.27 shows the forecast error of the best and the worst agents. The figure does not report observations on the forecast errors for each time period, but only for those days in which the agents were actually trading. The different forecasting abilities are apparent from the figure, with the best agent decreasing errors over time at a much higher rate.

These different forecasting abilities have consequences in terms of wealth accumulation (Figure 6.28), since the best gets richer and the worst gets poorer.

(c) Agent complexity and market complexity

In Figures 6.29 and 6.30 we compare prices, forecast errors and wealth dynamics for different hypotheses about the complexity of the traders' structure. In the first figure each agent processes information by means of two hidden nodes, while in the second there are ten hidden nodes. In the previous model we observed that increases in complexity of the structure added to the complexity of the market and prevented an actual improvement in the forecasts, as increased forecasting ability was more than compensated by increased market volatility. In this model we observe that difficulties in learning and in improving forecasts result not only from the complexity of the market but from the fact that learning happens less frequently: if an agent does not trade in a given period, no target is available for learning in the following one. These two factors must be considered in interpreting the dynamics of the relevant variables of the model. For wealth, we observe that differences between the best and the worst agent were more important when agents are simple. Agent complexity induces more complex dynamics and leads to a worse-performing best agent and to a better-performing worst agent.

(d) Learning rules

For a given set of parameters of the learning abilities and the structure of agents, we analyse the consequences of the different possible hypotheses about learning rules in terms of the quantity targets that they imply. The case where the target corresponds to risk neutrality is presented in Figure 6.31. In Figure 6.32 the target is equal to the simple average between the quantity that was described above and the one transacted in the previous period. Finally, Figure 6.33 presents a qualitative learning technique, where learning does not occur for the value but only for the sign of the quantity. The conclusions we can deduce from these results are that either the agent's individual behaviour or the global outcome of the system, especially in terms of volume, is very sensitive to the actual learning procedure. With the first method agents learn to become risk-neutral, and to sell all their shares or spend all their money in every transaction. Consequently volume is and remains high. Qualitative learning does not influence risk

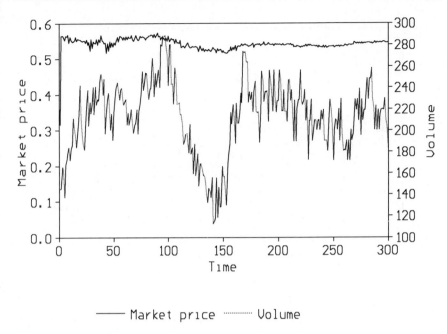

Figure 6.31 *Dynamics resulting from risk-neutral learning.*

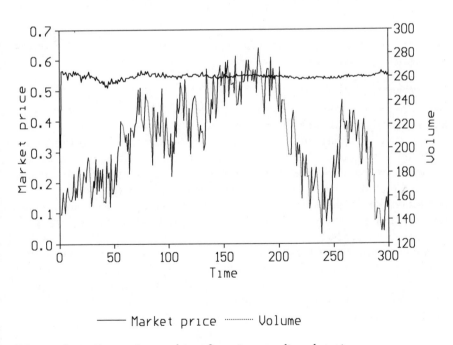

Figure 6.32 *Dynamics resulting from intermediate learning.*

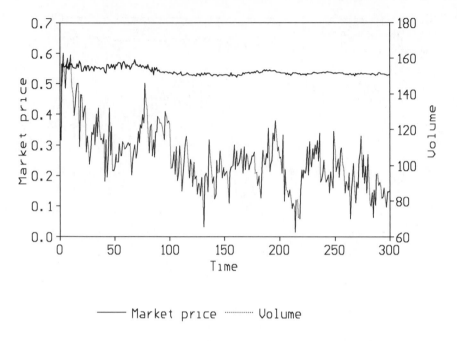

Figure 6.33 *Dynamics resulting from qualitative learning.*

aversion, and therefore allows more gradual behaviour in terms of quantity, which generates a lower volume.

(e) Implications of the model

In this second model we have considered ANNs as a tool that autonomously builds behavioural rules, on the basis of learning methodologies that take place within the framework of repeated interactions with the other agents and with the environment. These rules are used by the agents to optimize the quantity to trade over time. Although we did not attempt to interpret the rules which are embedded in the weights of the networks, this model gives an insight into more complex situations, where sets of rules evolve dynamically under the pressure of interactions with other similar agents.

A multi-population model of this application, in which technical and fundamental traders coexist, is presented in Margarita and Beltratti (1993).

The next chapter will examine not only interactions between similar agents but also those between heterogeneous agents in the framework of multi-population models.

7
Multi-population models

Outline of the chapter

In this chapter we present multi-population models by considering the main differences between the one-population models described in Chapter 6 and multi-population models and by stressing what are the dimensions of heterogeneity that induce us to classify certain models as multi-population rather than one-population.

The first of the models considered in the chapter has a theoretical structure similar to the one discussed in Chapter 6, except that agents belong to two populations differing in their computational abilities, information sets and procedures to interpret such sets. In the long run, the market endogenously determines the most effective type of agent.

The second model considers in more detail the institutional aspects of the market, and describes a situation where a dealer interacts with many traders. The heterogeneity is now of an institutional nature: the dealer has the task of buying and selling shares according to the desires of the traders at the prices he or she quotes. In this case the goal is again common, and consists of wealth maximization, but all the decision rules and instruments are fundamentally different between traders and the dealer.

In the third model we depart from the standard stock market simulations that were the basic framework of the other examples, in order to give some indications about the generality of the applications of multi-population models. We consider the interrelationships between a banking system and a productive system, which are related by the needs of the first to make a profit by lending credit to the second and the needs of the second to obtain financial support from the first in order to develop their activities. Firms are heterogeneous with respect to their productivity, so that banks have the task of assessing the creditworthiness of the various firms asking for financial assistance.

7.1 Multi-population models

7.1.1 Basic definition

Multi-population models represent situations where interacting agents may be structurally different, in the sense of having different goals and following different strategies for pursuing their goals. They can be defined as systems where agents, which are so heterogeneous as to be considered as different populations, interact in an environment which is influenced by the actions of the agents. Within each population, agents maintain the same characteristics of homogeneity found in one-population models. Heterogeneity is to be considered from one population to the others in the sense that agents belonging to different populations try to achieve possibly different goals by using decision rules implemented with different instruments and are endowed with different learning abilities.

We underline some important aspects of this definition.

1. Endogeneity of the environment: As in one-population models, the environment is highly influenced by both the behaviour and the interactions of the agents. From this specific point of view, there are no qualitative improvements in going from one-population to multi-population models, as the important change has already been made in moving from one-agent to one-population models.

2. Interactions of agents: Two levels of interactions may exist. In some applications, such as the one described in section 7.2, each agent may interact with every other, without considering the population he or she belongs to. In other applications, such as the ones described in sections 7.3 and 7.4, interaction is restricted to pairs of agents belonging to different populations.

3. Instruments: As defined in section 6.1, instruments include both the structure and the set of weights of the network. Weights vary from one agent to another due to the effects of initial assignment and learning. The structure remains the same within a single population, but varies from one population to another. Agents belonging to different populations may differ in one or more of the following aspects: information set, instruments, goals, decision rules and learning abilities.

    While one-population models are essentially defined by the use of the same decision rules on the part of all the agents, in multi-population models the decision rules and/or the goals may differ. It is apparent from the definition that the two classes of models may strongly overlap, since in both cases the system is composed of agents who differ with respect to one or more characteristics. The lines that divide the various agents or sub-populations may change from one problem to another, depending on the needs and goals of the researchers.

4. Learning: The transition from one-agent to one-population and to multi-population models corresponds to an increase in the complexity and richness of learning techniques. Whereas in one-agent models the only possibility is learning from the environment, in ways that can be more or less sophisticated, in one-population and multi-population models forms of collective learning may be considered (Margarita, 1992b). Some of these possibilities are presented in the applications described in this chapter: in the model of section 7.2 learning by imitation coexists with standard supervised learning; in

section 7.3 we present an application which is based on a mixed form of supervised and unsupervised learning.

5.   Competition versus cooperation: Population-based models can be classified into two categories, competitive and cooperative models, depending on the nature of the relations between agents. In the former, agents play individually one against the others for sharing resources. In the latter, agents may receive some benefits from acting collectively instead of individually towards the same (or a similar) goal. Clusters of cooperating agents may emerge within the populations as a result of these advantages. Although some aspects of economic systems can be described with cooperative models, here we mainly consider models of competitive agents.

6.   Other characteristics: All the other characteristics described in one-population models, like decision rules and information flow, are preserved in each population of multi-population models. Differences may derive from the extension of the scope of the model: for example, information flows multidirectionally, either between populations and the environment or among populations.

7.1.2 Financial markets as a two-population model

We believe that these models are important for studying social phenomena, even though some of the objects of analysis cannot be defined in general terms and vary from one situation to the other. Financial markets, the main object of interest of this book, are a good candidate because of some of their characteristics:

- a large number of agents;
- many repeated and often anonymous interactions;
- the use of particular strategies before taking actions;
- a clear way of evaluating the effectiveness of the strategies;
- the possibility of many different types of interactions, like imitation, pure competition or collusion.

A specific example of how a financial market may be analysed in the context of multi-population models may be useful to clarify the general meaning of such models. Suppose that traders in a stylized financial market can be subdivided into two populations, which differ in their trading strategies. A trading strategy may be informally defined as a set of variables and some methodologies to elaborate such variables that allow the information set of the trader to be mapped to his or her actions. Let us suppose that traders can be classified into fundamental and technical traders.

Fundamental traders look at variables such as interest rates, dividends and the balance sheets of the companies, and elaborate this information in such a way as to obtain a value for the available financial assets. This value is as close as possible to an 'objective' valuation, regardless of the most recent opinion of the market. Technical traders look mostly at the recent path of market prices, and use statistical techniques to extrapolate it into the future; for example, they compute various moving averages of past prices and try to obtain 'buy' or 'sell' signals. Technical traders do not really care about the 'objective valuation' of the asset, being mainly interested in the most forecastable short-run path of the price. In terms of the definition that was given earlier, fundamental traders and technical traders use different decision rules implemented with instruments (for example, the evaluation process) that may or may not be different to reach a common goal, for example wealth maximization.

Clearly, the strategies of the two populations will give rise to different actions even in the case where both populations are trying to achieve the same goal of wealth maximization. A prolonged period of rising market prices that is not justified by fundamentals will discourage the fundamental traders from continuing to buy, and may well induce them to sell part of their portfolio. On the other hand, technical traders may extrapolate the past increase and keep buying in the expectation of a future increase in the prices.

If the goal of the researcher is to understand the evolution of the market price, it is necessary to understand the market as a struggle between the two populations, since in general the change in the prices will depend on the proportions of the two populations. If, after a prolonged rise, fundamentals want to sell and technicals want to buy, the movement of the price will depend on the relative size of the two populations. Also, the possibility that the decision rules mapping information into actions are time-dependent is an element against the possibility of using constant-coefficient difference or differential equations to describe the dynamics in the proportions of the populations.

In order to predict the future it becomes necessary to know the proportions of the two populations and their respective trading strategies. It would be difficult to understand the situation without considering such interaction. The predictive task would be even more difficult as far as long-run results are concerned, since the proportion of the two populations is neither constant nor exogenous, but evolves endogenously. If trading strategies spread across traders as a function of their most recent performance, the stochastic process of the price will be history-dependent.

The division between technicals and fundamentals may be not so central when the goal is not to understand the dynamics of the market price, but for example to forecast which trading strategy (which instrument) dominates in the population of technicals. It may well be that the final outcome of the struggle among strategies is largely independent of the interaction with the other population. In this case a one-population model that analyses the evolution of the trading strategies of the technicals may be entirely appropriate for the purpose at hand.

7.1.3 Multi-population models and models of exhaustible species

A natural question that may come to mind is: what is the relationship between multi-population models and the multispecies models considered in mathematical bioeconomics? The answer that we suggest here is useful in discussing the differences between the approach we consider in this book and the one based on strictly analytical models.

In considering multispecies models, Clarke (1990) notes that 'A given biological population is merely one component of a complex ecological system that contains predators, prey, competitors, disease organisms, and other living things. Modelling the dynamics of a population by means of a single differential or difference equation implies a neglect of these ecological interrelations ... This neglect may be justifiable in some cases, particularly where only one species of an ecosystem is subject to exploitation. With ever-increasing demand on renewable resources, however, single-species models are becoming increasingly inadequate. Multispecies models, unfortunately, present significant theoretical and practical difficulties.'

There are three important elements in this discussion, namely specification, methodology and results. We now discuss each of them in turn.

(a) Specification

The literature mainly considers the case of interactions of different species of animals, and this allows an important simplification to the equations that are used to describe the dynamics. Animals in fact tend to behave according to mechanical rules that may easily be described in terms of deterministic, constant-coefficient differential equations. For example, Clarke studies Gause's model of combined harvesting of two competing populations, based on the following differential equations for the numbers of individuals belonging to populations x and y:

$$dx/dt = F(x, y) = rx(1 - (x/K)) - axy$$

$$dy/dt = G(x, y) = sy(1 - (y/L)) - bxy$$

where it is assumed that each population has a logistic growth equation, with different productivity rates r and s, but that change also depends on the level of the other population. The model may be written in this relatively simple form because no decision rules are explicitly described. The micro-behaviour of the animals belonging to the two populations is left unspecified. It is however implicit that the decision rules of the agents composing the population are either so simple as to be described by the two differential equations, or so complicated but interrelated in such a way as to produce a simple aggregate dynamics. Given the lack of plausibility of the latter hypothesis, the first explanation seems more likely, and therefore it is assumed that the actions of the populations are of a time-invariant nature that may be described quite easily.

This treatment of the problem appears to be way too simple for many of the issues that are relevant for the interactions of humans competing in social and/or economic battles. Arthur (1988), for example, notes that 'unlike the particles in physics, the particles in economics – the agents – act on the basis of expectations and of strategy. . . . We are immediately in some difficulty. There are several plausible ways to introduce expectations and strategy into economic problems, and choosing an appropriate one becomes a matter of some subtlety.' In fact we will explicitly show in this chapter how simple but reasonable models of human interaction give rise to dynamics that are much more complicated than those described by systems of deterministic, constant-coefficient equations. The approach we pursue with our models is related to ideas put forward in the AL literature, where the effort that is made by the researcher is to understand the complex aggregate dynamics of a system not by means of a complicated mathematical description, but by the attempt to see whether such aggregate dynamics can be replicated by a model based on repeated interactions of individual organisms behaving according to some simple rules.

(b) Methodology

The methodology used to solve these models is the analysis of differential equations. This has one advantage and one disadvantage. The advantage is the possibility of obtaining analytical results that shed light on the qualitative properties of the solutions. The disadvantage is the difficulty of solving systems of differential equations, as clarified by Clarke's remark on the 'theoretical and practical difficulties'. Very often, the researcher has to make very restrictive hypotheses in order to obtain results. Some variables may be ignored simply because it is difficult to obtain solutions for systems composed of more than two state variables. This however means that an imperfect description of the system may lead to misleading results, when the behaviour of the sub-system considered by the researcher depends on the evolution of variables that are left outside.

In contrast, even the simpler models that are considered in this book give rise to dynamics that are too complicated to be solved analytically, so that one has to perform simulations. This complication arises from the learning tasks which are performed by the agents in our models. Without the need to learn from the environment, it would certainly be possible to simplify the description of the systems and to solve some of them with analytical methods.

(c) Results

The results obtained by the systems of differential equations are usually based on the steady state solutions, which show what happens to the system once this reaches a state of quiet. The steady state is therefore the main object of interest. The models of this book instead usually give rise to dynamic paths that are both history-dependent and particularly interesting when looked at from the point of view of the transition towards the steady state. We refer the reader to Chapter 2 for the relationships between such modelling concepts and the models mainly used in economic theory.

7.2 A stock market model with imitation

7.2.1 Description of the model

This section presents a revised and extended version of the model described in Beltratti and Margarita (1992).

In accordance with the model described in the previous chapter, anticipation of a growth in prices induces the agent to demand shares, since this is more convenient than holding money. Agents who on average make few mistakes on the change in prices will tend to buy low and sell high, and to increase their total amount of wealth more than agents who on average make mistakes by buying high and selling low. The difference is that we now consider two populations of agents, differing in their architecture and endowed with different abilities to discover nonlinear relations in the variables in the information set. The first type of agent possesses superior ability to access and process data and pays a cost for this ability, while the second type of agent owns only simple instruments that can be used free of charge. Periodically, agents can imitate those agents who follow more effective strategies and as a consequence of this learning may swap from one strategy to another, choosing whether it is worth paying the cost for a sophisticated processing capability. In order to make this model comparable with the one previously described, we also maintain the different learning abilities resulting from initial endowments.

We consider an artificial stock market populated by two types of ANN-based agents, which we call smart (S-agents) and naive (N-agents), differing in their information sets and procedures to interpret such sets. We interpret the various procedures as different trading strategies in the sense that, given a specific information set, the action of the agent depends on such procedures. S-agents use a sophisticated methodology to make predictions of market prices, but to achieve this they have to pay a fixed cost every period. N-agents only look at the most recent market price for their forecasts and pay no cost. Within S-agents, we consider a sub-population of dumb agents (D-agents) with the same structure but with reduced learning capabilities, depending on the initial values of their weights (see section 6.2.5 for a detailed description of this characteristic).

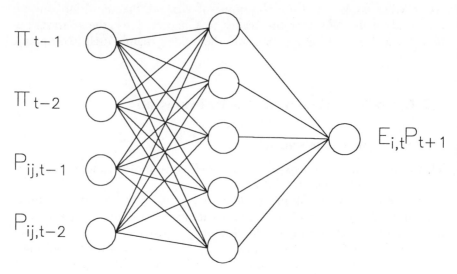

Figure 7.1 *The structure of S- and D-agents.*

7.2.2 The different types of agents

(a) Smart agents

We use the same structure described in section 6.2.4 for modelling S-agents: a neural network with four input, five hidden and one output neurons. For convenience, the structure is shown again in Figure 7.1.

The information set $I_{i,t}$ is a vector composed of the following inputs: π_{t-1}, π_{t-2}, $P_{ij,t-1}$, $P_{ij,t-2}$ while the output is again $E_{i,t}P_{t+1}$. We can write the following functional form for the output of the networks:

$$E_{i,t}P_{t+1} = g^i(I_{i,t}) = f[B_{i,t} \, f(A_{i,t} \, I_{i,t})] \tag{7.1}$$

Learning is based on the mechanism that has been described in section 6.2.5.

(b) Dumb agents

D-agents are structurally equal to S-agents, apart from one peculiarity, described in detail in section 6.2.5: they do not take the information provided from the outside world seriously, and always forecast an extreme value of the price, equal to either 0 or 1. The particular configuration of their weights induces them both to forecast extreme values and not to change their weights very much when comparing realizations and expectations: these are the cases in which BP does not allow agents to enter the morning of day t+1 with a better way of interpreting the information set and of using it to predict the price at time t+2. We are in the presence of networks which do not learn, and maintain a definite opinion about the evolution of the variable, always forecasting either 0 or 1.

(c) Naive agents

Finally, to describe N-agents we use a very simplified structure (Figure 7.2). The information set is restricted to the last value of the market price, π_{t-1}. There is one input node, no hidden layer and one output node, $E_{i,t}P_{t+1}$. A nonlinearity is introduced by means of the logistic function present in the output neuron. This structure should be less efficient than the others to uncover nonlinear regularities in the data.

Figure 7.2 *The structure of N-agents.*

The analytical formulation is simpler than formula 7.1:

$$E_{i,t}P_{t+1} = g^i(I_{i,t}) = f(A_{i,t}\ I_{i,t}) = f(a_{i,t}\ \pi_{t-1}) \tag{7.2}$$

where $a_{i,t}$ is a time-varying parameter.

7.2.3 Learning in artificial agents

(a) Learning by imitation

The marketplace where agents evolve is the same as the one described in section 6.2 as far as market rules and expectations formation are concerned. Learning is also similar for target building and BP technique but differs in two main aspects.

- S-agents learn faster than N-agents because they are endowed with more effective learning parameters (learning rate and momentum of the BP algorithm)
- Additionally, a form of learning by imitation is allowed, periodically inducing the agents to change their strategy by looking at the more profitable strategies followed by the other agents.

(b) Cost and computational abilities

As mentioned, the difference between the first two types and the third type of agents is justified by different information availability and abilities to analyse market data. S-agents (for example, money managers) look at a wide information set, and elaborate the information with a complicated structure. N-agents (for example, households investing in financial markets) do not have the time and ability for this and just look in a very naive way at the most recent market price.

But such different abilities are accounted for by a cost c, which is paid every period by S-agents to maintain their abilities. The combination of information processing complexity, cost and differences in parameters due to different learning paths are the elements which make agents heterogeneous, and induce them to assign different values to the assets they can trade. From now on we refer to a complexity/cost combination as a trading strategy followed by the agent. In the next sections we describe how our agents choose long-run forecasting strategies, in the sense of selecting an appropriate combination of complexity and cost.

(c) The dynamics of the model

From an analytical point of view, for given proportions of S-, D- and N-agents, the dynamics of the model can be described through the following equations:

$$\pi_t = J^{-1} \sum_{j=1}^{J} E_{j,t} P_{t+1}$$

If i is an S- or D-agent

$$E_{i,t} P_{t+1} = g^i(\pi_{t-1}, \pi_{t-2}, P_{ij,t-1}, P_{ij,t-2})$$

If i is an N-agent

$$E_{i,t} P_{t+1} = g^i(\pi_{t-1})$$

$$P_{ij,t} = 0.5 \ (E_{i,t} P_{t+1} + E_{j,t} P_{t+1}) \tag{7.3}$$

Note the importance of the proportions of the three types of agents in determining the dynamics of prices, due to the fact that the formation of expectations is type-specific. The larger the proportion of agents belonging to a type, the larger the impact of this type on the market price. Our model, however is more complicated than what is described by equation 7.3, since proportions themselves are endogenous to the model, as we describe in the next section.

7.2.4 Evolution of trading strategies

The last important feature of our model is that agents choose their type: is it worth paying the cost c to have more information and to process it in a more sophisticated way? To answer this question, strategies have to be endogenous in the long run. In the model in fact, agents are not stuck with a certain strategy, but periodically have an opportunity to switch to a different one, on the basis of imitation of the most profitable strategies. In order to simulate this swap mechanism, we use a modified version of GAs in the following way.

- Every T periods we randomly select in the population some strategies, with a probability directly proportional to the market value of the wealth of the agents
- We reproduce the chosen strategies subject to some random modifications
- We randomly assign the new strategies to the old traders, which begin a new race starting with the same amount of disposable wealth that they had immediately before the reshuffling of strategies.

In this way the strategies which work better (in terms of allowing accumulation of wealth) become more widespread among the agents, while those performing poorly are abandoned. Note that one agent can vary his or her strategy according to the general evolution of the environment. Under some conditions, depending on the strategies adopted by the majority of the other agents, it may be worth paying a cost for computational complexity, while in other circumstances, for example when prices are easy to forecast and most of the other agents adopt the no-cost strategy, it may be more profitable to be naive. The choice of a strategy is not a once-for-all decision, but has to be revised every T periods, as a function of the environment, that is, of the trading strategies adopted by the other agents.

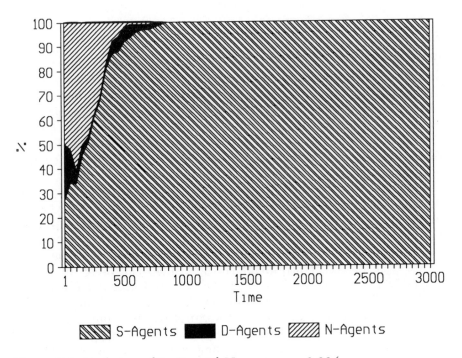

Figure 7.3 *Evolution of S- D- and N-agents, c = 0.004.*

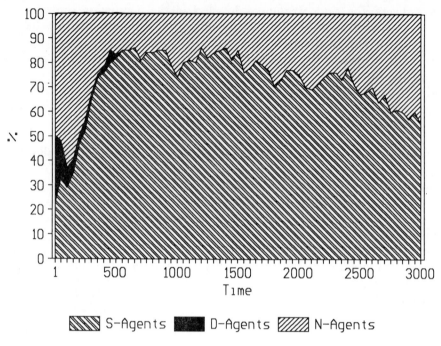

Figure 7.4 *Evolution of S- D- and N-agents, c = 0.01.*

7.2.5 Results

We performed simulations with a population composed of 100 networks, divided at the beginning into 50 N-agents and 50 split between S- and D-agents. Share prices are normalized between 0 and 1. The learning rate and momentum of S- and D-agents are 0.6 and 0.9; for N-agents the values are 0.3 and 0.0, in order to take into account the different learning abilities of the various types. We perform simulations with three values of the cost parameter c (0.004, 0.01, 0.02) in order to modify the comparative advantage of S- with respect to N-agents.

Figures 7.3 to 7.5 show the proportions of the types of agents over 3000 periods, for three values of c. It is shown that in each case D-agents disappear from the market after a few periods of time because of the low learning ability we have previously discussed, so that two types remain to interact in the long run. In the models of Chapter 5, non-learning agents prove to be the worst performers and lose more and more wealth, but remain in the market. In this model, the same conclusions can be drawn, with the difference that nobody imitates these agents and they disappear from the population under the mechanism of selective imitation.

The proportions of S- and N-agents are time-varying and depend crucially on the value of c. In the long run, if c is low (Figure 7.3), S-agents take over the market very quickly, while N-agents disappear. At

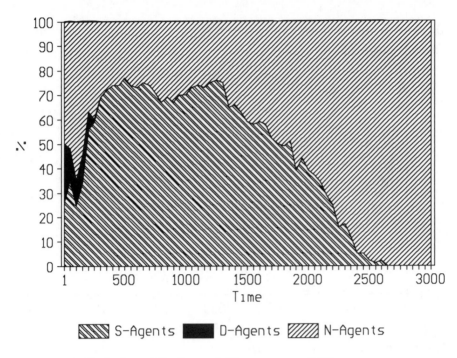

Figure 7.5 *Evolution of S- D- and N-agents, c = 0.02.*

the opposite extreme (Figure 7.5), if the cost is too high, it is more convenient to be of type N. When c = 0.01 no type can drive the other out of the market during the 3000 periods we consider, even if the path shows some trend against S-agents.

In conclusion, the market endogenously determines whether it is more effective to be of type S or type N in the long run. It turns out that the proportion of the two types depends on the history of market prices: in periods of turbulence the more complicated machinery used by S-agents is worth the cost, while in tranquil times N-agents do not have a comparative disadvantage and take over the market. It is noticeable that times become tranquil or turbulent as a result of the proportion of S-agents in the market: S-agents learn the model very quickly and stabilize the market, in this way preparing the ground for the expansion of N-agents. In the long run, however, the type taking over the market depends on the value of the cost of information. These different results can be understood by considering the effects of the strategies of the two types on market prices. At first the market price is very volatile (Figure 7.6 shows a typical plot), so that being a sophisticated analyst is very helpful in improving predictions. The endogenous increase in the proportion of N-agents, however, brings about a stabilizing effect on the price, making the computational comparative advantage less and less relevant. Figure 7.7 shows that the

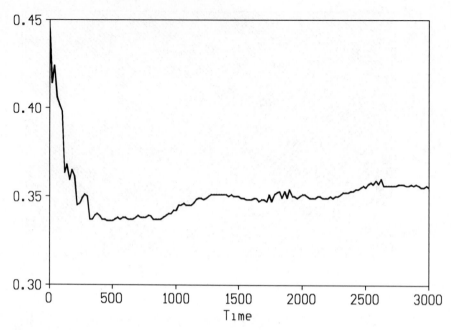

Figure 7.6 *Market price, c = 0.01.*

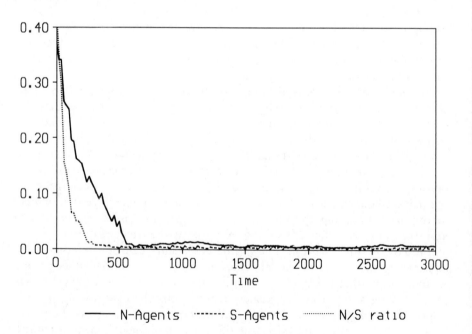

Figure 7.7 *Dispersion of forecasts, c = 0.01.*

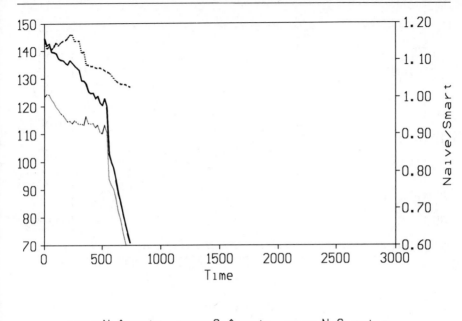

Figure 7.8 *Wealth of S- and N-agents, c = 0.004.*

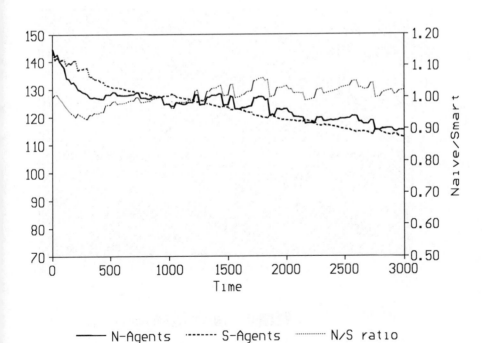

Figure 7.9 *Wealth of S- and N-agents, c = 0.01.*

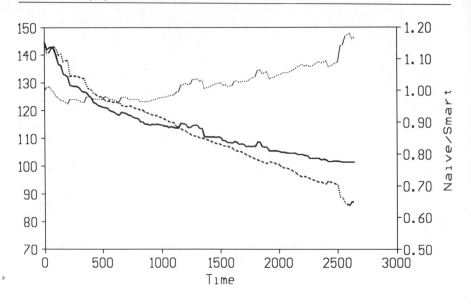

Figure 7.10 *Wealth of S- and N=agents, c = 0.02.*

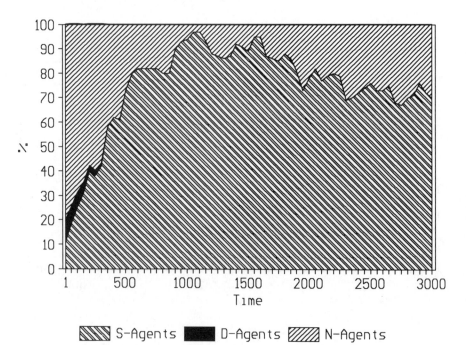

Figure 7.11 *Evolution of S- D- and N-agents, c = 0.01; initial proportions: 20 S- and D-agents, 80 N-agents.*

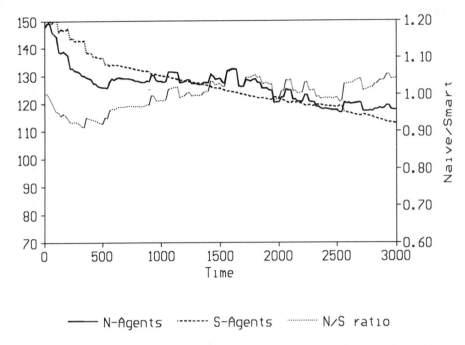

Figure 7.12 *Wealth of S- and N-agents, c = 0.01; initial proportions: 20 S- and D-agents, 80 N-agents.*

standard deviation of the forecasts of the various agents decreases over time, especially in the case of S-agents who come to agree on a conventional valuation. When the price is stable it is not worth paying a high cost for processing information more efficiently, since under these circumstances a naive forecasting rule works as efficiently as a more complicated one. When the price is stable, the combination of the cost c and the equalization of the forecasting rules across agents starts to deteriorate the wealth of S-agents, as shown in Figures 7.8 to 7.10.

   The fact that the long-run price is stable regardless of (but at a value depending on) the history of the process gives us few chances to observe more frequent changes in the type of agent dominating the market. It is likely that in a market hit by continuous exogenous shocks (unlike the model we are considering, where evolution is totally endogenous) the resulting volatility of the market price would make S-agents 'useful' even for a high cost c, since N-agents by themselves would not be able to understand and stabilize the price process. In fact in our last simulation (Figure 7.11) we start up the market with a proportion equal to 20% of S-agents and a relatively high cost of 0.01 (which according to Figure 7.5 would drive S-agents out of the market). The initial variability of price makes S-agents more apt to understand the environment, which increases their

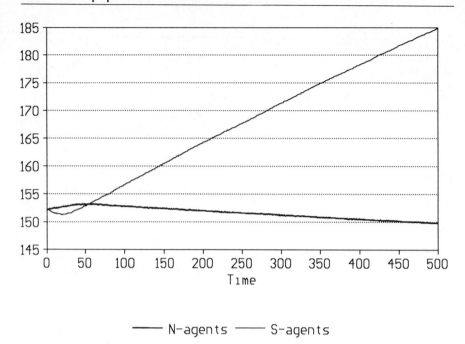

Figure 7.13 *Average wealth of the two populations.*

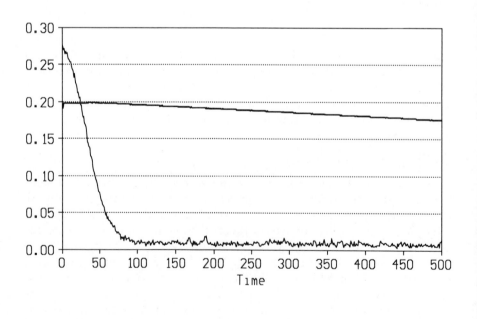

Figure 7.14 *Standard deviations of opinions in the two populations.*

proportion beyond 90% before the cost c drives down their wealth with respect to the wealth of N-agents (Figure 7.12). The rise of S-agents stabilizes the price, and their decadence is due to their own performance.

For confirming the interpretation we gave about populations' dynamics, we examine the evolution of wealth and forecasts of the two populations, under the same hypothesis of the previous example, that is, 20% of S-agents and 80% N-agents.

Figure 7.13 shows the dynamics of the average wealth of the two populations, showing the advantage of being able to forecast in a more accurate way. Figure 7.14 reports the dispersion of the opinions in the two populations, showing that neural networks reach a consensus about the forecast in a much shorter time period than is achieved by simpler forecasters. Again this is a proof of the learning ability of the neural network, and its superiority with respect to simple linear rules. In this case the profits from superior computational ability are large because of the small proportion of smart agents, which never substantially affect the price in a market dominated by inefficient linear forecasters.

7.3 Co-evolution of strategies in an on-screen stock market

7.3.1 Description of the model

We are interested in studying the dynamics of an 'on-screen' stock market, where all the traders can buy and sell shares from a dealer. The dealer is a price-maker and has the institutional purpose of buying and selling shares at the two prices that he or she decides at each point in time: the bid price, which is the price the dealer is willing to offer for buying shares from the traders, and the ask price, that is, the price the dealer is willing to ask for selling shares to the traders. The difference between the ask price and the bid price is the spread, giving the dealer a compensation for the job of operating the market. This is a centralized stock market, since at one moment of time all the traders buy and sell from the same source at the same prices. The prices, however, are not necessarily equilibrium prices, in the sense that at a given pair of prices the total demand may exceed the total supply of traders, the difference being absorbed by the dealer.

The interests of the two types of agents are therefore opposed: the larger the spread, the better off the dealer, and the worse off the traders. There is, however, a limit to how far the spread can go, since when the spread is too high, traders stop trading.

We consider only one dealer in order to simplify the simulation structure of our model, which would become very involved with more than one dealer, since each trader would need to compare the prices offered and asked by all the dealers before trading with the one offering the best conditions. In practice, competition between the dealers forces them to maintain prices in line with each other. To take this element into account we let the number of traders who join the market at any time depend negatively on the spread decided by the dealer. In such a way the latter faces a trade-off between earning more profit for each transaction and earning less unitary profit on a larger number of transactions. Although implemented in a simplified form (one of the populations contains only one individual), this model maintains the characteristics of multi-population models.

The timing of our model is the following: at the beginning of the period the dealer decides the bid and the spread, and then traders are free to buy from the dealer or sell to the dealer at these same prices. Traders have to respect a budget constraint that will be described later on. Both the traders and the dealer have the goal of maximizing wealth. The dealer absorbs every imbalance between supply and demand. The agents are different with respect to the institutional role they play in the market, so that it becomes essential, and this is the main goal of the application, to understand the evolution of the strategies adopted by each type of agent in order to understand the aggregate behaviour.

7.3.2 Biological analogies and ANNs

The structure of the model, heterogeneous agents competing for the appropriation of a resource by adopting various possible strategies, recalls the models and the theories presented in the biological literature. Biologists describe the evolutionary process in terms of co-evolution, a phenomenon that occurs when many different subjects compete for survival in a common environment. One may roughly say that co-evolution is a more general term than evolution, since the former considers subjects that evolve and affect the environment faced by the other agents, while in the latter there is a population that tries to adapt to a fixed environment. In the words of Koza (1992b) there is co-evolution when '... the environment of a given species includes all the other biological species that contemporaneously occupy the physical environment and which are simultaneously trying to survive'. Such a description seems appropriate for the economic problem we are studying. The idea of co-evolution has found important applications outside biology, especially in social systems that are characterized by the struggle of different classes of agents against each other. Miller (1989) uses co-evolution in a genetic algorithm to evolve a finite automaton as the strategy for playing the Repeated Prisoner's Dilemma game. Hillis (1992) uses co-evolution in genetic algorithms to solve optimization problems.

We relate the main features of our economic model to the basic insight of the AL literature (Langton, 1992), in the sense that we characterize our agents as neural networks operating according to simple behavioural rules, generating a complex outcome through many interactions. The model may be relevant for economists and for decision-makers, since it illustrates a process where imperfect knowledge about the general conditions of the market is of central concern. By recognizing that the dealer does not have knowledge of the demand function of the market, we point out the difficulty of measuring in precise terms the appropriate target in each period, and underline the importance of the hypotheses that are made about the learning process.

In this application we also want to consider the two main difficulties that arise when building ANN-based economic models: (1) it is not always possible to devise targets related to outputs of the network, in order to implement supervised learning and (2) it is often difficult to interpret in economic terms the decision rules adopted by the artificial agent, in other words to identify the factors that suggest taking one or another course of action.

Referring to point (1), one can say that building appropriate targets for supervised learning is the more involving task when using ANNs as a description of economic agents. It is here that the interconnection between the description of the trader as a network and the implications of economic theory must be very strong. In some cases, such as for the traders in our model, economic theory suggests a certain target, and at the same time helps to interpret the outputs of a network in terms of decisions taken by a rational agent. In other cases, such as for the dealer in our model, economic theory suggests a target that is well defined in theoretical terms, but that in practice would require an incredible amount of information and computational ability on the part of the agent. For example, the appropriate target for the dealer could be calculated after taking into account the demand functions of all the traders, clearly an impossible task in any practical situation. In the next sections we will point out the need to integrate the standard BP learning with elements that are typical of a reward and punishment methodology, in order to describe a learning process that is not exactly the one that should be followed in a perfect information environment, but at least has the merits of easy computability and of being close to a reasonable rule of thumb that may be followed in practice by agents with a limited computational ability.

Point (2) refers to the possibility of interpreting the input–output mapping of a given network in terms of strategies, that is, in terms of a time-invariant description of the reaction of a network to a given set of signals coming from the environment. In fact the structure of a network implies that inputs and outputs are real numbers: this is indeed one of the main advantages of using neural networks instead of classifier systems that may only consider discrete alternatives and are therefore less general from a computational point of view (see Chapters 1 and 3). This lower generality, however, also implies a better interpretability of the input–output mapping in terms of decision rules.

The approximation we use in this application, which is described in detail in the following sections, consists of interpreting inputs and outputs in terms of discrete choices (or actions) in order to classify the possible decisions. The discretization of the inputs and outputs space may be used to attain an approximate description of the decision rules of the traders without losing the benefit of modelling agents who can learn and act in a continuous space. Exactly how we explore this idea is explained in the next sections.

7.3.3 Dealer, traders and market rules

(a) Dealer

The dealer has the problem of choosing the bid and the ask prices, with the goal of increasing his or her wealth. The dealer's information set is composed of Q_{Bt-1}, Q_{St-1}, P_{Bt-1}, D_{t-1}, where Q_{Bt-1} (Q_{St-1}) is the total amount of shares that were bought (sold) by the dealer in day t–1, and P_{Bt-1} and D_{t-1} are respectively the bid price and the spread in t–1. The dealer has considerably more information than each single trader about the market, since only the dealer knows the total demand and supply at the end of each day, and can evaluate the imbalance between demand and supply. The output of the network representing the dealer is P_{Bt} and D_t, that is, the proposed bid price and spread in t (Figure 7.15).

The dealer's learning is difficult since the mapping between action and goal is not known: given an action in terms of choice of bid and spread,

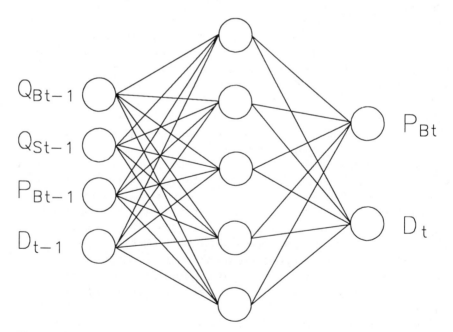

Figure 7.15 *Structure of the dealer.*

its consequences on the change in wealth are not defined since they depend on the reaction of the environment, that is, of all the traders. In this case, however, it is very difficult to understand what the trader should learn over time if the purpose is the maximization of wealth. For example, if the dealer decides to increase the bid price and the spread and his or her wealth decreases, it is not clear whether a decrease in prices would have increased wealth. The problem here is that the dealer does not know the relationship between actions and wealth. There is a double problem of learning the consequences of one's actions and of learning which actions, in a given context, actually increase wealth.

We choose the following setting: we consider four possible strategies, depending on the change in bid price and spread with respect to the previous period

Strategy number	Strategy vector	Bid price change	Spread change
1	$Z_{1,t}$	–	–
2	$Z_{2,t}$	–	+
3	$Z_{3,t}$	+	–
4	$Z_{4,t}$	+	+

so that one has the four possible time-dependent vectors:

$$Z_{1,t} = (-1,-1), \ Z_{2,t} = (-1,+1), \ Z_{3,t} = (+1,-1), \ Z_{4,t} = (+1,+1)$$

where the first element refers to bid price and the second element refers to spread.

A vector $P = (P_{1,t}, P_{2,t}, P_{3,t}, P_{4,t})$ is associated with the strategies and represents the probabilities of their adoption according to some lottery.

At each time t, on the basis of the processing performed by the ANN, the dealer decides a bid price and a spread. These values will be larger or lower than the ones prevailing in time t–1, so that the decision can be classified into one of the four possible strategies. Trading takes place at the resulting prices and the wealth of the dealer changes accordingly.

1. If the change in wealth is positive, there is an indication that the strategy that was selected was working in the right direction, so we increase the probability associated with this strategy. The targets for price and spread at time t, aimed at giving a reinforcement, are defined in the following way:

$$
\begin{aligned}
\text{Price target} \ &= P_{Bt} + \alpha(P_{max} - P_{Bt}) && \text{if } P_{Bt} - P_{Bt\text{-}1} > 0 \\
&= P_{Bt} - \alpha(P_{Bt} - P_{min}) && \text{if } P_{Bt} - P_{Bt\text{-}1} < 0 \\
\text{Spread target} \ &= D_t + \beta(D_{max} - D_t) && \text{if } D_t - D_{t-1} > 0 \\
&= D_t - \beta(D_t - D_{min}) && \text{if } D_t - D_{t-1} < 0
\end{aligned}
$$

where α (β) is an adjustment coefficient for bid price (spread), and P_{min} and P_{max} (D_{min} and D_{max}) are the minimum and maximum values used in bid price (spread) normalization.

2. If the change in wealth is negative, the strategy was wrong and the dealer changes strategy by randomly selecting a strategy from the other three, according to the vector of probabilities at time t. Then we decrease the probability of the strategy that has been abandoned by the dealer.

If the new strategy corresponds to the vector $Z_{j,t}$, we define targets for price and spread in the following way, in order to give a punishment:

$$\text{Price target} = P_{Bt-1} + \alpha(P_{max} - P_{Bt-1}) \qquad \text{if } Z_{j,t}(1) = +1$$

$$= P_{Bt-1} - \alpha(P_{Bt-1} - P_{min}) \qquad \text{if } Z_{j,t}(1) = -1$$

$$\text{Spread target} = D_{t-1} + \beta(D_{max} - D_{t-1}) \qquad \text{if } Z_{j,t}(2) = +1$$

$$= D_{t-1} - \beta(D_{t-1} - D_{min}) \qquad \text{if } Z_{j,t}(2) = -1$$

where $Z_{j,t}(1)$ and $Z_{j,t}(2)$ represent respectively the first and second component of vector $Z_{j,t}$.

In both cases, after building the targets, learning occurs through the BP algorithm.

The idea of the scheme is that the neural network acts by itself as long as the change in wealth is positive. The probability of the strategy that is providing this change in wealth is increasing at the expense of the probabilities of the other three, and the target is reinforcing the action that was actually taken: an increase in the price (spread) that brought about an increase in wealth is compared with a larger increase, to encourage the network to take a stronger decision in the same direction in the future. When the strategy fails, the dealer decides to change his or her strategy by choosing a new strategy with a probability proportional to its past success. It is worth noting that the lottery is used only for choosing the criterion for building BP targets and not for choosing the actual strategy of the dealer. The actual decision is taken by processing the information set through the ANN.

One of the advantages of using neural networks is the possibility of processing information in the form of real numbers, not simply integers. Our agents, for example, decide the exact quantity they want to transact, or the price at which they are willing to trade with others. If we used other technologies, for example a classifier system, then it would be impossible to determine these choices with such precision, and the agent would just give positive or negative signals, for example the willingness to buy or sell a fixed quantity. This advantage of neural networks becomes a disadvantage when it comes to interpreting the decisions that are taken. It is difficult to say that some of the traders adopt a certain strategy for buying or selling, since the decision space is continuous. In a sense, each trader is using a specific strategy defined by the vector of weights of the specific network.

In order to interpret the decisions of the traders we adopt the following description of the mapping between inputs and outputs based on four binary variables:

- the sign of the change in the bid price from t–1 to t;
- the sign of the change in the spread from t–1 to t;
- the sign of the net quantity traded in t–1;
- the sign of the net quantity traded in t.

We then define a decision rule as a mapping between the first three elements and the last.

In the results we will describe the proportion of the traders that follow one of the given strategies, and relate their strategy to the strategy chosen by the dealer, whose discretization has been previously defined. Note that with this methodology we can maintain the benefits of using neural networks to take decisions that are in a continuous space, while having the advantage of describing them with a discrete representation.

(b) Traders

Trader i enters the early morning of day t with a given amount of money $M_{i,t}$, a stock of shares $S_{i,t}$ and an information set $I_{i,t}$. The latter includes P_{Bt}, D_t, P_{Bt-1}, D_{t-1}, Q_{it-1}, $Z_{i,t-1}$, where P_{Bt} is the bid price decided by the dealer at the beginning of time t, at which it is possible to sell any amount of shares to the dealer; D_t is the spread decided by the dealer at time t, which drives a wedge between bid and ask prices, since $P_{At} = P_{Bt} + D_t$; Q_{it-1} is the number of shares transacted with the dealer in the last period; Z_{it-1} is the sign of the operation, equal to +1 for a purchase and –1 for a sale.

The outputs of the network representing the trader are Q_{it} and Z_{it} which define the amount and sign of the operation that the trader proposes to the dealer (Figure 7.16).

The trader has two choices for carrying his or her wealth forward to the following morning: money and shares, about which the trader will have to make a decision at noon of day t. Each day the trader can buy (sell) shares against money in a stock market, at a price P_{At} (P_{Bt}) which is decided by the dealer. Agents decide the number of shares they want to trade, with the purpose of increasing their wealth.

We now consider the learning of the traders. How do traders learn over time? Economic theory and common sense suggest that traders who maximize wealth try to buy before the price goes up, in order to have the option to sell at a higher price in the future, and sell before the price goes down, to perhaps buy in the future at a lower price. We follow this simple but rational rule and teach the traders to buy (sell) any time that the

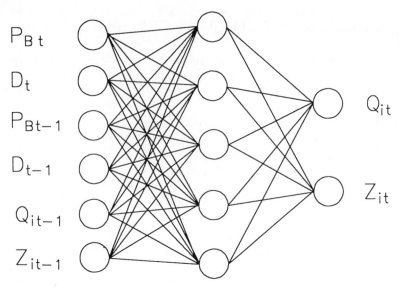

P_{Bt}

D_t

P_{Bt-1}

D_{t-1}

Q_{it-1}

Z_{it-1}

Q_{it}

Z_{it}

Figure 7.16 *Structure of the traders.*

information set signals a future increase (decrease) in market prices. This rule is similar to the one discussed in Chapter 6. Furthermore, we calculate the market price as the simple average between the ask and the bid at each point in time, and teach the trader to buy (sell) before an increase (decrease) in prices. Therefore we define $P_t = (P_{At} + P_{Bt})/2$, and compare the decision taken by traders at t–1 with the change $P_t - P_{t-1}$. If the change was positive we tell the trader that he or she should have bought more shares at the beginning of day t–1. We compare the buy/sell decision of the network at t–1 with the "right" one implied by the change in the future price. If the actual and the optimal action coincide, there is no error and no learning about this specific output, otherwise we signal to the network an error that gives rise to learning. For learning about the size of the transaction, the number of shares that the network decided to buy or sell, we compare the actual number of shares that were traded with the number that should have been traded in order to maximize wealth, taking into account the constraint that each agent can buy shares only if enough money is available, and cannot sell shares that are not already owned (no short-selling is allowed). This optimal number can be determined by considering the sign of the change in price from one period to the next.

- If the change in price between t–1 and t was positive, the optimal action in t–1 was a buy and the target is equal to the maximum trade that would have been allowed by the budget constraint in t–1, that is, M_{t-1}/P_{Bt-1}.

- If the change was negative, the optimal action in t–1 was a sale, and the target is equal to S_{t-1}, that is, the number of shares that were held at the beginning of day t–1, and that should all have been sold before a drop in price.

The behaviour we are teaching the trader is certainly a wealth-maximizing one: ideally the trader should learn to recognize that there is some nonlinear relationship between the information set and the future change in the market price, and that such a relationship is to be exploited to trade in a wealth-maximizing fashion.

In order to interpret the decisions taken by the traders in terms of time-invariant decision rules, we consider the decision to buy or sell as a function of the following inputs:

- change in bid from t–1 to t;
- change in spread from t–1 to t;
- decision (to buy or sell) taken in t–1.

This would yield a large number of possible decision rules, which are restricted to four when the decision of the dealer about the bid and the spread is announced at the beginning of day t. For example, if the dealer announced a bid that is larger than the one of period t–1 (positive bid change) and a spread that is lower than the one prevailing in t–1 (negative spread change), one has the following four possibilities:

Bid change	Spread change	Action at t–1	Action at t
+	–	buy	buy
+	–	buy	sell
+	–	sell	buy
+	–	sell	sell

In this way we can characterize four conditional strategies that show persistence or reversal of behaviour from one day to the next.

7.3.4 Results

Simulations are performed principally for investigating the co-evolution of the strategies of the two types of agents. Figures 7.17 to 7.21 describe the results of some simulations. Figure 7.17 reports the dynamics of the bid and ask prices, showing that there is much volatility in the dealer's decisions as far as the prices are concerned. There is much less volatility in the spread, the vertical difference between the two lines (note, however, that spread is constrained between 0.01 and 0.06). Figure 7.18 reports the

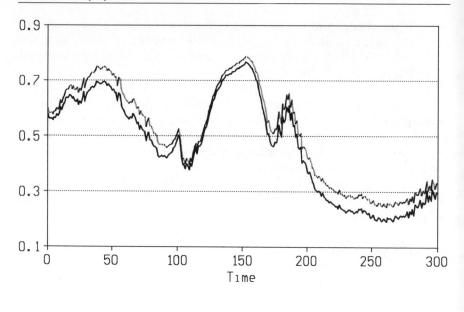

Figure 7.17 *Dynamics of bid and ask prices.*

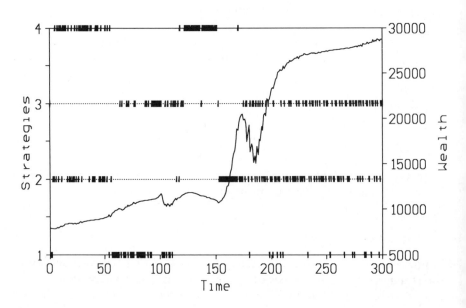

Figure 7.18 *Strategies and wealth of the dealer.*

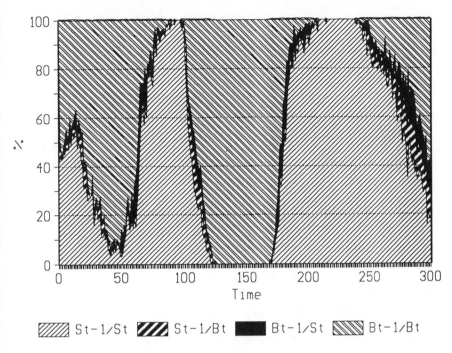

St-1/St   St-1/Bt   Bt-1/St   Bt-1/Bt

Figure 7.19 *Evolution of traders' strategies.*

strategy chosen by the dealer at each point of time, together with the evolution of his or her wealth. The dealer seems to use different pairs of strategies for different periods. From 0 to 50 the dealer alternates between strategies 2 and 4, uses 1 and 3 from 50 to 100, then switches decisively to 4 until 150, and then mostly uses 2 and 3, a pair that have never appeared before. There seems to be some relationship between the chosen strategy and the dynamics of wealth, with more experimentation with new strategies when wealth is more stable. Towards the end of the sample, for example, there is some experimentation with strategy 1. The strategy numbering system is defined in section 7.3.3.

Figure 7.19 reports the proportions of traders using the various possible strategies, that is, continue to sell, continue to buy, switch from buying to selling, switch from selling to buying.

There is a clear predominance of the strategies that suggest continuing to do the same thing from one period to the next. From 50 to 120 almost everybody keeps buying, while from 170 to 240 everybody keeps selling. What is the relationship between this pattern and the strategies chosen by the dealer? Figure 7.20 reports the bid price and the difference between the proportion of traders who buy (among those who trade on every given day) and the proportion of traders who sell (among those who trade on every given day). There is a strong co-movement between the two series:

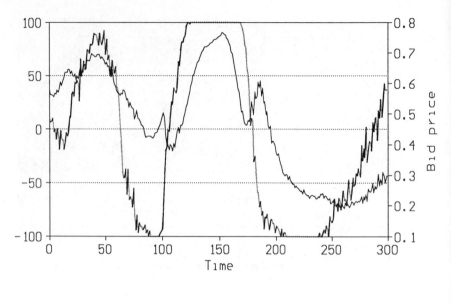

Figure 7.20 *Proportion of buying traders and bid price.*

most of the traders buy when the price is rising since their extrapolation of the past trend in prices suggests to them that there is persistency in the tendency of prices, so that when the price starts rising there are good chances that the price will keep on rising.

There are therefore clear relationships between the decisions of the traders and those of the dealer. Figures 7.21 and 7.22 show the co-evolution of the strategies of the dealer and of the population of traders. In order to simplify the figure we separately consider the dealer's price strategy (Figure 7.21) and spread strategy (Figure 7.22) versus the proportion of selling traders. In both figures, −1 corresponds to a decrease while 1 denotes an increase.

We can describe the mutual evolution of the dealer's and traders' strategies in the following way (for the sake of simplicity, we only focus on the dealer's price strategy, without commenting on the spread strategy).

1. Let us suppose that the dealer starts by following a successful strategy corresponding to an increase in price.
2. The dealer's wealth increases and the dealer does not change strategy.
3. Market prices tend to rise.
4. In response to the dealer's strategy, by the effect of learning rules, buyers overcome sellers in the population of traders.
5. The dealer is forced to increase sales and reduce purchases.

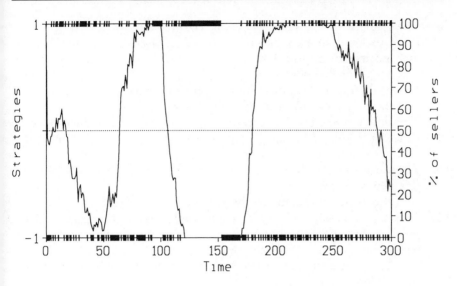

Figure 7.21 *Co-evolution of traders' and dealer's strategies (dealer's price strategy)*

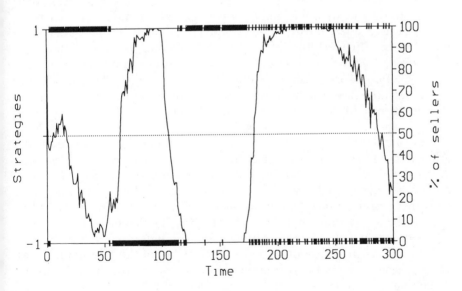

Figure 7.22 *Co-evolution of traders' and dealer's strategies (dealer's spread strategy)*

6. The amount of the dealer's wealth, computed as $W_{d,t} = M_{d,t} + S_{d,t}$ P_t, is exposed to two opposing forces: a positive one due to the increase in prices, and a negative one due to the reduction of the number of owned shares.
7. When all traders become buyers, the latter force becomes stronger and the dealer has to face a decrease in wealth.
8. The dealer reacts by changing strategy and begins to reduce prices.
9. Reacting to this new strategy, sellers reappear on the market and help to confirm the decreasing trend.
10. The wealth of the dealer increases and the dealer tends to maintain this new strategy.
11. Sellers become dominant in the market.
12. After a few periods, a phenomenon similar to the one described in point 6, but with the opposite sign, occurs which generates a new reversal in the strategy of the dealer.
13. The long-run dynamics of the system are generated by iteration of these steps.

Similar observations can be made about spread strategy. Interactions between price strategy and spread strategy have yet to be explored.

Two facts contribute to smoothing the dynamics of the system.

- The swaps that have been described refer to learning strategy, that is, to the one used for building the targets of the dealer. So they have a delayed effect on the strategy actually followed by the dealer.
- Traders often exhibit differences in individual behaviour (learning speed, reactivity to inputs) which can generate some spikes in the evolution of the dealer's wealth. In some periods in fact, the dealer does not use a single strategy but a couple of strategies, swapping frequently from one to the other.

Our simulations show that the strategies of the agents are mutually influenced and co-evolve over time in a manner that is related to the goal assigned to each agent, that is, the maximization of wealth. As in the models described in Chapter 6, it is important to analyse the strong influence that learning rules may have on the building of behavioural rules. Finally, the results show that the aggregate market outcome emerging from repeated interactions of these simple agents is indeed complicated, and difficult to interpret without an a priori knowledge of the behavioural rules of the agents. Such interpretation is made easier by our attempt at describing the structure of the various networks in terms of strategies defined on a discretized action space.

7.4 A model of a banking system

7.4.1 Description of the model

In this model we depart from the basic framework of the previous examples in order to give some indications about the generality of the applications of multi-population models. Two important aspects differentiate this model from the ones previously described.

- The system under analysis is no longer a stock market but a banking and productive system.
- Only one of the two populations is modelled by means of ANNs (banks) while the other (firms) is simulated through a stochastic process. The behaviour of firms is not adaptive but varies exogenously depending on the economic cycle.

The application that we present here is a revised and extended version of the model described in Margarita and Beltratti (1992).

We consider a banking system composed of artificial adaptive banks, which have to make decisions about the opportunity to lend money to prospective borrowers, which are risky firms whose value evolves stochastically over time according to a heterogeneous (across firms), time-varying probability. The banks' problem is to discriminate between good and bad borrowers on the basis of previous experience. Their incentive to discriminate depends on the possibility that borrowers with low productivity may not be able to repay the debt if they are hit by an unfortunate sequence of productivity shocks.

Banks decide whether or not to give out loans on the basis of an information set which is partly firm-specific and partly of a macroeconomic nature. The evaluation of such an information set takes place by means of neural networks which learn over time to distinguish between good and bad borrowers.

This issue is related to recent theories on financial intermediation stressing the role of banks as institutions that can efficiently evaluate the economic performance of those who ask for credit. In the recent literature, the very existence of financial intermediaries is no longer justified only by economies of scale, but also by their possibility of discriminating between good and bad borrowers. The point is well described by Santomero (1984): '. . . banks function as a filter to evaluate signals in a financial environment with limited information. Financial agents are either pathologically honest or dishonest, but due to imperfect information, participants find it difficult to evaluate the quality of signals or the honesty of agents. This gives rise to financial intermediation whose primary role is the evaluation and purchase of financial assets.'

The theoretical literature has also shown that the loan decision on the part of banks is difficult in an economy with incomplete information.

According to Stiglitz and Weiss (1981) there may well be equilibrium credit rationing, a term used to describe a situation where, in the face of excess demands, banks decide not to give new credit rather than lend out financial resources at a higher interest rate. The reason for such a behaviour is that a higher interest rate may dramatically increase the riskiness of the portfolio by inducing borrowers with worsening future profit prospects to accept a costly loan in the hope of an unlikely stroke of luck in the future. This is yet another example of the general principle according to which stockholders of leveraged firms gain when business risk increases, since they are gambling with the money of their creditors (Brealey and Myers, 1984).

In reality such an evaluation takes place through the collection of information and the analysis of a set of signals which are partly specific to the firm that is asking for credit and partly of a more general, macro-economic, nature. A firm asking for credit is supposed to provide evidence of its economic and financial situation by tangible actions such as giving the bank its balance sheet and providing information about the market in which the firm sells its usual products. The bank filters the information with general knowledge about the state of the economy and its influence on the activities of the firms. The size of the firm is also an important piece of information, as small firms tend to be more concentrated in one or a few activities, and are therefore more risky.

We are interested in studying this evaluation process, and the learning process by which banks start from a very incomplete knowledge of the productivity of the existing firms and arrive at decision rules according to which loans are given to borrowers with specific characteristics, given a certain state of the economy. Static models are not well suited to this task, which is dynamic. We model this evaluation process by means of neural networks, one for each bank, deciding the amount of credit to be given to a firm on the basis of an information set which includes some signals related to the economic situation of the firms. Our banks are therefore artificial adaptive agents in the terminology of Holland and Miller (1991). We are somewhat respectful of the theoretical literature in the sense that the interest rate is given and banks vary the amount of the loan which is accorded to firms. The value of firms, described by a stochastic process, can increase or decrease with certain probabilities depending on the business cycle. The task of banks is to distinguish between good and bad firms, and to decide the loan given to a firm. The aspects we want to stress are analysed by means of different simulations. It would be impossible to give analytical results, since the model is too complicated when learning is taken into account. In fact the learning performed by a given bank depends on the history of the firms that are met and on the bank's ability to discriminate. Learning takes place through a particular methodology described more precisely in section 7.4.3. The interest of this methodology lies in the possibility of having an agent, in our model a bank, learn even at times when no action is taken. In contrast to what happens in standard back-propagation algorithms, in our model agents act discontinuously but have the possibility of learning in every period.

7.4.2 Firms and banks

We describe the whole economic system by considering separately its three fundamental components: firms, banks and their interactions.

(a) Firms

Banks and firms are the agents that populate the model. Firms are represented as a stock of assets whose amount can increase or decrease according to an exogenously specified stochastic process. More precisely we assume that the value of firm i at time t is $V_{i,t}$, and that the expectation of such a value at time t+1 is given by:

$$E_t V_{i,t+1} = P_{i,t} V_{i,t}(1 + x) + (1 - P_{i,t}) V_{i,t}(1 - x) \qquad (7.4)$$

where x is the percentage amount of change in productivity of firm i and $P_{i,t}$ is the probability that the value of firm i at time t will be larger in the future. The cross-sectional initial variability of the different firms in our model depends on an extraction of probability $P_{i,0}$ from a uniform distribution between 0.1 and 0.9. Time variation is deterministic and is introduced with a function that simulates a parametric economic cycle, that is:

$$P_{i,t} = P_{i,0} + m \sin(k^{-1} 2\pi t)$$

where k is the periodicity, the length of the cycle, and m is a magnifying factor determining the amplitude of this cycle. In this way we model a set of firms which are heterogeneous with respect to the evolution of their value, and that also change according to economic conditions. The banks'

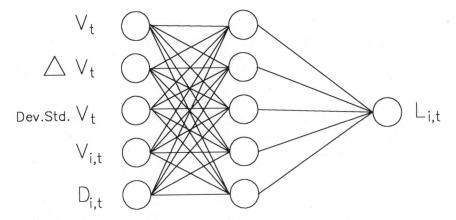

Figure 7.23 *The structure of the banks.*

task is to distinguish firms according to their unknown type and performance. Time variation of the productivity parameter complicates such a learning process.

(b) Banks

We model banks as adaptive agents by means of ANNs. The specific structure of the banks is reported in Figure 7.23. The information set of the bank, $I_{j,t}$, includes V_t and its standard deviation, ΔV_t, $V_{i,t}$ and $D_{i,t}$, where V_t is the average value of the firms, $V_{i,t}$ is the value of the firm asking for credit and $D_{i,t}$ is the total debt of the firm asking for credit.

The first three inputs are therefore of a macroeconomic nature, and can be interpreted as signals about the state of the economy (the third input in particular may be useful to evaluate the short-run cycle in economic activity). The last two inputs are specific to the firm asking for credit. A bank maximizing profit should learn that credit should be given to those firms presenting a good situation, that is, a high value and a low stock of debt. The first two inputs are useful for comparing a specific firm with all the other firms in the economy.

The output of the bank that results from the processing of this information set corresponds to the amount of the loan to give out, $L_{i,t}$, ranging between two exogenously specified minimum and maximum values, L_{min} and L_{max}.

(c) Interactions between banks and firms

The system evolves in discrete time. The interaction between banks and firms takes place every T periods. Every T periods, firms can apply for loans. A quasi-continuous process can be implemented when $T = 1$. The interaction among the agents occurs according to the following rules:

1. Among all the possible combinations of banks and firms we randomly consider p% of possible combinations. For example, 3 banks and 6 firms give rise to 18 possible combinations between a bank and a firm. If p = 50%, we consider 9 possible meetings. In such a way a randomly selected sub-sample of firms ask a randomly selected sub-sample of banks for a loan. Given that in our simulations the number of firms is much larger than the number of banks, a subset of firms interact with all the banks.
2. A given firm cannot receive a loan from a certain bank if it did not pay back the loan which was received previously from the same bank. It may of course happen that indebted firms receive loans from banks which are different from those that gave loans in the past. If a firm cannot repay in one period, then the debt remains and will have to be repaid in the future.
3. A firm asking for a loan may convince a bank to provide credit by showing a certain information set related to the economic conditions of the firm, its value and total debt.

4. The bank evaluates such firm-specific information together with information related to the general conditions of the economy, which may vary according to the business cycle.
5. If the bank decides to give out the loan, it must also decide the amount of the loan. Loans are paid back in N periods of time, with a constant repayment, at an interest rate j. N and j are exogenously fixed and are homogeneous across firms.

7.4.3 The learning of the banks

As described above, banks must learn to distinguish between good and bad borrowers. For the learning procedure, we use a methodology that is a form of on-line learning for time-dependent processes when a target is not available. This problem is a particular case of the temporal credit assignment problem, where rewards must be delayed in time with respect to the action. Why do we need to introduce this methodology in the context of our model? In our model banks evaluate the possibility of giving out loans only in periods T, 2T, 3T . . ., that is, on those days when the credit market is open and the firms may apply for credit. On the other days there is no loan request and therefore no output on the part of the network. Conversely, from periods T+1, 2T+1, 3T+1, . . ., until respectively T+N, 2T+N, 3T+N, . . ., firms may repay the loans and banks are aware of the actual repayments made by the firms. However, this does not mean that there are no learning possibilities when the market for new loans is closed. Banks may learn something from firms' debt repayment performance. This is particularly relevant when T < N, since then a bank may be called upon to evaluate a loan request before other loans are exhausted. If we used a standard back-propagation algorithm when T < N, banks would give sets of loans without learning anything from the observation of the repayment performance of their debts.

Our problem is therefore to model learning on days when the output of the network is 0. The method, based on the BP algorithm, allows a specific realization of a variable to be compared to a target which was supposed to be pursued by the agent. The basic idea of the algorithm is to create an appropriate target for each day of the repayment period, and use it to evaluate the initial decision. To illustrate the algorithm in the context of our model, let us suppose that a loan was given out in period T; the target of the bank for the periods between T+1 and T+N (the day when the loan is supposed to be repaid back completely) changes in such a way as to keep track of the past history of repayments for that loan. In T+1, for example, the target is set in the following way.

1. If there is a regular repayment of the part of the loan that was supposed to be repaid in T+1, the target is equal to the amount of the loan plus (1/N) times the difference between the largest loan that the bank could have given and the loan that the bank actually gave.

Therefore, assuming we can write, the hypothesis of complete regular repayment:

$$G_{T+i} = L_T + i \, (L_{max} - L_T)/N \qquad\qquad i = 1, 2, \ldots, N$$

where G_{T+i} is the target to use in period $T+i$, L_T is the amount of loan given out in period T and L_{max} is the maximum allowed loan (for the sake of simplicity we drop the index referring to the firm).

The procedure is repeated for $T+2$, $T+3$ ..., $T+N$. Thus the bank learns that it should have given a larger loan to a good borrower, which is repaying its debt according to the agreed schedule.

2.   If there is no repayment in $T+1$ the target is the amount of the loan minus $(1/N)$ times the difference between the loan that the bank actually gave and the lowest loan that the bank could have given (possibly 0).

Therefore we can write, assuming the hypothesis of complete absence of repayment:

$$G_{T+i} = L_T - i \, (L_T - L_{min})/N \qquad\qquad i = 1, 2, \ldots, N$$

where L_{min} is the minimum allowed loan and other symbols are as defined above.

Thus the bank learns that it should have given out a lower loan to a firm which is not repaying the debt according to the schedule. From $T+1$ to $T+N$ cases 1 and 2 can be mixed on the basis of the history of repayments. We can therefore write in a recursive form the general rule for building the target in each period from 1 to N:

$$G_{T+i} = G_{T+i-1} + R_i \qquad\qquad 1, 2, \ldots, N$$

with

$$G_T = L_T$$

and where

$$R_i \quad = (L_{max} - L_T)/N \qquad \text{if repayment occurs in period } i$$
$$= -\,(L_T - L_{min})/N \qquad \text{if repayment is missing in period } i$$

This learning mechanism allows banks to distinguish between good and bad firms with a simple system of reward and punishment, similar in spirit to the work of Arthur (1991). The bank learns over time to associate good decisions with an information set corresponding to a good general economic condition and to a good signal from those firms asking for credit. Note that only the information at T, $2T$, $3T$ ... is directly relevant to the loan decision taken in T, $2T$, $3T$ ..., since it is only on those days that the bank is making a decision. The target of the network for the days between $T+1$ and $T+N$ is strictly associated with the decision that was taken at T, and with the history of repayments.

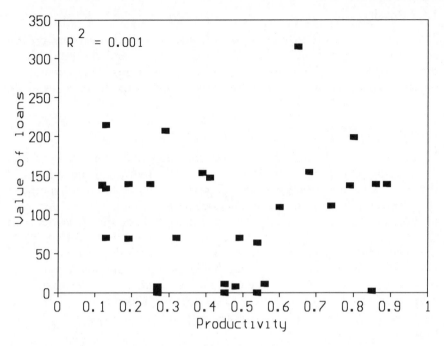

Figure 7.24 *Loans and probabilities, m = 0.0, t = 10.*

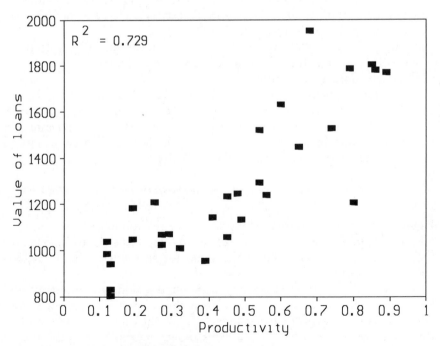

Figure 7.25 *Loans and probabilities, m = 0.0, t = 200.*

7.4.4 Results

The main aspects we analyse are the effectiveness of the learning process among banks as a function of the economic cycle, and the influence of the interest rate on the performance of banks and firms. The outcomes of the simulations relating to these three aspects are presented in Figures 7.24 to 7.38.

(a) Effectiveness of learning among banks

Figures 7.24 to 7.32 report the relationship between the probability $P_{i,t}$, which corresponds to a measure of firms' productivity, and the amount of the loans which are given by the banking system, under different hypotheses about the amplitude of the economic cycle. For each hypothesis, plots refer to three different time periods. The goal is to evaluate the effectiveness of the learning methodology: the more knowledgeable the banks are about the type of the various firms, the closer the relationship should be to a line with a slope equal to 1, since banks will give out loans mostly to those firms which are more likely to increase, rather than decrease, their value over time. The coefficient of determination is computed for the data corresponding to each plot, in order to quantify the degree of the relationship.

Figures 7.24 to 7.26 consider the case where the probabilities for each firm are time-independent, that is, there is no cycle in the economy. They show that learning is indeed effective. As time goes by, the relationship between loans and productivity becomes closer and closer to the one that would hold under perfect information.

Figures 7.27 to 7.29 consider the case where the magnifying factor is equal to 0.1, so that there is a weak cycle in the system. The results are qualitatively similar to the previous ones.

The same happens in Figures 7.30 to 7.32, where the factor is 0.3, corresponding to a stronger cycle in general economic activity. This time it takes longer before the learning actually takes place. We can interpret this phenomenon by saying that the economic cycle and heterogeneity of firms interfere and make learning more involved.

(b) Influence of the interest rate on the performance of banks and firms

Figures 7.33 to 7.37 consider the problem of the influence of the interest rate on the performance of banks and firms. Figures 7.33 to 7.35 report the average value of the assets of the banks for an interest rate of 3%, 5% and 7% per period.

It is shown that the relationship between the value of the banks and the interest rate is not monotonic. When the interest rate increases from 3% to 5% the value of the banks increases, but the opposite happens when the rate increases from 5% to 7%. This shows the existence of some kind of complementarity between the banking sector and firms. A moderate

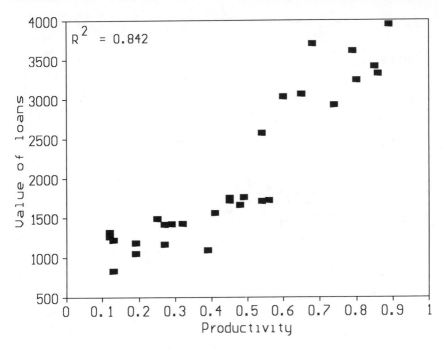

Figure 7.26 *Loans and probabilities, m = 0.0, t = 400.*

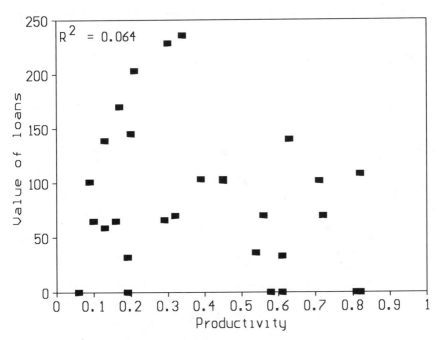

Figure 7.27 *Loans and probabilities, m = 0.01, t = 10.*

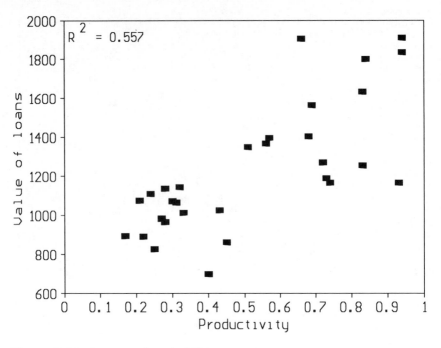

Figure 7.28 *Loans and probabilities, m = 0.1, t = 200.*

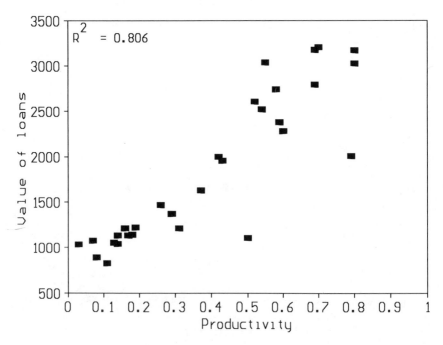

Figure 7.29 *Loans and probabilities, m = 0.01, t = 400.*

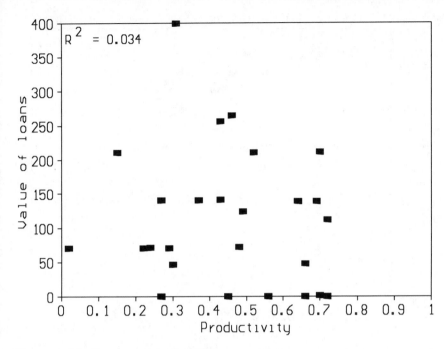

Figure 7.30 *Loans and probabilities, m = 0.3, t = 10.*

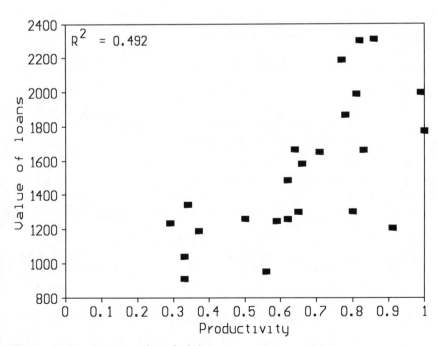

Figure 7.31 *Loans and probabilities, m = 0.3, t = 200.*

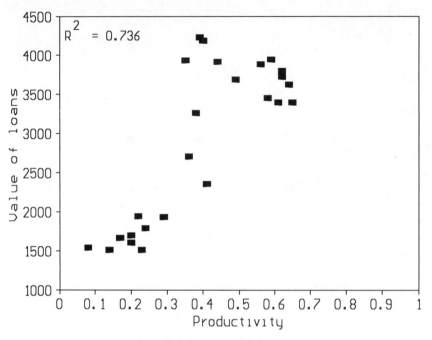

Figure 7.32 *Loans and probabilities, m = 0.3, t = 400.*

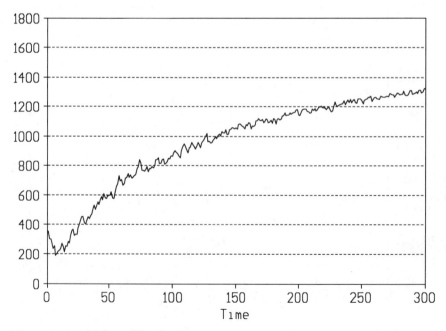

Figure 7.33 *Value of banks, j = 0.03.*

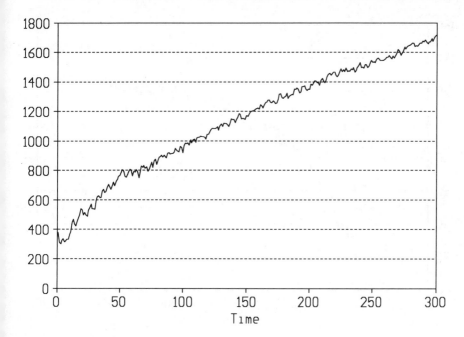

Figure 7.34 *Value of banks, j = 0.05.*

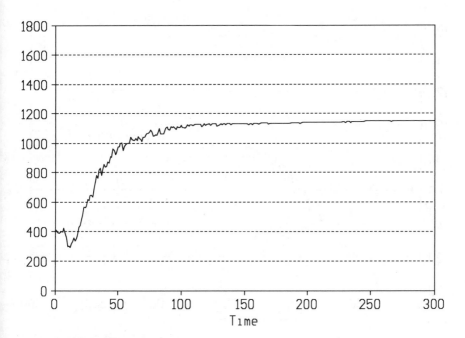

Figure 7.35 *Value of banks, j = 0.07.*

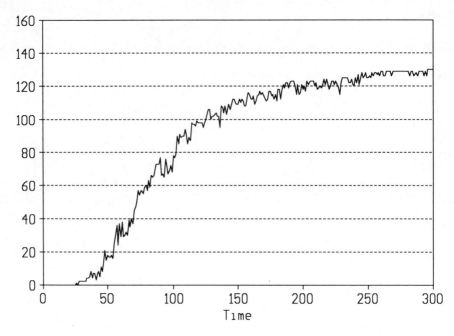

Figure 7.36 *Bankruptcy index, j = 0.03.*

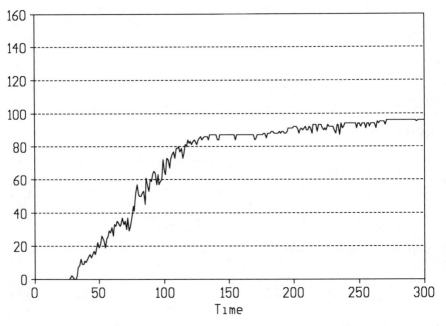

Figure 7.37 *Bankruptcy index, j = 0.05.*

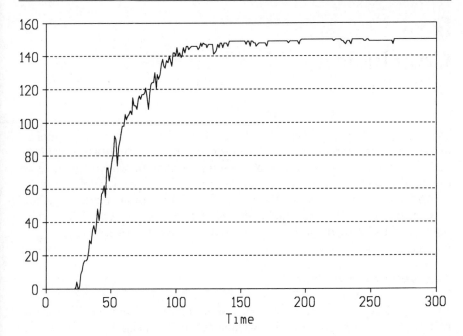

Figure 7.38 *Bankruptcy index, j = 0.07.*

increase in the cost of credit is beneficial to the banks and harmful to firms; a larger increase is harmful to everybody, as the value of banks starts to decrease due to the failures of some of the firms. We find a confirmation of this interpretation in the plots of Figures 7.36 and 7.38, which show the increase in what we call the bankruptcy index, that is, the number of firms that are not able to repay their debt, as the interest rate increases. The minimum value of this index corresponds to an interest rate of 0.05.

These simulations show that after a certain number of periods, banks learn to discriminate among the types of borrowers; the time it takes for such learning to occur depends on the time-variability of the economy. Learning is more difficult when a cycle in the system is superimposed on the heterogeneity among firms. It is also shown that an excessive increase in the rate of interest is harmful to both firms and banks due to the increase in the bankruptcies of firms which are unable to repay their debt.

8
Conclusion

The various chapters have considered such diverse issues as economic models, artificial intelligence, artificial life and financial markets. Given the vastness of the material, we find it useful to sum up the main ideas in this final chapter. Beyond reviewing the ground that we have covered, we also offer some discussion of the material we have not covered, but which may turn out to be important for future research projects. The various points discussed below are not presented in a specific order.

The structure of learning

As pointed out in Chapter 2, many dynamic economic models assume that agents possess structural knowledge about the economy. In such cases learning is not even considered as a relevant issue. Only in a few cases is it assumed that agents do not have such knowledge from the very beginning, but act on the basis of models which are recursively estimated as more and more data become available. In these cases learning is central to the analysis, but extremely restrictive assumptions are made. In particular, learning behaviour is associated with econometric algorithms. For example, most of the theory analysing the convergence of models with learning agents to rational expectations equilibria assumes that agents estimate linear regression models on which to base forecasts and decisions. Convergence takes place when the true and estimated models become the same in the long run. This approach completely ignores any structural explanation of learning behaviour. The identification of learning with linear econometric models may be useful for proving theorems, but seems to be overly restrictive. As we have discussed throughout the book, individuals and institutions seem to gain experience in a variety of ways which are certainly not well described by the fiction of the econometrician recursively adapting his or her models as new data become available. ANNs may be a useful tool for developing microfoundations of learning behaviour. We have also developed a way to deal with a type of learning founded upon the development of consistency in agents' behaviour, without a priori economic assumptions. We have observed that simply by applying some consistency requirements it is possible to reproduce complex behaviours of economic agents on the basis of simple endogenously developed internal rules.

ANNs resemble many of the characteristics associated with real learning and reasoning schemes. For example:

- the association between inputs and outputs in an ANN is usually robust with respect to small changes in the structure of the network and to the presence of noise in the inputs;
- learning takes place by induction, after repeated observations of sets of examples;
- learning is adaptive, as new learning and behavioural rules are developed in order to adapt to a changing environment.

In the book we have only started to tackle the issue of how such learning takes place, and we have mostly pushed the analysis of the interactions of learning agents in various market contexts. Some experiments have, however, been performed with ANNs and with genetic algorithms, even though understanding more deeply the structure of how agents learn and behave is a promising direction for future research. A way to evaluate the validity of different learning models may well be in terms of their effects on the aggregate behaviour studied with the adaptive simulated model. This may seem far-fetched, but is exactly what happened with the rational expectations hypothesis, which gained wide diffusion among economists after its relevance to macroeconomic models had been shown in a number of cases.

The interaction between the practitioners' approach to financial markets and applied uses of artificial neural networks

Financial markets are a clear example of the divergence between theoretical models and the real world. The theory of efficient markets with rational expectations suggests that traders should not use the information contained in past prices and returns for devising trading strategies, even though most traders do look at charts and other technical analysis indicators. Economic theory therefore suggests that most traders are wasting their time; they should not be concerned with finding ways to beat the market, since nobody can obtain excess returns without running compensatory extra risks. This theoretical implication is very strong: even if one were ready to admit that economic theory is basically right in rejecting technical analysis, it still follows that the theoretical models have little to say about how to approach the issue of stock evaluation in practice. This may be a reason why practitioners are not satisfied with the analyses proposed by academics. Artificial neural networks may be used to obtain a positive analysis of financial markets, as we have tried to show in our artificial markets models.

Effectiveness of trading strategies

One important conclusion that we draw from the models is that trading strategies that work under certain market conditions may not work so effectively under other market circumstances, as the success of a strategy may depend on the strategies adopted by the other traders in the market, with various degrees of complementarity or substitutability. For example, a strategy may work well when few other traders use it, but may become self-defeating when adopted by the majority of the market. These insights, which we believe are familiar on intuitive grounds to many traders, may receive a proper treatment in the context of the models we have developed.

Clearly, a precise evaluation of the effects of different strategies may take place only when an artificial financial market is fully developed, and we are still far from that objective. However, our exercises show that such an enterprise is possible and worth the effort. When an adaptive financial market model is developed to a further stage (and see below for what we regard as the most essential steps in terms of basic research for achieving such a purpose), there will certainly be no lack of practical applications.

- Traders might evaluate strategies in the artificial markets first, and assess their characteristics in terms of mean return, volatility and so on.
- Artificial markets may be used by financial intermediaries, e.g. mutual funds and pension funds, to interact with their clients. It would be possible to show the potential performance of various techniques of managing investors' money directly to the final investors, and the latter could communicate to the managers their preferences for one strategy or another given the level of risk that they want to take.
- The effects of different institutional regimes and economic policy measures might be evaluated within the simulation models. This may be relevant, for example, for assessing the effects of taxes, which are sometimes suggested as an instrument for decreasing the volatility of financial markets, on trading volumes and prices.

The interaction of adaptive agents in market contexts

The book has developed the analysis of several situations of markets characterized by interactions of learning agents, where the latter learn from an environment which they themselves contribute to shape. In general the cases we have considered involve financial markets, but an extended example has been given of how to use this approach to analyse the interactions between a banking sector and various firms applying for credit. The dynamics evolving from the interactions of such agents are sometimes complex, even in cases where such dynamics simply originate from the learning process itself.

One important insight obtained from these models is that different learning abilities may dramatically affect the dynamics of the market as well as the welfare of each single participant in the market. It has been seen that using sophisticated nonlinear models to form expectations may be worthwhile only when market conditions are turbulent, but also that continuous interactions between sophisticated traders may stabilize the market price, making the same models which helped the stabilization process less useful.

In some cases sophisticated traders stabilize the market and prepare their own way out of the market, as in stable conditions it becomes more profitable to use less complex forecasting techniques.

Clearly, such results were obtained in the context of highly stylized models that need more research, mainly in terms of specification, in order to understand to what extent they may be generalized. However, these examples provide some benchmark against which to evaluate future projects.

The description of artificial models

One fundamentally important research project concerns the criteria used by the experimenter to describe the results obtained by the models. Indeed, we have noticed that it is sometimes difficult to describe in synthetic but meaningful ways the products of the simulation models. There is a real need for a set of diagnostics, similar perhaps to the set of standard tests used to evaluate econometric regressions, on which different researchers can agree, in order to have a common way to compare the outputs of different models. Lacking such a common ground, it may be difficult to convey important messages to the community of researchers in the field.

To face this problem we have mainly used diagrams consisting of time paths for relevant variables, for example, market price and dispersion of opinions, and empirical distribution to approximate the steady state of the model. Another interesting area of research that we have not yet pursued, but is very important, lies in the calibration of the artificial models to real data. This in some sense goes back to the same problem we were discussing before about the diagnostics; to the extent that it is possible to single out a few key parameters of each artificial model, it is then useful to calibrate the model to see whether the output of the model is close, according to some metrics, to some stylized facts one is willing to consider as a relevant benchmark for assessing the validity of the model. There are many dimensions along which artificial financial markets can be calibrated, for example one can evaluate the markets in terms of volatility of prices, predictability of returns, trading volume, frequency of large crashes, and so on. Researchers should agree on a set of relevant stylized facts which represent the structure of the markets.

Decision rules

Another point which deserves discussion is the interpretation of the actions suggested by the ANN in terms of simple decision rules, relating observable variables to the suggestions provided by the network. This is an extremely relevant problem, especially when it comes to proposing concrete applications to the practitioners, who may not like the black-box approach often associated with ANNs. The book has provided both theoretical discussions and concrete examples of how one can face this problem. At the theoretical level, we have discussed various possibilities of interpreting the structure of the network, for example by means of derivatives between the output and the inputs, or by discretizing the space of inputs and outputs. For example, the actions of the dealer have been interpreted in this light, and it has been possible to show that to some extent one can interpret the situation of both the agents and the market as a whole in intuitive terms. Developing this line of research more precisely would also allow a stricter connection between artificial economic models and the co-evolution literature, which indeed interprets the strategies of various actors in interactive terms. This is another avenue for potentially fruitful research, which promises to extend to economics some of the insights that have been obtained in the Artificial Life literature. It is still an open question whether it is more useful to adopt the continuous approach of ANNs, followed by discrete interpretation of the input–output space, or whether it is more useful to start by immediately constraining the actions that can be taken by the artificial agent in terms of a discrete number of alternatives, for example by using classifier systems.

Complexity of the strategies

Trading strategies obtained from technical analysis of asset prices may sometimes be very complex, requiring the simultaneous use of different indicators. Artificial neural networks promise to be a useful instrument in the evaluation of such strategies. To understand the importance of studying automated trading systems one need only think of the possibilities that are open when traders evaluate various intertemporal strategies, that is, strategies which are not simply based on buy or sell each period, but for example imply buying in one period, then staying out of the market for a few periods, and then selling. In this case the space of possibilities is truly immense, and it is unlikely that it can be efficiently explored by simple systems. Sufficiently complex ANNs may generate insights that may prove to be profitable. This was analysed in Chapter 5, when the genetic trader was used to evaluate complex strategies that had been devised by the researcher. However, there is an even deeper possibility, which is that by observing an artificial financial market a trader may observe the artificial agents endogenously developing useful strategies that may have some relevance to the true markets.

Modelling behaviour

At the level of modelling individual behaviour, we have found out how difficult it is to provide a 'realistic' description of some problems that in standard economic theory are simplified by the assumption of structural knowledge of the economy. In the case of the dealer considered in Chapter 7, for example, it has been shown how difficult it is, for a dealer acting with an information structure resembling that found in real markets, to devise proper strategies. The dealer has to understand the reaction of the traders to any change in pricing policy, and also the effects of such reactions on the dealer's wealth dynamics.

The book has also highlighted the importance of the validation process imposed on the agent, and the connection between the implicit assumptions made in the training and the results in terms of rules. For example, teaching the agent to fully anticipate the trend in price might generate a risky behaviour that may not be appreciated by a risk-averse user. However, the attempts at tuning the implicit amount of risk aversion imputed to the artificial trader to reflect the needs of the user is not an easy matter, as shown by the results obtained in Chapter 6. On the other hand, the models of Chapter 6 had the ambitious purpose of building a whole market of completely autonomous traders, both forecasting future prices and deciding the appropriate trades. For more applied purposes, it may be worth exploring a partial equilibrium approach first, like the model of a genetic trader that was discussed in Chapter 5.

Implications for the efficiency of financial markets

Some relevant points can be made about the definition of market efficiency. The definition offered in the literature roughly says that a market is efficient when traders process the information according to a 'correct' model of the world, and this implies that excess returns are unpredictable, given the present information set. As the information set includes previous prices and returns and other information of a macroeconomic nature, one can test market efficiency by looking for a relation between future returns and past variables. The forecastability of returns that is found in practice may be interpreted either as inefficiency or as time variation in risk premia. There are many implicit assumptions in this view of financial markets, but perhaps the most fundamental is that there exists only one true model of the world. While this is being disputed by some theoreticians (see Chapter 2), there is also day-to-day evidence of financial markets that are largely populated by traders who: (1) actively trade every day, contrary to the implications of many rational expectations models, which imply complete lack of trading and (2) use technical analysis to evaluate prices. These agents behave in a way that is not consistent with the models based on true economic structures; but if we look at financial markets from the point of view of the artificial models we have considered in Chapters 5 and 6, we realize that the traders populating our financial markets do in fact trade and do in fact use past prices and returns to forecast the future. Our assumption of imperfect knowledge about the environment and of limited computational abilities may justify the choices of agents who do not find it optimal to search for all possible correlations in the space of future and past returns.

The use of sophisticated technical trading is equivalent to the use of complicated nonlinear forecasting techniques. These forecasting techniques may well beat the market for some periods of time, given the configuration of strategies used by the other agents in the market. However, they may become useless as other agents change their own strategies as a response to their inferior past performance. This continuous sequence of adoption and modification of strategies forms an evolving nonlinear universe which, when tested *ex post*, may well leave some traces of correlations that, however, do not have much to do with inefficiency, when by inefficiency one means the existence of unexploited trading opportunities.

It is therefore the very notion of market efficiency that has to be rethought, to come to a definition that is more operational and takes into account computing abilities.

References

Ackley, D. and Littman, M. (1991) Interactions between Learning And Evolution, in *Artificial Life* II, *SFI Studies in the Sciences of Complexity*, vol X, (eds C.G. Langton, C. Taylor, J.D. Farmer and S. Rasmussen), Addison-Wesley, Redwood City, CA.

Albin, P. and Foley, D.K. (1992) Decentralized, Dispersed Exchange without an Auctioneer. A Simulation Study. *Journal of Economic Behaviour and Organization*, **18**, 27–51.

Allais, M. (1953) Le Comportement de l'homme Rationnel devant le Risque: Critique des Postulats et Axiomes de l'école Américaine. *Econometrica*, **21**, 503–46.

Anderson, J.A. and Rosenfeld, E. (eds) (1988) *Neurocomputing, A Reader*, MIT Press, Cambridge, MA.

Anderson, P.W., Arrow, K.J., Pines, D. (eds) (1988) *The Economy as an Evolving Complex System*, Addison-Wesley, Redwood City, CA.

Arrow, K. (1986) Rationality of Self and Others in an Economic System. *Journal of Business*, **59**, S385–S399.

Arrow, K. and Debreu, G. (1954) Existence of an Equilibrium for a Competitive Economy. *Econometrica*, **22**, 265–90.

Arrow, K.J. and Hahn, F. (1971) *General Competitive Analysis*, Holden-Day, San Francisco, CA.

Arthur, W.B. (1988) Self-reinforcing Mechanisms in Economics, in *The Economy as an Evolving Complex System*, (eds P.W. Anderson, K.J. Arrow and D. Pines), Addison-Wesley, Redwood City, CA.

Arthur, W.B. (1989) The Economy and Complexity, in *Lectures in the Sciences of Complexity*, SFI Studies in the Sciences of Complexity, (ed D. Stein), Addison-Wesley, Redwood City, CA.

Arthur, W.B. (1990a) Positive Feedbacks in the Economy. *Scientific American*, February.

Arthur, W.B. (1990b) *A Learning Algorithm that Mimics Human Learning*, Santa Fe Institute Working Paper 90–026.

Arthur, W.B. (1991) Designing Economic Agents that Act like Human Agents: A Behavioural Approach to Bounded Rationality. *The American Economic Review*, **81**(2), 353–9.

Arthur, W.B. (1992) Information Contagion, Structural Change and Economic Dynamics, 4, 81–103.

Arthur, W.B. (1993) On Designing Economic Agents that Behave like Human Agents. *Journal of Evolutionary Economics*, **3**, 1–22.

Arthur, W.B., Holland, J.H., LeBaron, B. *et al.* Asset Pricing under Inductive Learning in an Artificial Stock Market. SFI Working Papers.

Arthur, W.B. and Lane, D.A. (1991) Information Constriction and Information Contagion, SFI Working Paper 91–05–026.

Axelrod, R. (1984) *The Evolution of Cooperation*, Basic Books, New York, NY.

Banerjee, A.V. (1992) A Simple Model of Herd Behavior. *Quarterly Journal of Economics*, 77, 797–817.

Barto, A.G., Sutton, R.S. and Watkins, C.J.C.H. (1990) Learning and Sequential Decision Making, in *Learning and Computational Neuroscience*, (eds M. Gabriel and J.W. Moore), MIT Press, Cambridge, MA.

Battiti, R. (1992) First- and Second-order Methods for Learning: between Steepest Descent and Newton's Method. *Neural Computation*, 4, 141–66.

Baum, E.B. (1988) Neural Nets for Economists, in *The Economy as an Evolving Complex System*, (eds P.W. Anderson, K.J. Arrow, D. Pines), Addison-Wesley, Redwood City, CA, pp. 33–48.

Beer, R.D. (1990) *Intelligence as Adaptive Behavior – An Experiment in Computational Neuroethology*, Academic Press, San Diego.

Beerel, A. and Horwood, E. (1993) *Expert Systems in Business: Real World Applications*, Ellis Horwood, Chichester.

Belew, R.K. and Gherrity, M. (1989) Back propagation for the Classifier System, in *Proceedings of the Third International Conference on Genetic Algorithms*, (ed. J.D. Schaffer), Morgan Kaufmann, San Mateo, CA, pp. 275–81.

Beltratti, A. and Margarita, S. (1992) Evolution of Trading Strategies among Heterogeneous Artificial Economic Agents, in *From Animals to Animats 2*, (eds J.A. Meyer, H.L. Roitblat and S.W. Wilson), MIT Press, Cambridge, MA.

Beltratti, A. and Margarita, S. (1994) An artificial adaptive speculative stock market, in *Financial Modelling*, (eds L. Peccati and M. Virén), Physica Verlag, Heidelberg.

Bikhchandani, S., Hirshleifer, D. and Welch, I. (1992) A Theory of Fads, Fashion, Custom and Cultural Change as Informational Cascades. *Journal of Political Economy*, **100**, 992–1026.

Bourgine, P., Walliser, B. and Lemoigne, J.L. (1991) An Interdisciplinary Research between Economic and Cognitive Sciences, in *Economics and Cognitive Science* (eds P. Bourgine and B. Walliser), Pergamon Press, Tarrytown.

Bray, M. (1982) Learning, Estimation, and the Stability of Rational Expectations. *Journal of Economic Theory*, **26**, 318–39.

Brealey, R. and Myers, S. (1984) *Principles of Corporate Finance*, McGraw-Hill, New York, NY.

Carpenter, G. and Grossberg, S. (1986) Neural Dynamics of Category Learning and Recognition: Attention, Memory Consolidation, and Amnesia, in *Brain Structure, Learning and Memory*, (eds J. Davis, R. Newburgh and E. Wegman), AAAS Symposium Series.

Carpenter, G. and Grossberg, S. (1987) ART 2: Self-organization of Stable Category Recognition Codes for Analog Input Patterns. *Applied Optics*, 26(23), 4919–30.

Caudill, M. and Butler, C. (1990) *Naturally Intelligent Systems*, MIT Press, Cambridge, MA.

Caudill, M. and Butler, C. (1992) *Understanding Neural Networks: Computer Explorations*, Vol. 1 and Vol. 2, MIT Press, Cambridge, MA.

Clarke, C.W. (1990) *Mathematical Bioeconomics*, John Wiley and Sons, New York, NY.

Cliff, D., Harvey, I. and Husbands, P. (1992) *Incremental Evolution of Neural Network Architectures for Adaptive Behaviour*, University of Sussex Cognitive Science Research Paper n. 256, Brighton.

Connell, J.H. (1990) *Minimalist Mobile Robotics – A Colony-style Architecture for an Artificial Creature*, Academic Press, San Diego.

Conslik, J. (1988) Optimization Cost. *Journal of Economic Behavior and Organization*, **9**, 213–28.

Davis, L. (ed.) (1987) *Genetic Algorithms and Simulated Annealing*, Pitman, London.

Davis, L. (1989) Mapping Neural Networks into Classifier Systems, in *Proceedings of the Third International Conference on Genetic Algorithms*, (ed. J.D. Schaffer), Morgan Kaufmann, San Mateo, CA, pp. 375–8.

Davis, L. (ed.) (1991) *Handbook of Genetic Algorithms*, Van Nostrand Reinhold, New York, NY.

Debreu, G. (1959) *Theory of Value*, Wiley & Sons New York.

Dreyfus, H.L. and Dreyfus, S.E. (1986) *Mind over Machine*, Free Press, New York, NY.

Ellison, G. and Fudenberg, D. (1993) Rules of Thumb for Social Learning. *Journal of Political Economy*, **101**, 612–43.

Emery, F.E. (1967) The next thirty years: Concepts, Methods and Anticipations. *Human Relations*, **20**, 199–237.

Feldman, J.A. and Ballard, D.H. (1982) Connectionist Models and Their Properties. *Cognitive Science*, **6**, 205–54.

Fontana, W. (1992) Algorithmic Chemistry, in *Artificial Life II* (eds C.G. Langton, C. Taylor, J.D. Farmer and S. Rasmussen), Addison-Wesley, Redwood City, CA, pp. 159–210.

Friedman, M. (1953) The Methodology of Positive Economics, in *Essay in Positive Economics*, University of Chicago Press, Chicago, pp. 3–43.

Gallant, S.I. (1993) *Neural Network Learning and Expert Systems*, MIT Press, Cambridge, MA.

Garbade, K.(1982) *Securities Markets*, McGraw-Hill, New York, NY.

Goldberg, D.E. (1989) *Genetic Algorithms in Search, Optimization and Machine Learning*, Addison-Wesley, Redwood City, CA.

Goldberg, D.E. and Holland, J.H. (1988) Genetic Algorithms and Machine Learning. *Machine Learning*, **3**, 95–9.

Goodman, R.M., Higgins, C.M., Miller, J.W. and Smyth, P. (1992) Rule-Based Neural Networks for Classification and Probability Estimation. *Neural Computation*, **6**, 781–804.

Goodman, R.M. and Smyth, P. (1993) Automated Induction of Rule-based Neural Networks from Databases. Intelligent Systems. *Accounting, Finance and Management*, **1**, 41–54.

Grefenstette, J.J., Davis, L. and Cerys D. (1991) *GENESIS and OOGA: Two Genetic Algorithm Systems*, TSP, Melrose, MA.

Grossberg S., (1982), *Studies of Mind and Brain*, Boston Studies in the Philosophy of Science, D. Reidel Publishing Company, Boston.

Grossman, S. and Stiglitz, J. (1980) On the Impossibility of Informationally Efficient Markets. *American Economic Review*, **70**, 393–408.

Hahn, F.(1973) *On the Notion of Equilibrium in Economics*, Cambridge University Press, Cambridge.

Haltiwanger, J. and Waldman, M. (1985) Rational Expectations and the Limits of Rationality: An Analysis of Heterogeneity. *American Economic Review*, **75**, 326–40.

Hebb, D.O. (1949) *Organization of Behaviour*, Science Editions, New York, NY.

Hecht-Nielsen, R. (1987) Counterpropagation Networks, in *Proceedings of the IEEE First International Conference on Neural Networks* (eds M. Caudill and C. Butler), SOS Printing, San Diego, CA.

Hey, J.D. (1991a) Copying with Dynamic Decision Making under Uncertainty, in *Handbook of Behavioral Economics*, vol. 2B, Behavioral Decision Making, (eds R Frantz, H. Singh and J. Gerber), JAI Press, London, pp. 295–307.

Hey, J.D. (1991b) *Experiments in Economics*, Blackwell, Oxford.

Hillis, W.D. (1992) Co-evolving Parasites Improve Simulated Evolution as an Optimization Procedure, in *Artificial Life* II, (eds C.G. Langton, C. Taylor, J.D. Farmer and S. Rasmussen), Addison-Wesley, Redwood City, CA.

Hinton, G.E., McClelland, J.L., Rumelhart, D.E. (1986) Distributed Representations, in *Parallel Distributed Processing*, (eds D.E. Rumelhart and J.L. McClelland), MIT Press, Cambridge, MA, pp. 77–109.

Holland, J.H. and Reitman, J.S (1978) Cognitive Systems Based on Adaptive Algorithms, in *Pattern-directed Inference Systems*, (eds D.A. Waterman and F. Hayes-Roth), Academic Press, New York, NY.

Holland, J.H. and Miller J.H. (1991) Artificial Adaptive Agents in Economic Theory. *American Economic Review*, **81**(2), 365–70.

Holland, J.H. (1992) *Adaptation in Natural and Artificial Systems*, 2nd edn, (1st edn, 1975), MIT Press, Cambridge, MA.

Hornik, K., Stinchcombe, M. and White, H. (1989) Multilayer Feed-forward Networks are Universal Approximators. *Neural Networks*, **2**, 359–66.

Hornik, K., Stinchcombe, M. and White, H. (1990) Universal Approximation of an Unknown Mapping and its Derivatives using Multilayer Feed-forward Networks. *Neural Networks*, **3**, 551–60.

Jordan, M.I. (1986) Attractor Dynamics and Parallelism in a Connectionist Sequential Machine, in *Proceedings of the 8th Annual Conference of the Cognitive Science Society*, Lawrence Erlbaum Associates, Hillsdale, NJ.

Kahneman, D. and Tversky, A. (1979) Prospect Theory: An Analysis of Decision under Risk. *Econometrica*, **47**, 363–91.

Kauffman, S.A. (1989) Adaptation on Rugged Fitness Landscapes, in *Lectures in the Sciences of Complexity*, (ed D. Stein), Addison-Wesley, Redwood City, CA.

Kauffman, S.A. and Johnsen, S. (1992) Co-evolution to the Edge of Chaos: Coupled Fitness Landscapes, Poised States, and Co-evolutionary Avalanches, in *Artificial Life* II, (eds C.G. Langton, C. Taylor, J.D. Farmer and S. Rasmussen), Addison-Wesley, Redwood City, CA.

Kelsey, D. and Quiggin, J. (1992) Theories of Choice under Ignorance and uncertainty. *Journal of Economic Surveys*, **6**, 133–53.

Kephart, J.O., Hogg, T. and Huberman, A. (1990) Collective Behaviour of Predictive Agents. *Physica D*, **42**, 48–65.

Keynes, J.M. (1936) *The General Theory of Employment, Interest and Money*, Macmillan, London.

Kirman, A.P. (1992) Whom or What does the Representative Individual Represent? *Journal of Economic Perspectives*, **6**, 117–36.

Knight, F. (1921) *Risk, Uncertainty and Profit*, Houghton Mifflin, New York, NY.

Kohonen, T. (1984) *Self-organization and Associative Memory*, Series in Information Sciences, Springer-Verlag, Berlin.

Kosko, B. (1992) *Neural Networks and Fuzzy Systems: A Dynamical Systems Approach to Machine Intelligence*, Prentice Hall, Englewood Cliffs.

Koza, J.R. (1992a) *Genetic Programming: On the Programming of Computers by means of Natural Selection*, MIT Press, Cambridge, MA.

Koza, J.R. (1992b) Genetic Evolution and Co-evolution of Computer Programs, in *Artificial Life* II, (eds C.G. Langton, C. Taylor, J.D. Farmer and S. Rasmussen), Addison-Wesley, Redwood City, CA.

Kurz, M. (1974) The Kesten-Stigum Model and the Treatment of Uncertainty in Equilibrium Theory, in *Essays on Economic Behavior under Uncertainty*, (eds M.S. Balch, P.L. McFadden and S.Y. Wu), North Holland, Amsterdam, pp. 389–99.

Kurz, M., (1994a) *Asset Prices with Rational Beliefs*, CEPR Publication No. 375, Stanford University.

Kurz, M., (1994b) On the Structure and Diversity of Rational Beliefs. *Economic Theory*, 4, 877–900.

Kurz, M., (1994c) On Rational Belief Equilibria. *Economic Theory*, 4, 859–76.

Lane, D.A. (1992) *Artificial Worlds and Economics*, presented at the Workshop on Nonlinear Dynamics in Economics, European University Institute, Florence.

Lane, D.A. (1993a) Artificial Worlds and Economics, part I. *Journal of Evolutionary Economics*, 3, 89–107.

Lane, D.A. (1993b) Artificial Worlds and Economics, part II. *Journal of Evolutionary Economics*, 3, 177–97.

Langton, C.G. (ed.) (1989) *Artificial Life*, Addison-Wesley, Redwood City, CA.

Langton, C.G. (1992) Life at the Edge of Chaos, in *Artificial Life II*, (eds C.G. Langton, C. Taylor, J.D. Farmer and S. Rasmussen), Addison-Wesley, Redwood City, CA.

Langton, C.G., Taylor, C., Farmer, J.D. and Rasmussen, S. (eds) (1992) *Artificial Life* II, Addison-Wesley, Redwood City, CA.

Le Cun, Y. (1985) Une Procédure d'Apprentissage pour Réseau à Seuil Asymétrique, in *Proceedings of Cognitiva*.

Lee, T., White, H. and Granger, C.W.J. (1989) *Testing for Neglected Nonlinearity in Time Series Models*, UCSD Discussion paper.

Levitt, B. and March, J.G. (1988) Organizational Learning. *Annual Review of Sociology*, **88**, 319–40.

Lindgren, K. (1992) Evolutionary Phenomena in Simple Dynamics, in *Artificial Life* II (eds C.G. Langton, C. Taylor, J.D. Farmer and S. Rasmussen), Addison-Wesley, Redwood City, CA, pp. 295–312.

Looney, C.G. (1993) Neural Networks as Expert Systems. *Expert Systems with Applications*, **2**, 129–36.

Lucas, R.J. (1980) *Studies in Business Cycle Theories*, MIT Press, Cambridge, MA.

Machina, M. (1987) Choice under Uncertainty: Problems Solved and Unsolved. *Journal of Economic Perspective*, **1**, 121–54.

Machina, M. (1994) *Non-expected Utility and the Robustness of the Classical Insurance Paradigm*. Presented as the Geneva Risk Lecture at the 21st Seminar of the European Group of Risk and Insurance Economists, Toulouse, France.

Machlup, F. (1967) Theories of the Firm: Marginalist, Behavioral, Managerial. *American Economic Review*, 57, 1–33.

MacKay, D.J.C. (1992a) Bayesian Interpolation. *Neural Computation*, **3**, 415–47.

MacKay, D.J.C. (1992b) A Practical Bayesian Framework for Backpropagation Networks. *Neural Computation*, **3**, 448–72.

Marcet, A. and Sargent, T.J. (1989) Convergence of Least Squares Learning Mechanisms in Self Referential Linear Stochastic Models. *Journal of Economic Theory*, **48**, 337–68.

Margarita, S. (1991) Neural Networks, Genetic Algorithms and Stock Trading, in *Artificial Neural Networks*, (eds T. Kohonen, K. Mäkisara, O. Simula, J. Kangas), North-Holland, Amsterdam.

Margarita, S. (1992a) Genetic Neural Networks for Financial Markets: Some Results, in *Proceedings of the 10th European Conference on Artificial Intelligence*, (ed. B. Neumann), John Wiley & Sons, Chichester.

Margarita, S. (1992b) Interacting Neural Networks: An Artificial Life Approach to Stock Markets, in *Artificial Neural Networks 2*, (eds I. Aleksander and J. Taylor), North-Holland, Amsterdam, pp. 1343–6.

Margarita, S. and Beltratti, A. (1992) Credit Risk and Lending in an Artificial Adaptive Banking System, in *Adaptive Intelligent Systems*, (ed. SWIFT), Elsevier Science Publishers, Amsterdam, pp. 161–176.

Margarita, S. and Beltratti, A. (1993) Dynamics of a Neural Network-based Financial Market, in *Proceedings of the International Conference on Artificial Neural Networks*, (eds S. Gielen and B. Kappen), Springer-Verlag, Berlin.

Marimon, R., McGrattan, E. and Sargent, T.J. (1990) Money as a Medium of Exchange in an Economy with Artificially Intelligent Agents. *Journal of Economic Dynamics and Control*, **14**, 329–73.

McClelland, J.L. and Rumelhart, D.E. (1986) *Parallel Distributed Processing: Explorations in the Microstructure of Cognition, Vol. 2: Psychological and Biological Models*, MIT Press, Cambridge, MA.

McClelland, J.L. and Rumelhart, D.E. (1988) *Explorations in Parallel Distributed Processing: A Handbook of Models, Programs, and Exercises*, MIT Press, Cambridge, MA.

Mel, B.W. (1990) *Connectionist Robot Motion Planning – A Neurally-Inspired Approach to Visually-Guided Reaching*, Academic Press, San Diego.

Miller, J.H. (1989) *The Co-evolution of Automata in the Repeated Prisoner's Dilemma*, Santa Fe Institute Report 89–003.

Minsky, M. and Papert, S. (1969) *Perceptrons – An Introduction to Computational Geometry*, MIT Press, Cambridge, MA.

Minsky, M. and Papert, S. (1988) *Perceptrons – An Introduction to Computational Geometry* (Expanded edition), MIT Press, Cambridge, MA.

Mühlenbein, H. and Kindermann, J. (1989) The Dynamics of Evolution and Learning: Towards Genetic Neural Networks, in *Connectionism in Perspective*, (eds R. Pfeifer, Z. Schreter, F. Fogelman-Soulié and L. Steels), North-Holland, Amsterdam, pp. 173–97.

Muth, J.F. (1961) Rational Expectations and the Theory of Price Movements. *Econometrica*, **29**, 315–35.

Nelson, R. (1995) Recent Evolutionary Theorizing about Economic Change. *Journal of Economic Literature*, **33**, 48–90.

Nelson, R. and Winter, S.G. (1982) *An Evolutionary Theory of Economic Change*, Harvard University Press, Cambridge, MA.

Newell, A. and Simon, H.A. (1972) *Human Problem Solving*, Prentice-Hall, Englewood Cliffs, NJ.

North, D.C. (1991) Institutions. *Journal of Economic Perspectives*, **5**, 97–112

Nottola, C., Leroy, F. and Davalo, F. (1992) Dynamics of Artificial Markets, in

Towards a Practice of Autonomous Systems, (eds F.J. Varela and P. Bourgine), MIT Press, Cambridge, MA, pp. 185–94.

Nowlan, S.J. and Hinton, G.E. (1992) Simplifying Neural Networks by Soft Weight-Sharing. *Neural Computation*, 4, 473–93.

Parisi, D., Cecconi, F., and Nolfi, S. (1990) Econets: Neural Networks that Learn in an Environment. *Network*, 2, 149–68.

Parker, D.B. (1985) *Learning Logic*, MIT Center for Computational Research in Economics and Management Science, T.R. 47.

Pigou, A.C. (1922) Empty Economic Boxes: A Reply. *Economic Journal*, 32, 458–65.

Prigogine, I. (1993) Bounded Rationality: From Conventional to Socio-economic Models, in *Nonlinear Dynamics and Evolutionary Economics*, (eds R.H. Day and P. Chen), Oxford University Press.

Prigogine, I. and Stengers, I. (1984) *Order out of Chaos*, Bantam, New York, NY.

Rasmusen, E. (1989) *Games and Information*, Basil Blackwell, Cambridge, MA.

Rawlins, G.J.E. (ed.) (1991) *Foundations of Genetic Algorithms*, Morgan Kaufmann, San Mateo, CA.

Ray, T. (1992) An Approach to the Synthesis of Life, in *Artificial Life* II (eds C.G. Langton, C. Taylor, J.D. Farmer and S. Rasmussen), Addison-Wesley, Redwood City, CA, pp. 371–408.

Refenes, A.N. and Azema-Barac, M. (1993) Neural Network Applications in Financial Asset Management. *Neural Computing & Applications* (to appear).

Rigler, A.K., Irvine, J.M. and Vogl, T.P. (1991) Rescaling of Variables in Back Propagation Learning. *Neural Networks*, 4(2), 225–9.

Rosenblatt, F. (1958) The Perceptron: A Probabilistic Model for Information Storage and Organization in the Brain. *Psychological Review*, 386–408. Reprinted in Neurocomputing: Foundations of Research (eds J.A. Anderson and E. Rosenfeld) (1989), MIT Press, Cambridge, MA.

Rosenblatt, R. (1959) *Principles of Neuro-Dynamics*, Spartan Books, New York, NY.

Rumelhart, D.E. and McClelland, J.L. (1986) *Parallel Distributed Processing: Explorations in the Microstructure of Cognition, Vol. 1: Foundations*, MIT Press, Cambridge, MA.

Santomero, A.M. (1984) Modeling the Banking Firm. *Journal of Money, Credit and Banking*, 4(16).

Sargent, T.J. (1993) *Bounded Rationality in Macroeconomics*, Clarendon Press, Oxford.

Shiller, R.J. (1987) Investor Behaviour in the October 1987 Stock Market Crash: Survey Evidence, in *Market Volatility*, (R.J. Shiller, 1989), MIT Press, Cambridge, MA.

Shiller, R.J. (1989) *Market Volatility*, MIT Press, Cambridge, MA.

Simon, H.A. (1957) *Models of Man*, Wiley & Sons, New York, NY.

Simon, H.A. (1969) *The Sciences of the Artificial*, MIT Press, Cambridge, MA.

Simon, H.A. (1979) Rational Decision Making in Business Organizations. *American Economic Review*, 69, 493–513.

Simon, H.A. (1984) On the Behavioral and Rational Foundations of Economic Dynamics. *Journal of Economic Behavior and Organization*, 5, pp. 35–55.

Simon, H.A. *et al.* (1992) *Economics, Bounded Rationality and the Cognitive Revolution*, (eds M. Egidi and R. Marris), Elgar, Aldershot.

Smith, A. (1776) *An Inquiry into the Nature and Causes of the Wealth of Nations.*

Smith, M. (1993) *Neural Networks for Statistical Modeling,* Van Nostrand Reinhold, New York, NY.

Stiglitz, J.E. and Weiss, A. (1981) Credit Rationing in Markets with Incomplete Information. *American Economic Review,* 393–410.

Sutton, R.S. (1984) *Temporal Credit Assignment in Reinforcement Learning,* Ph.D Thesis, Dept. of Computer and Information Science, University of Massachusetts.

Sutton, R.S. (1988) Learning to Predict by the Methods of Temporal Differences. *Machine Learning,* 3, 9–44.

Sutton, R.S. (1990) Reinforcement Learning Architecture for Animats, in *From Animals to Animats,* (eds J.A. Meyer and S.W. Wilson), MIT Press, Cambridge, MA, pp. 288–96.

Terna, P. (1991) Labour, Consumption and Family Assets: A Neural Network Learning from its own Cross-Targets, in *Artificial Neural Networks,* (eds T. Kohonen, K. Mükisara, O. Simula, J. Kangas), Elsevier Science Publishers B.V. (North-Holland), Amsterdam, pp. 1759–62.

Terna, P. (1992a) Artificial Economic Agents, in *SPIE Vol. 1709, Proceedings of Applications of Artificial Neural Networks III,* pp. 1003–14.

Terna, P. (1992b) Microeconomic Experiments by Neural Networks, in *Artificial Neural Networks 2,* (eds I. Aleksander and J. Taylor), Elsevier Science Publishers B.V. (North-Holland), Amsterdam, pp. 1339–42.

Terna, P. (1993a) Artificial Interacting Agents for Stock Market Experiments: the Cross-Target Method, in *Proceedings of ICANN 93,* (eds S. Gielen and B. Kappen), Springer-Verlag, Berlin.

Terna, P. (1993b) Randomness, Imitation or Reason to Explain Agents' Behaviour into an Artificial Stock Market, in *Advances in Artificial Intelligence* (ed P. Torasso), Springer-Verlag, Berlin.

Tesauro, G. (1992) Practical Issues in Temporal Difference Learning. *Machine Learning,* 8, 257–77.

Townsend, R. (1983) Forecasting the Forecasts of Others. *Journal of Political Economy,* 91, 546–88.

Trippi, R. and Turban, E. (1990) *Investment Management: Decision Support and Expert Systems,* Body & Fraser Div., Southwestern Publishing Co., Boston.

Tversky, A. and Thaler, R.H. (1990) Preference Reversals. *Journal of Economic Perspective,* 4, 201–11.

van Ooyen, A. and Nienhuis, B. (1992) Improving the Convergence of the Back-propagation Algorithm. *Neural Networks,* 5(3), 465–71.

Varian, H.R. (1992) *Microeconomic Analysis,* 3rd edn, W.W. Norton, New York, NY.

Waldrop, M.M. (1992) *Complexity,* Simon & Schuster, New York, NY.

Walras, L. (1954) *Elements of Pure Economics,* Allen and Unwin, London.

Wasserman, P.D. (1989) *Neural Computing: Theory and Practice,* Van Nostrand Reinhold, New York, NY.

Watkins, C.J.C.H. (1989) *Learning from Delayed Rewards,* Ph.D Thesis, King's College, Cambridge.

Weigend, A.S., Huberman, B.A. and Rumelhart, D.E. (1992) Predicting Sunspots and Exchange Rates with Connectionist Networks, in *Nonlinear Modeling and Forecasting – SFI Studies in the Science of Complexity,* (eds M. Casdagli and S. Eubank), Addison-Wesley, Redwood City, CA.

Weisbuch, G. (1991) *Complex Systems Dynamics*, in *SFI Studies in the Sciences of Complexity*, Addison-Wesley, Redwood City, CA.

Werbos, P. (1974) *Beyond Regression: New Tools for Prediction and Analysis in the Behavioral Sciences*, unpublished Ph.D. Dissertation, Harvard University, Department of Applied Mathematics.

White, H. (1982) Maximum Likelihood Estimation of Misspecified Models. *Econometrica*, **50**, 1–25.

White, H. (1987) *Some Asymptotic Results for Learning in Single Hidden Layer Feed-forward Network Models*, UCSD Discussion paper.

White, H. (1988) *Multilayer Feed-forward Networks can Learn Arbitrary Mappings: Connectionist Nonparametric Regression with Automatic and Semi-Automatic Determination of Network Complexity*, UCSD Discussion Paper.

White, H. (1991) Learning in Artificial Neural Networks: A Statistical Perspective. *Neural Computation*, **1**, 425–64.

White, H. (1992) *Artificial Neural Networks: Approximation and Learning Theory*, Blackwell, Oxford.

Whitley, L.D. (ed.) (1993) *Foundations of Genetic Algorithms II*, Morgan Kaufmann, San Mateo, CA.

Widrow, B. and Hoff, M. (1960) *Adaptive Switching Circuits*, 1960 IRE WESCON Convention Record, Institute of Radio Engineers, New York, NY.

Williamson, O.E. (1975) *Markets and Hierarchies: Analysis and Antitrust Implications*, Free Press, New York, NY.

Windsor, C.G. and Harker, A.H. (1990) Multi-variate Financial Index Prediction: A Neural Network Study, in *Proceedings of the International Neural Network Conference*, Kluwer Academic, Dordrecht.

Würtz, D., de Groot, C., Wenger, D., Unseld, S. and Schütterle B. (1993) A Neural Decision Support System for Predicting Currency Exchange Rates, in *Proceedings of the Second International Conference on Artificial Intelligence Applications on Wall Street*, (ed. R.S. Freedman), Software Engineering Press, Gaithersburg, MD.

Index